A Post-Western Account of Critical Cosmopolitan Social Theory

Radical Subjects in International Politics

Series Editor: Ruth Kinna

This series uses the idea of political subjection to promote the discussion and analysis of individual, communal and civic participation and activism. "Radical subjects" refers both to the character of the topics and issues tacked in the series and to the ethic guiding the research. The series has a radical focus in that it provides a springboard for the discussion of activism that sits outside or on the fringes of institutional politics, yet which, insofar as it reflects a commitment to social change, is far from marginal. It provides a platform for scholarship that interrogates modern political movements, probes the local, regional and global dimensions of activist networking and the principles that drive them, and develops innovative frames to analyze issues of exclusion and empowerment. The scope of the series is defined by engagement with the concept of the radical in contemporary politics but includes research that is multi- or interdisciplinary, working at the boundaries of art and politics, political utopianism, feminism, sociology and radical geography.

Titles in Series

A Post-Western Account of Critical Cosmopolitan Social Theory

Being and Acting in a Democratic World

Michael Murphy

ROWMAN & LITTLEFIELD

Lanham • Boulder • New York • London

Published by Rowman & Littlefield
An imprint of The Rowman & Littlefield Publishing Group, Inc.
4501 Forbes Boulevard, Suite 200, Lanham, Maryland 20706
www.rowman.com

6 Tinworth Street, London SE11 5AL, United Kingdom

British Library Cataloguing in Publication Information Available

Library of Congress Cataloging-in-Publication Data

Library of Congress Control Number: 2020948890

ISBN 9781786615527 (cloth)
ISBN 9781538149935 (paperback)
ISBN 9781786615534 (Electronic)

To Watsuji Tetsurō and Chris Rumford

Contents

Acknowledgments

Despite what many would tell themselves, no intellectual journey is taken alone. I have been privileged to have discussed the ideas contained in this book with many, many people, to whom I am sincerely grateful. And although the ideas contained within this book have been part of my life for longer than I can remember, I have needed to eat, to be reassured, to be calmed, to be made to see the bigger picture, and to be encouraged. I am humbled by the support that I have been given during the life of this project. There are far too many people to thank. However, there are a number of people who I would like to take this opportunity to thank. My mum who always believed in her son and to my dad for showing me that through compassion openings can occur. My aunt, Ellen Mangan, for her continuous support and love. To Anton Luis Sevilla, whose act of intellectual generosity gave momentum to this project. I wish that one day I can pay-on the debt. To Professor William Mander, Harris Manchester College, University of Oxford, who has been a wonderful mentor and friend for me and this project. To Mrs. Janet Smith who has been such a wonderful and incredible person to me and my project. To Mike Smart who for over thirty years has been a thorn in my intellectual pride and the genesis of so much creativity. Also, to Richard Shipp and Laurence Keynes for their conversations which have enriched my own understanding of the potential of the dialogue between Watsuji's ideas and the work of Gerard Delanty and Walter Mignolo's; a big thank you. Importantly, I would like to thank the Institute of Modern and Contemporary Culture, University of Westminster, and in particular, Professor John Beck, for their support during a visiting research fellowship. I would like to extend my sincerest thanks to Dr. Aurélia Mouzet, University of Arizona, for taking the time to comment on the draft manuscript which has been invaluable; thank you so much Aurélia. Of course, any shortcomings in the work are a result of my own hand. Lastly, to my wife, Kate. Kate, it is impossible to put into words what you have given me. You brought light into my wounds and I thank you for the creation of our new *aidagara*. I promise that for the next project I will get a cottage and take the dog with me.

Part I

DRAMA AND PROTAGONISTS

Introduction

Cosmopolitanism: Enabling Knowledge Cocreation and Translation Toward Social Change

The first part of this book introduces the theoretical landscape of cosmopolitanism, its connection to the world, and the protagonists whose work that the book will draw from. In the first chapter, we will discuss the notion of cosmopolitanism and specifically the idea of a critical cosmopolitan social theory. Our primary aim in the first chapter is to argue that cosmopolitanism's fundamental premise of incompleteness, as an example of reflexive negation, entails that for it to maintain its critical function that it must be carried out as a process of critique and cooperation with other relational sociologies. The second aim is the outline of a relational account of personhood as the ultimate unit of analysis of post-western critical cosmopolitan social theory. However, this is not an essentialized account of relationality, but an account that focuses on relationality being part of the "deep structure" of being human. The second chapter introduces the reader to the tradition of critical theory. However, rather than provide the usual rendition of critical theory as a uniquely Western tradition, this chapter will bring it into conversation with the tradition of decolonial thought. The point of the chapter is not to present a staid antinomy between the European and Latin American accounts, but to operate through a dialogical principle of critique and cooperation, deconstruction and reconstruction. Through such a method of dialogue, the aim is to draw on the positive aspects of both traditions within the setting of a conceptually interconnected world. Chapter 3 introduces the reader to the work of Watsuji Tetsurō. Watsuji's work is only beginning to be recognized in the West. However, Watsuji was a remarkable thinker who through his incorporation of Confucius, Buddhist, and Heideggerian studies, developed one of the first examples of a cosmopolitan global philosophy. Importantly, his work also represents a form of proto-decolonial thought, that has the capacity to provide novel and innovative resources for today's decolonial struggles.

COSMOPOLITANISM: ENABLING KNOWLEDGE COCREATION AND TRANSLATION TOWARD SOCIAL CHANGE

This book begins with a story:

> In a "developing" country, an academic trained in the Western academy enters the office of a government official. Armed with the moral clarity that can only come through an expensive intellectual effort and the canon of Western political thought she tells the official the story of Cosmopolitanism and its vision for a global future. She tells of how the Greeks had a vision of looking beyond one's own horizon; of how we are all citizens of the world. She tells of how in this world of interconnected concerns we should grasp the spirit of Cosmopolitanism. The government official has listened. She sits back, laughs and says, "My friend, when your people first came to my land you brought us civilization as we were not civilized but lived in a world of myths and religion, you raped the lands of its riches and its people. Then you fought your 'cold war' but it was my children who died for you to maintain the myths of your people. Then you told us that we needed to be democratic, so you brought your stories of democracy based on your religion and myths, but it was my children who died. You tell my people that the world needs free trade, but it is I and my husband that must look into our children's eyes as they starve. You have placed our bodies in bondage, our minds in shackles and stilled our voices. Now, you tell me that we are sisters. Tell me my sister, during all your learning did it not occur to you that after the many years that your people have known my own that my people may have had thoughts of their own on our encounter? During your education, was your curiosity not raised as to whether we have asked questions such as what is a human being, of how to live a good life, on justice, or of how to live with our neighbours? Have you ever thought that the *barbarism* of my people's tongue may also capture some scent of the adventure of being human? Now, as the world once more shifts, you bring me a new myth, a myth that you hope to make real in the world. You now tell me that we are sisters. Well, would you do something for me, my sister? Let us sit humbly together and see what the stories of *all our peoples* can bring to humanity's house, before more of our children die."

In *A Post-Western Account of Critical Cosmopolitan Social Theory* we have two aims. The first is to set out an account of post-Western critical cosmopolitan social theory as a process of critique and cooperation. I will argue that cosmopolitanism can only maintain its critical edge if it reaches out to other relational sociological cosmopolitan projects. At the level of intercultural exchange, through an engagement of mutual humility, in celebrating the global resources of cosmopolitanisms not as particularities, each vying for attention, but as a reciprocal phase of development, holds out the potential to rejuvenate world philosophies and to break through internal boundaries and limitations. This provides space for a new language of acting and being in the world through providing an "opening" within one's own consciousness to allow for new affirmations within a vibrant democratic community.

Drawing on this methodological approach our second aim is to provide radical account of being and acting the world to populate our language of critical cosmopolitan social theory. This will be achieved through applying our methodology to the works of the critical theorist Gerard Delanty, the decolonial theorist Walter Mignolo, and the Buddhist, Confucian, and Phenomenological inspired work of the Japanese thinker Watsuji Tetsurō. In the following pages, we do not aim to set out an illumination of the contradictions and antimonies of modernity for the sake of a sedate antinomy. Instead, our work is concerned with providing a spatial evacuation of the temporal-spatial modalities of modernity, the ideals of modernity. These dichotomize the relationship between self, other, and the world. This is motivated by the consideration that the problems that we face as local communities, internationally, and as a species in an interconnected and entangled world cannot be effectively addressed if we maintain the boundaries set up by the spatial-temporal modalities of modernity. In short, the story that we have told ourselves about who we are is causally part of the problems that we face personally, societally, and as a species, and are unlikely toprovide any realistic solutions. This broad synthesis of philosophical traditions, combines attention of social organisation, cross-issue comparative studies, critical multicultural perspectives, and the study of social practices to execute an account of a conceptually post-western centric critical cosmopolitan social theory as an ethico-political policy and research agenda.

In *A Post-Western Account of Critical Cosmopolitan Social Theory*, our objective is, by necessity, to achieve three distinct but interrelated tasks which correspond with the fundamental contradictions of political life: unity and diversity, inside and outside, space and time.[1] These tasks are to provide a means of cosmopolitan intercultural exchange, intracultural analysis, and the mechanism of change for the self. The vehicle for accomplishing these tasks is to move beyond current accounts of critical and decolonial theory. Both perspectives maintain the possibility of a radical approach to social theory. This is based on the interdisciplinarity required to explore the global consciousness of the relationship between self, other, and the world, though both accounts aim to provide a critical perspective on the problems of modernity. However, these accounts provide an understanding of the cosmopolitan

---

[1] For excellent discussions on attempts to articulate answers to these contradictions see Walker 1991 and 1992.

imagination based on the temporality of modernity—for Delanty this is the autonomous and distinct self, for Mignolo this is the mirror image of a totalizing other. The work of Watsuji allows us to step out of temporality. With his emphasis on the space of actual existing social relations, when brought together in the process of critique and cooperation with Delanty and Mignolo will allow us to reimagine ourselves, our relationship to the other, being and acting in a democratic world through points of critique within the practices of life.

INTRODUCING GERARD DELANTY AND WALTER MIGNOLO

In a series of publications, Delanty has developed a theoretical position that he describes as "Critical cosmopolitanism" (Delanty 2006, 2009, 2011, 2012, 2014). For Delanty "a non-Eurocentric approach [to Critical cosmopolitanism] would thus aim to identify those features of modernity than [*sic*] can be found in non-Western parts of the world and where the explanation of the phenomenon in question does not lie in Western influences" (Delanty 2009). Through such a framework, he hopes to overcome the intellectual and normative residues of conceptual Eurocentrism. For Delanty, such a critical cosmopolitanism is created between the global and local because of an open encounter between the imaginary of cultures and societies. In such an account, cosmopolitanism exists within all societies and is a transformative process of *transcendental immanence*. In this sense, cosmopolitanism is not a description of a local given state or an aspiration for a specific situation, but rather an imaginary situation that can take different forms according to the historic context and social circumstances. At the moment of this transformative dialogue, maintains Delanty, newness is created; a third culture of transcendence. Through the heuristic processes within "global history" and the dialectic between "structures of consciousness," Delanty argues that space has been created within global consciousness at the local level that have been influenced by Western concepts through which these have now lost their Western specificity with the potential to overcome not only objections of Eurocentrism but also all ethnocentric methods.

Walter Mignolo passionately challenges a benign view of modernity as containing the origins of cultural translation and transcendence. Drawing on the intellectual legacy of thinkers such as Enrique Dussel, Emmanuel Levinas, and Aníbal Quijano, the decolonial project that Mignolo is an influential figure has sought to provide connections between peoples who live, today, with the effects of colonialism. For Mignolo, though theorists of modernity may cherish the emancipatory effects of the temporal movement, for him such an account omits an important aspect: the dark-side or under-side of modernity. Mignolo aims to develop a critical cosmopolitan account that firmly addresses the "imperious" account of universal knowledge with its accompanying assimilation of otherness. This epistemological critique links the epistemic location, the localized conditions through which reality is understood, with the subject. This challenges the myth of universal, absolute, and passive knowledge and truth. Instead, it looks toward using the relative experiences of local populations, *relative universalism*, to generate new ways of being and acting in the world. In the decolonial project, the experiences of the colonialized provides the basis for social, political, and economic renovation and rejuvenation within and between people's who have suffered the trauma of colonialism and neocolonialism. This, it is claimed, rather than being simply a rejection of the ideals of modernity, aims to undermine these ideals through the enunciation of injustices, to then proclaim new affirmations of the human condition.

However, as will be demonstrated over the next two chapters, the theoretical limits that Delanty and Mignolo impose of the imaginative potential of their projects mean that they, even when applied collegiately are unable to escape the loop of totality through their own resources. Though the theoretical encounter between these two thinkers' work reveals a rupture in both accounts, what is required is an account of multidimensional space that can draw on cosmopolitan resources to deconceptualize the world to express the multimodality of being human. This book's primary aim is to set out a vocabulary of critical cosmopolitan social theory. Such a vocabulary is spatial as this allows us to undermine the claims of necessity that the temporal, modernity, or age of empires for instance, make. In examining the effects on the space of people's lives, understanding our bodies as the interconnected contact with the world, allows us to provide a critical perspective on the present. It is into this space of our consciousness that *A Post-Western account of Critical Cosmopolitan Social Theory* aims to provide a new language of cosmopolitan critical social theory for a more democratic way of acting and being in the world.

To achieve this, our engagement with the critical and decolonial traditions will be carried out through Watsuji Tetsuro's[2] concepts of emptiness, *fūdo*, and *aidagara*.[3] These allow us to create a "border" between critical and decolonial theory, to step outside of the temporal-spatial modalities of modernity to then return with new affirmations of the being in the world. The cosmopolitan practice of bringing the north, south, east, and west together, to overcome our partialities, enriches the critical theorist's world with an encounter with

---

[2] We will follow the Japanese convention of using the family name Watsuji throughout this book.
[3] We will be returning to these three concepts shortly.

the practices of life, and imbues the imagination of our Buddhist philosopher with the criticality required for being and acting in a democratic world. This overcomes the present restrictions placed on the possibilities of the cosmopolitan imagination through expanding agency and nourishing individuality as an interconnected social endeavour. That is, it is through the recognition of our interdependence between self-other-world that offers our only protection against our own vulnerability.

To begin this journey, we need to set out how we perceive and conceive of reality. What is real, rational, and achievable, is provided through the temporal-spatial modalities of modernity. This defining of "I" as the rationality of an autonomous and distinct unit of analysis is meant to provide a series of answers to the fundamental contradictions of political life: unity and diversity, space and time, inside and outside. Modernity provides our interpretive space and emphasizes the transitive nature of being, *to be*, as a singularity. You rationally understand yourself as a singularity, your nation is a singularity, and the human species is a singularity. However, this has created the means for the dichotomization of self and other, modernity and tradition, human and nonhuman worlds, as absolute and abstract terms.

Through interaction and exchange with other and the world, a society's chosen outcome to these contradictions is central to the maintenance of a people, a community, a nation, for identity, security, and internal solidarity. Modernity's answer to the contradictions of being human is the creation of identity tied to the rationality of authority. This provides a narrative of a "peaceful" inner identity that is opposed to an anarchy of the outside. This formation and maintenance "I"s' obligation to the state, as a citizen, places blockages to "I"s' relationship to otherness, of a wider humanity. This creation of abnormal "otherness" has the benefit of favoring the state or authority as the authentic expression of reason and efficiency within and beyond its territorial boundaries. The state's authority across political, cultural, and social institutions provides it with an unassailable position in respect of agenda-setting, deliberation, and decision-making. The resulting tension between the abstraction of the individual as an autonomous and distinct entity and the state as *constituted power* of existing sociopolitical arrangements, leads to the neglect of the creativity of the "local," of existing *constituent power*: proper politics is carried out at the national level, the local is not important.

Concealed behind the language of neoliberal triumphalism and cosmopolitan aspiration after the fall of the Berlin Wall and collapse of the Soviet Union was an antinarrative of truth. For the neoliberal, the victory of universal individualism over universal socialism was first and foremost a victory for the individualization of ethics. It is important to remember that any discussion of the totalizing and dehumanizing effects of neoliberalism must begin with an acceptance that it begins with an ethical claim of freedom. This appeal to an abstract "freedom," disembodied as an ultimate unit of analysis, blind to social existence, has provided the means to establish financial, economic, and political, national and global institutions. For the cosmopolitan, their aspiration imagined that old ways of seeing the world would be dispensed with so that the relationship between self, other, and the world could be transformed. Ostensibly capable of providing a critique of the spatial implications of globalization, of how the temporality of globalization has effected lives, cosmopolitanism claims to hold the capacity to respond to the ideas that now normalize the lives of the global population.

But for those that live within the cavernous ravine of existential threats as a daily reality, within and on the edges of modernity, their antinarrative to the claims of modernity can be articulated with a declarative, "you've just noticed that liberal ideals conceal an underside?" The three recent shocks to the neoliberal view of the world—the financial crisis of 2008, the United Kingdom's referendum decision to leave the European Union, and the election of Donald Trump to the presidency of the United States of America—have revealed a battleground for the rationality the political between "populist" and "established" political identities. This battle for the image of being and acting in a democratic world has coincided with the belief among many citizens within Western democracies of the emergence of a gap between themselves, as embodied citizens living contextualized lives, and centers of power. Here, the citizen perceives that they lack control of and access to democratic agenda-setting and decision-making. This, they feel, has the effect of over-riding the social and political concerns at the level of the *familiar*, the local and every day, with power being corralled within the confines of a circle of political and economic elites. This leads to a democratic sentiment that the outcome of democratic deliberations is neither fair or true, in the sense of being a representation of their concerns. The political life of the local is subsumed to the project. The underlying point here is that the projects of globalization, and in respect of Europe, the EU, have been carried out with an eye to the project rather than a deep consideration of the effects of these processes on the lives of the people in those communities.

For those espousing populist agendas, the response to these concerns, despite the irony that it is elites that are calling for the rejection of a different set of elites, an appeal has been made to the fundamental values of a "people," however one may wish to define such a term. While for the most part, these appeals have been based on vacuous and opaque policy agendas, they do benefit from resonating as an emotional response to having a process distort the fabric of one's life and which is seemingly outside one's control. For this part of the population, the forces of globalization and unity in diversity which is implied by this process are applied to them and their lives, without reference to themselves.

Established political figures do recognize that globalization, the cosmo-politanization of the everyday, and democracy is perceptively not working for the majority. They do understand that a way forward needs to be found to address the unequal distribution of resources. This, is it hoped, would improve the life conditions and opportunities for the billions of people that have been left behind by the current phase of globalization. However, all they have to offer is to argue for change in order for things to remain the same. While Emmanuel Macron and other statesmen and women concede that the system is broken, that there is a need to "reinvent" ourselves through reinventing our societies and the relationship between the individual and the institutions of the community, they are incapable of enunciating a *familiar* vocabulary of change, a vocabulary that people locally would recognize. The cause of this is a political and social vocabulary that our politicians must draw on, which stems from the emergence of the European enlightenment, which appreciates the world in terms of absolutes and subsumes difference. Of course, and as the experiences of colonialism affirm, it is a mote point whether power was ever meant to reside in the hands of the "masses" in the representative democracies that slowly emerged from the events of the American and French revolutions.

While populist and established political figures are fighting over the ratio-nality of the political sphere, both sides are doing so through maintaining old ways of seeing the world—the temporal-spatial modalities of modernity. Though both sides prescribe different approaches, both rely on the creation of "I" as both a preformed and preforming being, a transitive being, through its relationship to the state or a people. In the case of the populist, this identity, *to be*, is created in context of a national or ethnic identity, which understands its roots as a historic project. In the case of the established figures, they have no choice but to rely on old ways of seeing the world. The state here is under-stood as the concrete, material, and symbolic manifestation of rationality with the context of a wider interstate realm. The "I" of the democratic nation-state is preformed, a transitive being, through its relationship to the state and oper-ates in support of settled interests or identities. This approach to the social and political does simplify reality as rational, or rational from a chosen perspective at least. However, this construction of the social and political world understands intransitive preferences as irrationality, and not amend-able to logical engagement or analysis. As such, the "I" of modernity was always only a partial account which fails to provide a dynamic account of a culture's internal heterogeneity, its *constituent power*, the intransitivity of our relational mode of being. This process of the identity-formation of the citizen places blockages on "I"s' relationship to otherness, of a wider humanity.

And then the shock of SARS-CoV-2 emerged from the world. Many have maintained an enthusiasm or concern about the disruptive potential of new technologies and artificial intelligence. However, three aspects of the public's response to the SARS-CoV-2 outbreak have revealed the anomalies and inadequacies of our current social, economic, and political systems. Viewed positively, this awareness could, in the long term, provide the positive disruptive potential that shakes a society out of its complacency. First, after a *century of the self*, humanity revealed itself not in the staid duality of the individual or the community, but in the relationship *between* the social and the individual, the socioemotional scaffolding that links one human being to another: social environment mattered. It was the expression of local population's everyday humanity, in the everyday kindnesses between peoples and local creativity that contained the worse of the effects of COVID-19. It was real human contact from the doctors, nurses, care-workers, cleaners, and the immigrant that provided the medical necessity for many thousands of people to survive. Also, and maybe more importantly, it was these people, that held the hands of those who died in isolation, that allowed our friends and loved ones to share their final moments through that most human of desires, contact with another.

Second, our communities were not saved from imploding by the *Masters of the Universe*. It was the people who take our bins away, who deliver our mail, who stand for hours behind a till, or stack shelves, or clean our hospitals, the immigrants within our communities that allowed us to avoid close contact with the real world. With neoliberalism's emphasis on human capital, the decolonialist has rightly drawn our attention to the dehumanizing effects of colonialism and the need for it to be linked with its prehistory of racialized commodification of people. These are the forgotten faces of modernity that allowed us to feel a sense of personal distance and impunity in the challenge of a competitor that adapted and improved itself. However, this sense of personal impunity coexists with the knowledge that for the most disadvantaged, life is dominated with a struggle against stagnating wages and who teeter on the precipice of poverty. This antinarrative of truth reveals an underside of modernity as their practical connection with democracy being enhanced through the recurring supplication of a "X" and the knowledge of a triptych of suffering. They know that compared to those predestined to practice social and economic advantage, that the education that they receive will be poor and instrumental. They know that the societies in which they reside will restrict the opportunities that their lives encounter. As well as knowing that their lives will be "poor, nasty, brutish," they know that compared to those with social and economic resources that their lives will be short. They know these facts because they encounter them every day as social freedoms.

Third, the horizon of democracy that we have created for ourselves understands the cultural, societal, economic, and political institutions that constitute the state, as being the arbiter of identity, rationality, and method of reasoning. However, for many, the space of democracy, globally and locally, is divided. Formed through the imaginative horizon of reformation theology and a pessimistic portrayal of what it is to be human, there is a space of democracy that predestines socioeconomic advantages to those with existing socioeconomic advantage. Existing alongside this, there is another space of democracy, connected as a mirror image, connected but closed, for those predestined to be without such advantages.

This antinarrative of the ideals of modernity is strongly enunciated through the decolonial project, but this is also experienced in the capitals, major cities, towns, and villages of the "West." However, what gave succour to our communities globally was the mobilization of the locality of politics. This was brought about through a dynamic critical cooperation between the state, the local, individuals, and collaboration between regions. What our communities' reactions to the SARS-CoV-2 pandemic demonstrated was that intelligent problem-solving directed at a problem of common concern is achieved not just by the individual, solely, or by the community, solely. Rather, intelligent problem-solving *emerged* as a function of the *betweenness* of individual and the community, locally, to provide a means of *familiar*, real-world solutions. Drawing on the *familiar*, the ontic, and the epistemic resources of communities allowed people to address this problem of common concern. This process allowed them to recognize themselves as legitimate independent sources of rationality.

If there is to be any benefaction to these recent events, it is that can provide the ground for reconsidering and renovating how we think about the relationship between institutions and the individual. Not as the redundant dichotomized duality between self and institutions, self and the other, and self and the world. This does offer the hope of the creation of "open," less concrete and distinct communities, to provide a pluralistic, relational, creative, embodied, and independent source of legitimate rationality for a more democratic way of being and acting in the world. However, while this does offer a route to living in a more democratic way, the societal dynamics that SARS-CoV-2 has revealed also contain the dangers of more authoritarian ways of being in the world.

COSMOPOLITANISM

Cosmopolitanisms emerge as one response of the human desire to reconcile the interconnected contradictions of being a social (infinite) and finite being: space and time, unity and diversity, inside and outside. It represents a self-awareness of our finite totality through the realization of what one does not share with those outside of one's own totality. However, cosmopolitanism does not begin in the word, a discipline, or doctrine, but through our enactive engagement with the world. Cosmopolitanism is concerned with how the interactions between cultures, or peoples, are a reciprocal phase of societal development which provides a means of internal transformation. Here the emphasis is on transcending the limits, boundaries, of internal approaches, through the recognition of mutual influencing, shared or unbalanced experiences, and entwined processes, to arrive at new affirmations of the human condition. Rather than understand the state, the society, or the individual as an autonomous and distinct sole legitimate source of rational legitimacy, cosmopolitanism tries to provide another pool of resources to answer the contradictions of the human condition: inside and outside, unity and diversity, space and time.

Intertwined with a foreground of demographic changes, international terrorism, environmental concerns, and questions of political and economic legitimacy, cosmopolitanism has come to play an important role in the debate concerning the supposed deficiencies of the nation-state as well as concerns over the effects of unfettered neoliberal globalization. As a critique of globalization, cosmopolitanism claims to respond to the ideas that now normalize the lives of the global population. So far, the theoretical possibilities of the cosmopolitan imagination have been explored mainly through a supposed unique Greek genealogy of the sentiment. For the "standard narration" (Inglis 2014), in the Western tradition, cosmopolitanism's philosophical and etymological roots lie in the Greek idea of "a citizenship of the world." In this narrative, the concept of cosmopolitanism has a rich theological, philosophical, and political lineage. This is most associated with, and draws on, the Stoics, Pauline Christianity, and Enlightenment thinkers such as Immanuel Kant. In its usage, we find cosmopolitanism being expressed as mobility not only in travel but also in respect of the imaginative potentiality for social reflexivity. It is also used to express a global openness that can appreciate other cultures and traditions. This, so the argument goes, leads to cultural and individuals enriching their social reflexivity in their encounter with the other. As will be apparent this involves self-transformation that recognizes incompleteness both societally and in the individual.

Finally, and more recently, we find it being regarded as a multidisciplinary and interdisciplinary movement. Cosmopolitan understanding in the fields of political and social theory calls for a deeper engagement with civilizations other than our own. This recognizes that the field can no longer afford to remain disconnected from the practices, lives, and worldviews of others. As an approach, it calls for a fusion of horizons that encourage us to consider ourselves as citizens of the world and to take this allegiance to the world community as relevant in our moral deliberations. Here, rather than being characterized as a specific doctrine or fixed idea, cosmopolitanism has come to be understood as a generalized common research agenda, the ambition of which is to structure a non-Western centric approach to social theory. Such an approach represents an emerging paradigm of social and political analysis that draws on the recognition of global entanglement and diffusion to describe an evolving and multifaceted social reality. As a non-Western centric social science, it would seek to identify those features of all civilizations and societies that display internal logics of development and is characterized by a new role for the imagination in social life. This it would do without privileging Western perspectives. This orientation toward world openness can be regarded as central to the cosmopolitan imagination. It is the interplay between self, other, and world, and a third-space which emerges between through this interconnection, that the cosmopolitan moment becomes evident. In such a process of encounter, we find the opportunity not only to correct our own self-understanding, but to engage in creativity when we consider these challenges. At the moment of this transformative dialogue, newness is created. Multidisciplinary and transdisciplinary by instinct, prominent examples of such an approach to imaginative global research are the works of the Gerard Delanty and Walter Mignolo, which this book will be exploring.

CRITICAL COSMOPOLITANISM AS CRITIQUE AND COOPERATION

Many have criticized the Western cosmopolitan project, as described by the "standard narrative." Such criticisms have focused on its abstractness, its disembodiment, and its inclination to seek only values in other traditions that resemble its own, and its inability, beyond platitudes, to use other perspectives to reflect on the relationship between self, other, and the world. While methodologically cosmopolitanism would support the vital critical claim of incompleteness, in the rejection of exclusive oppositions, in terms of its research commitments, it is dedicated to accepting the limitations of its own social consciousness. That is, rather than being an attitude of "openness" and form of dialog capable of acknowledging the agonistic dimension of the social, as well as the contingent nature of any type of social order, cosmopolitanism is reliant on its own bias and prejudice. Here it is understood that such an account of cosmopolitan reason does not cherish a dialogic understanding of reasoning and communication. Instead, it clings to argumentative strategies that only find confirmation bias in the values of other cultures. While the Western cosmopolitan imagination looks to new ways of being and acting in the world, in its projection onto the world of its assimilatory values, values that are myopic to the dark side of the moral history of the West, it is neither based in the real world nor can it provide a means of imagining a new-world-to-come. A corollary of this is the willful blindness to the long-term consequences of "our" engagement with the "rest" in terms of our own psychosocietal identity and on the blockages to resilience of colonialized and exploited communities around the world. While the cosmopolitan imagination of the "West" does cherish a view of the world as diverse, in failing to account for the question of race and colonialism to extend beyond its own theoretical horizon, it is neither immanent nor can it provide the means of transcendence.

Yet the human sentiment that gives cosmopolitanism its appeal has not only been expressed as an exclusively Western universalistic phenomenon. Non-Western traditions have nurtured and articulated these sentiments through multifaceted approaches to reason, reasoning, concepts of the human condition, and methods of inquiry from those that have been appropriated by Western theorists. These traditions have generated conclusions as to nature of humanity, its relationships not only among itself but also to other inhabitants of the planet as well as to the planet itself. For instance, in his *Geography of Human Life*, the Japanese thinker Makiguchi "taught the importance of realizing that the individual human being is more than just citizen of a nation state" (Henderson and Ikeda 2004). Desmond Tutu has also brought a similar perspective from the African tradition of Ubuntu, the self existing within a field of connections, where "my humanity is caught up and inextricably bound up in yours" (Tutu 2005). Similarly, from the Indian subcontinent, Rabindranath Tagore challenged us to overcome uncritical loyalty to nationalism and build a world not broken into fragments. As a result, it would not be wrong to refer to "cosmopolitanisms" rather than "cosmopolitanism."

I am mindful of the opportunities for the development of a theoretical position capable of undermining the abstractness of the temporal available through the great philosophical or theological practices of the world. These do offer the potential, through their emphasis on the relational nature of being human, to enrich the personal, intracultural, and intercultural psychosociological imagination. However, while one must recognize the importance of Western, Confucius, or African universal expressions of cosmopolitanism, caution must be maintained as they, like the "standard narrative," are only particular manifestations of the sentiment of cosmopolitanism.

The global family of cosmopolitanisms, Western, the Asian branches, Islamic, African, and Latin American, stand within a marketplace of convergent ideas, each vying for the attention of enthusiastic enunciators. The initial concern of this current work is that such projects lead to a replication of the domineering and lack of contextuality that has rightly taxed post/decolonial thinkers in terms of the imposition of Western-derived social sciences. Though non-Western forms of cosmopolitanism stress the relational, the intransitive nature of being, they do so as an axiomatic claim. If cosmopolitanism is enunciated as a self-evident truth of being human, no matter how

appealing a contraposition, this represents the closure of fundamental questions concerning the human condition and signifies a claim of completeness.
This excludes internal heterogeneity and reduces relationality to the reification of *to be* as singular expressions of how communities have reconciled the
tension between relationality and individuality. As such, the same arguments
and concerns that have been raised against the dominance of Western-derived
social science could be applied to the imposition of a system of social thought
generated from one or other of the world's great systems of practice. This
is not to say that global traditions do not cherish the diversity of the human
condition. Neither is this to suggest that how global communities have reconciled the tension between individuality and community is of no interest
to the cosmopolitan theorist. However, in the essentialization of identity it
recognizes human diversity as a mirror image and against the background of
human history, of relative closure; fundamental truths have been answered.
Like the critique of the "standard narrative," it seems difficult to understand
the imaginative possibilities of relational modalities as both immanent and
with the potential of transformation if it cannot escape the theoretic horizons
of its life-world.

If the "standard narrative" of cosmopolitanism is tied to its own prejudices, and we have similar concerns about the efficiency of drawing on other
cosmopolitanisms, at the exterior to Eurocentrism or alterior, how are we to
proceed to fulfill the promise of cosmopolitanism: to think the unthinkable.
How are we to provide a language of fluid geotheoretical boundaries for critical dialogue? Cosmopolitanism, as a critical resource of society, cannot be
reified through institutions, texts, political parties, traditions, or expressions
of temporal certainty. As a traveling theory, it is capable of descending into
the historical conditions to which all human understanding is subsumed, in
the relationship between self, other, and the world, to then ascend to a critique
of ideology of the present? It is against the background of the plurality of
cultures, our self-awareness of finite totality, that begins to reveal the critical
transcultural potential of incompleteness, in the "gap" in-between in which
different cultures meet, of a self-revolutionizing logic for *becoming*.

However, before we engage in our tasks, we need to consider how does
a cosmopolitan think? This may seem such a naive question. And yet, the
answer to it is only assumed in the literature and lies at the heart of the problem of cosmopolitanism. Is one a cosmopolitan because one moves thought
beyond the confines of methodological nationalism or is one a cosmopolitan
through engaging with the consciousness that arises at the border where
different forms of consciousness meet? These may or may not be cosmopolitanisms. In our examples, Western and other forms of cosmopolitanism,
thinking like a cosmopolitan becomes a treacherous endeavour, leading to
external assimilation, and a means of internal control, if based on axiomatic

self-evident truths. These self-evident truths are prejudiced through a reliance on temporal moments of clarity, of beginnings, and of uniqueness. This fails to recognize thought's own incompleteness and sociohistorical interconnectedness across and between multiple sources of creativity. Both fail to return thought from "out-there" to "in-here," through which to provide for internal transformation—being cosmopolitan. Remaining "out-there" leads to assimilation and the reification of "in-here."

Therefore, if an account of critical cosmopolitan social theory is to overcome the frustrated potential of both the critical and decolonial projects, but which draws on their positive aspects and the relationality of other cosmopolitanisms, it must necessarily be inclined to endlessly shatter the meaning of reality and legitimize practical creativity. This follows from the fundamental proposition of cosmopolitanism, our incompleteness. As a form of reflexive negation, incompleteness alerts us to the danger of understanding the human condition as merely *to be* or of essentializing our being through our multitudinous, relational, and interconnected ways of being in the world. Rather, cosmopolitanisms should recognize that creativity emerges as a critical function of the enactment between the finiteness of our existence and the infinite otherness of our nature as a social being. Not beginning in the temporal, *to be*, in the transitivity of the cultural, social, political, and economic world, or as identified as the imposition of preforming relational roles, in *A Post-Western account of Critical Cosmopolitan Social Theory* I am concerned with *becoming* through the creativity of the "deep structure" of self and its relationality with other and the world. This links and intertwines endogenous and exogenous sociohistorical experiences and provides points of critique from outside the dominant modes of social, economic, and political conventions through which new affirmations can be created. Though there are different forms of reflexive negation open to global theorists, one could look to Hegelian or Jainian systems of logic, for example, in our work this will be carried out through the application of emptiness, from the work of the Japanese philosopher, Watsuji Tetsurō. Emptiness, rather than being an account of absolute skepticism will function in our work as a reflexive negation, negating the absoluteness of *constituted reality*, but allowing for new spaces to be formed through the articulation from the *constitute space of reality*.

This re-evaluation of how a cosmopolitan thinks becomes manifest when we try to understand the space of the interstate, the intrastate, and the personal. The first and most obvious task of critical cosmopolitan social theory is to provide a method of intercultural critique and cooperation. Reflexive negation, as a relational logic in the realm of the inter-national, accommodates the observation that a finite state, though immanent, cannot form an identity without the mediation of the plurality historical finite agents. For critical cosmopolitan social theory, this is beyond notions of comparative philosophy. This penetrative and honest stance, understood as reciprocal transactions between different intercultural communities, aims at the development of new affirmations of the relationship between self, other, and the world. This is not the rejection of ideals, per se, only that these should not be taken to mean more than conditional affirmations. Instead, through critique and cooperation as a heuristic tool, against the background of the historical "openness" of communities, assumed interconnection and cultural entanglement, cosmopolitan social theory represents the possibility of the reimagining conventional truths through the exposure of self, other, and the world to a logic of reflexive negation.

Such intercultural dialogue can only be considered authentic and productive if it is carried out from the level of intracultural analysis which enunciates from the meeting point of the axes of the ideals of a society and the multifarious conditions of individual life-worlds. This provides a "pluralist" vision of collective agency which moves away from claims to access to a "context-transcendent" system of principles and requires that we have in place a less distinct notion of inside and outside. Instead, this book looks to the local within an open community of *shared consciousness* to provide multiple loci of enunciation as independent sources of rational legitimacy within communities. Such a scheme demands the inclusion of multiple sources of reasoning, reason, agenda-setting, and decision-making processes. It looks to the revalorization of the "local" as a site of grassroot intra- and inter-state democratic social and political creativity and for the articulation of injustices as a spatial phenomenology.

If change is possible, if limitations are to overcome at the level of the inter- and intracultural exchange, then personhood also needs to be part of the process. In understanding collective agency as pluralistic, open, incessant, and creative, rejects the closure of political identity. This requires an account of being human that does not reduce existence to passivity, through abstraction or essentialization. In refocusing analytical attention on to the practices of everyday life, offers a way of understanding being human as creative, enactive, and generative within the fluidity of space.[4] Temporal claims have tied human agency to the confines of the state, a nation, or a "people" as the sole arbiters of reason and rationality. In moving away from perceptual, conceptual, and linguistic reification, requires that the subject must gain independence from not only external coercion, *negative liberty*, but that a society must provide the structures or conditions that would be required for self-realization to be expressed, *positive liberty*. However, in the account of human agency that I will put forward in *A Post-Western account of*

---

[4] See also Parr, T., & Friston, K. J. (2018).

Critical Cosmopolitan Social Theory, the concern is not the support of rights, per se, but with the articulation of negative and positive rights as points of critique. The move away from the reification of social ontology as a neutral space toward an understanding of human agency as creative and enactive begins with an embodied subject. This subject constantly and generatively, theory-forming of their world, engages with their world which is understood spatially. Appreciating the circular relationship between our bodies, our thoughts, and our actions with the social and natural environment provides for a political ontology in which the role between power and the individual becomes immediate. Though we are immersed in our social and natural worlds, through disabling the neutrality of social space allows us to turn our attention to the enunciation of injustices rather the articulations of "neutral" ideals. Rather than rely on the staid antinomy of self and other, this allows for not only the infinity of otherness but also infinity of self:self and society are offered the space for change.

The final task of this introduction is to introduce cosmopolitan space. This requires that we initiate into the debate two heuristics devices for cosmopolitan space; the space in which cosmopolitan communication takes place. Our spatial heuristic devices are diametric duality and concentric duality.[5] We will go into more detail about these devices in the next chapter, but for now, I want to outline briefly what they are and what role they play in this book. Cosmopolitanism, as it is presently practiced, structures space as a diametric duality. Diametric dualities represent the closure of fundamental questions concerning the human condition and signify a claim of completeness. The distinctive characteristics of such a space are the assumed separation between systemic parts, the symmetry as a mirror image, and against the background of human history, a relative closure. This represents notions such as that of modernity versus tradition, or self versus other, and men versus women. Importantly, though connectedness between self and other is recognized, structural blockages to individual and societal openness are evident with no internal mechanism for change because the "ideal" of self is complete. Why would "I" in my encounter with other need to change if I am complete. While they do represent an articulation of a particular expression of the cosmopolitan ideal, in their concreteness they can only ever be partial. The result of this is the proliferation of cosmopolitanisms which fail to productively engage with each other. By engaging productively, we understand as the practical

---

[5] I would like to note my indebtedness to the work of Dr. Paul Downes for his work on Lévi-Strauss which this project has applied to the relational sociology of Watsuji, See Downes, 2012. It is important to note that, following Lévi-Strauss, in human societies diametric and concentric relational structures coexist. However, I am concerned with providing an account of critical cosmopolitan thought. Therefore, the emphasis will be on in understanding human space as a means of overcoming the obstacles to political and theoretical experimentation.

activity of cosmopolitanism that transcend the limits, boundaries, of its internal approach, through the recognition of mutual influencing, shared or unbalanced experiences, and entwined processes, to arrive at new affirmations of the human condition.

Such an approach is made possible through understanding social space through the heuristic device of concentric dualities. The fundamental claim of cosmopolitanism is the notion of incompleteness. If epistemic and ontic diametric dualities represent blockages in terms of the creation of knowledge, concentric dualistic social structures acknowledge our incompleteness. This is to accept that our relations within social space are less concrete and that the production of knowledge is based on cooperation and critique, rather than certainties that set up diametric dualities, that is, cosmopolitan versus noncosmopolitan. In recognizing incompleteness allows for a mechanism of epistemic change that leads to ontic transformation-changes in the production of knowledge within a pluralistic community, constitutive power, will lead to changes in constituted arrangements. What we are proposing in this book is that cosmopolitanism can only fulfill its function as a critique of the present if we understand the activity of critical cosmopolitan thought within social space as a concentric duality. If we understand the relationship between self-other-world as an assumed connection, then an epistemic and ontic landscape is revealed in which actors within different spaces act upon each other, individually or societally, as a phase of reciprocal development. This should not be understood as some sort of denunciation of tradition. Such schemata are not contrary to conventional experience, only in the claims of closure in respect of conventional fictions. In such an approach, the cosmopolitan theorist, when considering matters of common concern, would collaborate across borders and transdisciplinary in bringing together, at the point, where ideals meet the practices of life, to bring about epistemic and ontic synergies.

As we will explore in the first two chapters of this book the role that diametric dualities play in the cosmopolitan imagination at present is the process of assimilation and the eradication of difference. Nevertheless, the illumination of diametric dualities such as in the decolonial project's denunciation of injustices, in the face of the projection of Western ideals, does offer an the opportunity for their articulation. In this sense, consciousness relates to social reality by limiting possibilities through the adoption of certain objects that are "convenient fictions" (diametric dualities) in respect of problem-solving. However, when combined with our creative notion of concentric dualities, this identification of injustices provides for the new affirmations of the relationship between self, other, and the world. To do otherwise is to retreat within one's own sense of completeness.

INTRODUCING WATSUJI TETSURŌ

In 1889, in the Japanese Prefecture of Hyogo, a remarkable man was born. The second son of a physician, Watsuji Tetsurō, would spend a life accumulating and engaging with knowledge of the human condition from around the world to produce possibly the first account of global philosophy. That is an account of the human condition, of the relationship between individuality and human communities, with all their tensions, opportunities, and contingences that this brings, and which was capable of drawing on all cultural enunciations.

If the decolonial cosmopolitan project aims at overcoming the universalizing tendencies of modernity, then the thought contained within Watsuji's work is representative of decolonial cosmopolitanism. Of course, a prominent strand of interpretation of Watsuji's work, and that of the twentieth-century Kyoto School of philosophy of which he was on the fringes, is that their work exhibited a tendency toward *nihonjinron*. These are theories that focus on the "uniqueness" of Japanese national and cultural identity and how Japan and the Japanese should be understood. Such critical tendency has continued in works on Watsuji and the Kyoto School such as those produced by Bernard Bernier (2006) and Chiara Brivio (2009) who both argued that Watsuji's ethical system merely represented a reflection of the imperial Japanese state's eschatological image of being human. Of the critical writings, Sakai Naoki's *Translation and Subjectivity* (1997) presents an important critique of Watsuji's work which is perceived as cultural essentialism. In an earlier work, Sakai had argued that Watsuji's ethics sanctioned a "blind leap into the destiny of the community," (Sakai 1993: 266), which had resulted from the construction of the totality as both immanent in and anterior to individual consciousness. In this reading of Watsuji, the dialectic between the individual and the collective represents the tyranny of the collective over the individual. Against such a scholarly and historical background, it would seem difficult to argue that Watsuji could be a decolonial cosmopolitan thinker.

However, it is possible to provide a reading of Watsuji that acknowledges the tensions within his work, but which in identifying these draws out its potential to contribute to global social theory. Just like the decolonial and cosmopolitan projects, Watsuji was concerned with the effects of modernity on colonized nations. Rather than proposing an ontic and epistemic account aimed at grounding thought on a new, Japanese account, Watsuji, as I will discuss in the following chapters, was looking for connections between East and West. Such an account was focused on intercultural learning and the identification of limitations. As such, contrary to Sakai, the account that will be put forward in this book acknowledges the historical-social nature of knowledge production-ontic and epistemic location. Such an understanding, to draw on Castoriadisian[6] terminology, views the "social imaginary" as having the characteristic of openness and creativity which would allow for continual alteration of the given meanings and the innovation and change of significations. This is not to set aside ontic and epistemic location and its importance for subjectivity, but only to weaken their claims, and to therefore identify cultural limitations. Such a reading suggests that for Watsuji communities are, far from being hermitically sealed designators, fluid and interconnected. Furthermore, it is this interconnectedness that is necessary for intracommunal transformation. This, as will be developed in the third chapter, suggests that Watsuji is positing a relative universalism as opposed to an absolute universalism of modernity: an account of multiple modernities, though an account that does not set out ideals, such as European modernity.

Rather than present the individual as the homo economicus, or as the norm-following and role-playing actor of the homo sociologicus, Watsuji was instead concerned with exploring how ethical practice is enacted within concrete human relationships. Watsuji's two-stage social-epistemology of *fūdo* and *aidagara* stresses the interdependence of the individual and society.[7] Watsuji's concepts of *fūdo* (milieu) and *aidagara* (betweenness) gives a two-stage account of a relational socioepistemology. Drawing on the Sino-Japanese linguistic tradition, *fūdo* literally means wind and earth. In the concept of fūdo Watsuji aimed to "uncover" the fundamentally social and intersubjective nature of human existence, and the resulting definition of human existence, *Ningen Sonzai*, as inextricably both individual and social. Watsuji did not treat fūdo as solely the natural environment, but as a concept in which biological, physical, and geographical features exert forces on human living and through which human beings in turn transform the environment. In this view *fūdo* is a relational web in which life unfolds.

Watsuji stresses how *aidagara* involves not merely reason, but the body, feelings, the will, everyday action-connections, gestures, vocal and bodily expressions, and that these are mediated through concrete things (*fūdo*) and practical act-connections. He argues that the immediate connection with another is possible because the physical body is an expressive vehicle that externalizes, via "practical act-connections," aspects of another's subjectivity in such a way that I have immediate perceptual and emotional access to them: we share consciousness. Though aspects of their subjectivity stay transcendent, it is the case that the body, as a communicative modality,

---

[6] This is referring to the important work of Cornelius Castoriadis.
[7] It is important to stress that though fūdo and aidagara must be understood together, this understanding must be accompanied by an appreciation of the societal dynamics of emptiness (reflexive negation).

makes manifest other aspects of subjectivity within the *aidagara* of social interaction. This is not a merely cognitive account but indicates for Watsuji the "subjective extendedness" of the social self.

Here we return to the question of how does a cosmopolitan thinker and the third of Watsuji's concepts to be used in this book, emptiness. In the second part of the book, emptiness will be fulfilling the role of reflexive negation for the cosmopolitan imagination. Derived from the contribution of thinkers such as the second-century (CE) Nāgārjuna, the concept of emptiness appears in Watsuji's scheme as double negation, or the two negations that characterize the structure of being human. Watsuji writes:

> We cannot first presuppose individuals, and then explain the establishment of social relationships among them. Nor can we presuppose society and from there explain the occurrence of individuals. Neither the one nor the other has "precedence." (Watsuji 1996 [1938]: 102)

Watsuji's purpose in applying emptiness to social and personal analysis was his desire to overcome what he saw as the one-sidedness of other ethical systems, say of the individual or of community. Emptiness allowed him to consider key structures of human existence, subject versus object, individual versus totality, as nondualities. Here what we would now understand as a postfoundational approach to social science does not attempt to erase completely such ontological categories such as the individual or community but only to weaken their ontological status and to stress their reciprocity. This ontological weakening does not lead to the assumption of the total absence of all grounds, but rather to the assumption of the impossibility of a final ground and an awareness of contingency. As will be discussed below there are issues with Watsuji's presentation of emptiness. However, it is possible to provide a reading of emptiness as a critical epistemic tool for social analysis and normative struggles that delivers the epistemic basis for a postfoundational account of critical cosmopolitan social theory not as a metaphysical account but as a basis for a nondualistic heterogeneous method of social analysis.

Delanty's and Mignolo's accounts of critical cosmopolitanism are formed through triadic models. However, though Mignolo and Delanty do emphasize the critical aspect of thought these are only partial accounts. To overcome this, following our process of critique and cooperation, Watsuji's account of social ontology is introduced to the positive aspects of critical theory, the protection of the individual, and decolonial theories of sociohistorical identity and the promise of decolonial heterogeneity. Watsuji's work lacks critical perspective through which to enunciate an account capable of robustly critiquing over-positioning of individuality or the over-positioning of sociogenic norms.

The introduction of the individual of critical theory and the sociohistorical identity of decolonial theory to *aidagara* provides a substantive critical perspective of how inside and outside are interconnected. The outcome of this synthesis is similarly a triadic model. This is composed of an ultimate unit of analysis being a post-individual subjectivity, that the encounter occurs within a concentric understanding of space, a relative immanent universalism, and the result of this encounter is a radical cosmopolitan imagination focused on matters of common concern. Rather than a grand projection of ideals onto the world, this overcomes the present restrictions placed on the possibilities of the cosmopolitan imagination through expanding agency by safeguarding the infinity of otherness and simultaneously requiring the opening of infinity within self.

CHAPTERS

As may be already be apparent to the reader, there can be no denying that the subject matter of this book is difficult. While it could not be described as light-reading, I have endeavoured to make the book accessible to the general reader. To this end, I have included a glossary of frequently used technical terms. I have also structured and written the book in a way that makes clear technical terms. This may make the prose, at times, repetitive or drawn out, but my intention is for the book to be available as a resource to people who are quaintly described as "normal." Considering that the subject focus of this book is "normal" people, I feel that this is appropriate.

Chapter 1 is intended to introduce the general reader to a range of perspectives on the cosmopolitan imagination. However, unlike most works of cosmopolitan critical theory, it also provides alternative accounts from the decolonial movement, the Buddhist tradition, and the Chinese tradition of Confucius. The point of the introduction of these accounts is to illustrate that the ultimate unit of analysis of cosmopolitanism, who you are, need not be the abstract individual of "Western" accounts of the concept. The third aim of the chapter draws on the central proposition of cosmopolitanism, our incompleteness, to discuss how this entails that if cosmopolitanism is to remain critical, relevant, and *familiar*, then it must engage with other global relational sociologies through the process of critique and cooperation.

Chapter 2 begins to focus on the critical nature of cosmopolitan thought and will develop as follows. The first section is concerned with setting out the theoretical landscape of critical theory for the general reader. This is important as it will give you a broad introduction to the development of critical theory through which to situation the proposed synthesis of Delanty's and Mignolo's work. The decolonial critique represents a significant challenge not only to critical theory, but also to the future of democracy, the international order, environmental studies, and capitalism. Compassion for the other is central to Mignolo's work. The concluding section begins the process of developing a new affirmation of critical theory and will provide the basis of what will be developed fully in the second part of this book.

Chapter 3 aims to introduce his ideas and his contribution to global thought. To achieve these goals, the chapter will present key concepts from Watsuji's ethical vocabulary and highlight the cultural roots from which he draws on. Within the circles of Japanese philosophy, Watsuji and his work, is a divisive figure. However, what we will attempt to demonstrate in this chapter is that Watsuji's work represents a proto form of decolonial theory. As such, this chapter suggests that he offers intellectual resources for the practical activity of decolonialism.

The first part of this book is concerned with largely deconstructive activities. Chapter 4 begins the process of reconstruction through presenting the concept of emptiness as the epistemic basis, a form of self-revolutionizing logic, for a post-Western cosmopolitan social theory. How does a cosmopolitan think? The answer to this is not as straightforward as one may imagine. What we are looking for in this chapter is an account of emptiness, as used by Watsuji, that can perform the function of cosmopolitanism's fundamental premise of incompleteness. Derived from the contribution of thinkers such as the second-century (CE) Nāgārjuna, the concept of emptiness appears in Watsuji's scheme as double negation, or as the two negations that characterize the structure of being human, individuality and society. This does not lead to the assumption of the total absence of all grounds, but rather to the assumption of the impossibility of a final ground, or teleology, and an awareness of contingency and contestation.

In chapter 5, we will explore the cosmopolitan tasks of inter- and intracultural analysis. This will be carried out through bringing together the relative universalism of the decolonial theorist and the first part of Watsuji's socio-epistemology, *fūdo*. Such a spatial perspective provides a means to critique the normativity of temporality to develop new forms, new temporalities, of social and political experimentation. Here we will outline the potential for a model of participatory democracy as critique and cooperation that operates within the social spatial dynamics of nullification by jury. This provides a localized and grounded locus of enunciation capable of undermining the one-directionality of power between ruler and ruled.

Chapter 6 looks to provide an account of agency as an enactive being. The last chapter has seen the individual immersed within their society. Though we suggest that existent social spatial dynamics could be exploited to provide pluralistic sources of rational legitimacy, this requires a pluralistic account of agency. To achieve this, rather than essentialize individuality or sociohistorically, informed identity, "docks" the critical and positive elements of Delanty's and Mignolo's unit of analysis within Watsuji's account of *aidagara*. This allows us to understand creativity of the infinity of otherness and self as the outcome of the collision between the cultural, social, political, and economic world with our multitudinous and interconnected ways of being.

Chapter 1

Doing Cosmopolitanism

INTRODUCTION

On June 14th at the Prague European Summit 2017, the Czech Republic's minister of foreign affairs, Lubomír Zaorálek, told a remarkable story about how things have come to be (Wintour 2017; Zaorálek 2017). He began his speech by conceding that he was speaking to a room full of the elite and that "[Europe] was segmenting . . . in which different categories of Europeans are growing further apart. There is a Europe of Erasmus educated people who reap the benefits from economic integration and freedom of movement. And those who struggle against stagnating wages and teeter to the precipice of poverty. For whom economic integration is an existential threat." This, as he notes, carries with it threats to social cohesion and threats to political stability. Here he noted the failure of the inside of Western politics. This, he argued, was caused by the failure of politics to discuss the concerns raised by globalization. This was because at times he felt that the main problem was ourselves.[1] Therefore, what was required to address such concerns was the establishment of a "new equilibrium between Market liberalisation and social justice for all Europeans." The underlying point here was that the projects of globalization and the European Union (EU) have been carried out with an eye to the project rather than deeply considering the effects on local communities and the lives of the people in those communities.

However, he also noted that this was only one side of the debate concerning radicalism and discontent. To explore the other side Zaorálek drew on the works of the Czech philosophers Jan Patočka (1907–1977) and Zbigniew

---

[1] Of course, Zaorálek was referring here not just to the West, geopolitically, but to the economic and political elites of the West.

Brzezinski (1928–2017). As he explained, for Patočka, radicalism is a modern openly progressive gesture, and the point was how to acknowledge it and harness it. "For the first time in history," citing Patočka, "we have huge amount of people, conscious, more and more educated, informed, equipped with new expectations. This . . . mass of people, unstoppable energy, uncontrollable movement . . . world of lifting barriers . . . between countries and civilizations . . . a new openness on this planet . . . at the same time the propensity to violence chaos . . . the question is how to harness this movement of this power." Speaking of Brzezinski this represents "a waking that we are facing now . . . we should be focussed on the non-Western world's newly politically aroused masses. Long repressed political memories are fuelling in the large part the sudden and very explosive awakening energised by Islamist extremist in the Middle East. But what is happening in the Middle East today might be just as the beginning of a vital phenomenon to come out of Africa, Asia and even the pre-colonial peoples of the Western hemisphere in the years ahead . . . [this] something new, this delayed political self-assertion enhanced by delayed outrage and grief . . . which is surfacing for revenge . . . what we are facing now is the return of our colonial past."[2]

The primary aim of this chapter respond's to Zaorálek's concerns and recalls our discussion about the relationship between inside and outside, the past and present, unity and diversity, and how the changes of the last thirty years have effected spaces inbetween that we live in. We aim to move beyond both Western cosmopolitan theory's obsession with the rational actor or accounts that rely on an absolute sense of otherness to instead focus on the relational nature of being human as an enactive and generative agent. However, this is not to simply move to another existing paradigm of cosmopolitan thought. Though relational accounts are provided from non-Western sources, in their insistence of a foregrounding of identity, they fail to provide a means for internal change offered in the encounter with the other, inside or outside. Instead, we will suggest that cosmopolitanism is a movable site of ideas whose loci of enunciation are a pluralistic account of the agent. Rather than a simply intersubjectivity that ends at the body, I am concerned to explore the potential for radical social theory of the "deep structure" of the self and its reciprocal relationship with society. Such an account, we will argue provides the resources for intracultural transformation and intercultural exchange not reliant on the objectivity of necessity.

As I suggested in the introduction, cosmopolitanism represents one form of question through which to provide a series of answers to these contradictions

---

[2] I would not like to give the impression that, only in the twenty-first century, colonialized peoples are only now finding the resources to battle against colonialism. See Gopal (2019), for a superb and accessible history of resistance to colonialism.

of the human condition. It also represents a question of what story about ourselves we want to tell ourselves. There is something of the "magical realism" of Gabriel García Márquez (1927–2014) about the cosmopolitan imagination.[3] Just as García Márquez's writing shifts the reader's view to allow them to travel into the magical of everyday life, so too with the cosmopolitan imagination.[4] Cosmopolitanism purposely distorts spaces and times and highlights a commutation to something strange but strangely familiar: real and imagined. Cosmopolitanism provides a space from which "I" can enunciate from the in-betweenness of the cavernous ravine of the imaginary of *becoming* and what "I" experience as reality. It is an unsettling reminder of the necessarily incompleteness of how we experience ourselves, others, and the world. In the glare of our everyday reality, the images perceived through the cosmopolitan imagination appear ephemeral, to be somehow between here and somewhere beyond. And yet far from the abstraction of methodology individualism or the essentialization of identity, cosmopolitanism demonstrates a commitment to the sensuous nature of our reality. In linking the ideation of an essential humanity and the possibility of critical transformation, cosmopolitanism offers the opportunity to reimagine our relationship to ourselves, others, and the world. It is a commitment to engage with the lives and experiences of people which recognizes the precondition of the nonuniversal nature of my own development and values and how this can contribute to the greater good. In terms of the twenty-first-century consanguineal encounter of self, other, and the world, cosmopolitanism's reminder of our own incompleteness provides the opportunity to reimagine the rules of what could be. But when we critically ask from where could we draw on the cosmopolitan imagination, we are faced with the question of what "it" is?

Though this book is not meant as a history of cosmopolitanism, I shall first introduce the reader to the theoretical/historical terrain of debates surrounding the sentiment of cosmopolitanism. Alternative accounts from the decolonial movement, the Buddhist tradition(s), and the Chinese tradition of Confucius will allow the reader to see that the ultimate unit of analysis of cosmopolitanism, who we are, need not be the abstract individual of "western" accounts of the concept. I hope to show that cosmopolitanism is only ever

---

[3] Some Latin American writers have argued that magical realism could not be transposed to Western imaginaries because it is geographically/culturally anchored. See, for example, Takolander (2007: 213); Chanady (1995: 125–144). For a history of magical realism see Zamora and Faris (1995).

[4] The German art critic Franz Roh is credited with coining the phrase "magical realism" which he used to define the baroque or exotic elements in realistic paintings. However, the use of the term as a narrative strategy only emerged in the work of the Cuban writer Alejo Carpentier (1949) who called it "real maravilloso," but theorized the concept as it pertained to literature. Therefore, while Marquez, in the popular literary imagination, has become synonymous with the term, its theoretical foundations were laid by Carpentier.

cosmopolitan if it engages with other relational ontologies through which it maintains its critical perspective.

After the collapse of the Soviet Union, the cosmopolitan approach became popular in the academic literature in part as a response to the omnipresent discourse of globalization which followed it. With the premature end of history proclaimed and in the aftermath of the events of September 11, 2001, the ideological struggle between the individualist universalism and a socialist universalism became a search for a response to growing global conflicts which could challenge the clash of civilizations thesis of Samuel Huntington.[5] Advocates of cosmopolitanism hope that it would have the potential to draw on the concrete experiences of communities globally to provide a means to address these concerns by acknowledging our interconnectedness. That by doing so it would be possible to go beyond the strategy of projected globalized fear that carries over the stasis of the cold war through to the new century. This could also provide a nonuniversalizing critique of the inhumanity of the inverted totalitarianism of the neoliberal agenda.

So far, the theoretical possibilities of the "standard narrative" (Inglis 2014) of the cosmopolitan imagination have been explored mainly through a supposed unique Greek genealogy of the sentiment. In the Western tradition, the concept of cosmopolitanism has a rich theological, philosophical, and political lineage. It is most associated with the Stoics, Pauline Christianity (Richter 2011; Carter 2001), and Enlightenment thinkers such as Immanuel Kant (Fine and Cohen 2002; Held 1995; Nussbaum 1997). The primary focus of theory has been on a formalist account that emphasizes the moral and legal demands of a world citizen. Diogenes of Sinope, the founder of Cynic philosophy, when asked where he belonged, is reported to have replied, "I am a citizen of the world." The core of the Cynic philosophy was to live in concord with the "law of nature" outside of conventional societal models. However, the idea of the Cosmopolis only begins to emerge in Stoic philosophy during the Greek and Roman Empires of the Mediterranean world. Stoic cosmopolitanism provides modern cosmopolitan researchers with not only the notion of "cosmos in which human kind might live together in harmony," but also, to some extent, the idea of "world citizenship" (Held 2005: 18; Couture and Nielsen 2005: 183).

However, in beginning the cosmopolitan project with the "standard narrative" of being a "citizen of the world" confines the cosmopolitan imagination. These are projects that have appropriated a human sentiment through a sleight of the etymologist's hand: the ancient Greeks invented the word, therefore, we will confine ourselves, substantively, to the Greek account. Doing so

---

[5] On this subject, see Huntington, Samuel P. (1993). The clash of civilizations? *Foreign Affairs*, 72(3), 22–49. Retrieved May 26, 2020 from *JSTOR*: www.jstor.org/stable/20045621.

perpetuates a characterization of understanding social and political phenomenon through the history of Western conceptual thought. Such a history has developed through a particular way of understanding the nature of the self, the world, and the universe. This is an understanding which itself was linked to the ascendency of particular groups to political, economic, social, and military power. However, if it is a claim of cosmopolitanism that the encounter with the other reveals one's own limitations, one's own incompleteness, and offers to expand one's own imaginative capabilities, restraining the cosmopolitan imagination within the European experience confines it within its own geo-theoretical horizon which subsumes it creative potential. In a world of conceptual interconnectivity, it seems to lack theoretical ambition not to productively engage with the imagination of the other, an imagination which has been developed through mutual phases of development with the self. This has the potential to illuminate the shadows within our own thought?

Being cosmopolitan is not a merely a "Western" preserve. Less widely reported iterations of non-European cosmopolitan thought are recognized in the diverse ancient works of numerous Egyptians, Hebrews, Chinese, Ethiopians, Assyrians, and Persians, where moral duties beyond the immediate community were advocated (see Brown and Held 2010: 3–4; for a wideranging discussion of non-Western and premodern forms of cosmopolitanism see Webb 2015). For instance, the ontology and axiology of the self and individual found in early Buddhist, African, and Confucian traditions differ considerably from those associated with European humanism. As Vinay Dharwadker (2001: 7) states the Buddhist tradition of cosmopolitanism foreshadows the Greek one in interesting ways. In the early Brahmanical social order, there was no way to be fully human except to belong by birth to a particular varna (caste group). Much as the Greeks had treated "barbarians" as outsiders, and as deficient in terms of humanity, so too did the Hindu system of embossed genealogical identities discriminately exclude the untouchables, those of indeterminate genealogy and foreigners. What both the Stoic and Buddhist examples demonstrate are ancient examples of open, inclusionary, and heterogeneous societies, as opposed to the closed, exclusionary, and self-homogenizing societies of the Greeks and Indo-Aryan peoples. What this suggests is the possibility of not one but many humanisms and that alternatives to the formalist vertical accounts of the political and the social are accessible.

These non-Western resources are worthy of our attention. As we shall explore in this chapter, one can find substantive capital from within these world views to address new questions for the exploration of our social and natural worlds. This is especially true when we consider the different processes of reasoning and methodologies that these traditions apply. These offer the opportunity to explore new questions on how we understand ourselves and our communities in the face of existential threats such as global warming. What I am suggesting is that cosmopolitanism finds its criticality in the "gap" between forms of consciousness. It is within this "gap" between what is, *to be*, and what could be, *becoming*, that the cosmopolitan imagination has the potential to spread new light on one's own limitations.

Being Cosmopolitan

In the opening sentence of Kant's "An answer to the question: what is enlightenment?" (1784), he wrote that "Enlightenment is man's emergence from his self-incurred immaturity. Immaturity is the inability to use one's own understanding without the guidance of another." This "attempt to define, explain, and deal with the human predicament through science as well as achieve mastery over it through the use of social technology" evolved in the ferment of eighteenth-century philosophy in Europe and provided the certainty of modernity (Kalekin-Fishman 2012). Modernity, characterized as a realization of the Enlightenment project, produced "a radicalized consciousness [detaching] itself from all previous historical connections and [understanding] itself solely in abstract opposition to tradition and history as a whole" (Habermas 2007 [1980]: 363–364). For Kant,

> The peoples of the earth have entered in varying degrees into a universal community, and it is developed to the point where a violation of laws in *one* part of the world is felt *everywhere*. The idea of a cosmopolitan law is therefore not fantastic and overstrained; it is a necessary complement to the unwritten code of political and international law, transforming it into a universal law of humanity. (Kant 2010 [1795])

From this perspective, modernity and human emancipation have identifiable temporal and spatial origins. This view of modernity sees the causal nature of modernity as a continuation of the universalizing progress of a "of logic and rationality the West inherited from ancient Greece" (Jahn 2012: 690). This has swept through a European mind, and now the rest of humanity and is rooted in a universalizing interpretation of history and subsequently of "progress."

Early Christianity is commonly seen as a secondary cosmopolitan source, with its stress on the equality of all human beings before a transcendent God. However, it was not until the thirteenth and fourteenth centuries that this Christian interpretation of Greco-Roman universalism began to flourish again in Europe (Carter 2001; Heater 1990). Yet, it was only as a consequence of the intellectual revolution, in Europe, initiated by Descartes and Spinoza that Enlightenment thinkers began to substitute the transcendent God that underpinned Christian conceptions of cosmopolitanism with the transcendence of history, science, and the modern subject (Vaughan-Williams 2007: 44). Following on from the Greco-Roman and Renaissance formulations of cosmopolitanism, this third generation of cosmopolitans assimilated the previous features of the ideal while grappling with its further implications in science, politics, and economics (Schlereth 1977: xxv).

Though there were many Enlightenment cosmopolitan thinkers, it is widely accepted that the legacy of Immanuel Kant is the most significant in terms of the cultivation of an enduring cosmopolitan ideal. *Perpetual Peace*, which famously promoted the idea that all rational beings are potential members of a single moral community, was based on the (presumed) values shared by "citizens of the world" (Kant 2006; Kleingeld 1998; Schlereth 1977; Vertovec and Cohen 2002: 10).

For Kant:

> The peoples of the earth have entered in varying degrees into a universal community, and it is developed to the point where a violation of laws in one part of the world is felt everywhere. The idea of a cosmopolitan law is therefore not fantastic and overstrained; it is a necessary complement to the unwritten code of political and international law, transforming it into a universal law of humanity. (Kant 2010 [1795])

Kant's cosmopolitanism reveals itself through a complex web of seven systematically discrete senses of cosmopolitanism: knowledge, morality, education, history, the order of "nature," local legal order, and federal/global legal order. Kant had sought a solid basis for cosmopolitanism to meet the criticisms directed against his predecessors such as the Abbé de St Pierre and Jean-Jacques Rousseau. A common understanding of Kantian cosmopolitanism rests on his account of hospitality, that is, the welcoming of distant strangers into ones' home, as the individual embodiment of his otherwise macro-politically oriented cosmopolitanism. For Kant, all men have a right to reciprocal hospitality anywhere in the world, "by virtue of their right to communal possession of the earth's surface" (Kant 1990: 106). And as a moral being, each individual has a duty to obey and understand the bonds and principles that unite him or her with other humans (Vaughan-Williams 2007: 44). On this interpretation, the borders of political communities do not bound moral duties but are universally applicable.[6]

---

[6] However, critiques of Kant note the limitations to who is included in, and excluded from, European understandings of humanity. Kant's understanding of racial hierarchies excluded those he understood to be less than human from his moral frames and therefore from ethical treatment and cosmopolitan engagement (see Charles W. Mills 1997). However, while I am not advocating on

However, as Hans Reiss has argued, the Kantian account of politics forms part of a multifaceted ontology of morality, since "the principle of universality demands that our social and political institutions should be governed and our public conflicts settled in a universal manner" (Reiss 1990: 20). In turn, this requires the existence of universally valid law, which should govern the realm of the political. Kant found such a basis in a teleological theory of nature. For Kant, the principal purpose of nature was a "universal cosmopolitan existence" through which all the "original capacities of the human race may develop." While the individual human being and community may believe that they are pursuing their own projects they are all along being "unwittingly guided in their advance along a course intended by nature" (Kant 1992: 41).

As would be expected moral cosmopolitanism has significantly informed the formulation of the various cultural and political cosmopolitanism approaches. The expansion of cultural diversity due to immigration, the rise in ethnic multiculturalism, and the blurring between international and national rights, has brought cosmopolitanism into the discussion about general citizenship (Cheah and Robin 1998; Eder and Giesen 2001). While rejecting both cultural relativism and ethnocentrism, cultural cosmopolitanism approaches are concerned with the problem of the recognition of difference and the respect for the variety of cultures (Kleingeld 1999). As Delanty points out (2009: 57), "cosmopolitan citizenship is understood in terms of a cultural shift in collective identities to include the recognition of others." Such a shift in cultural boundaries and identities vary in their application from the modification of the traditional definition of citizenship within the borders of the nation-state to global citizenship and various forms of transnational (Ong 1998) and post-national societies (Smith 2007). This multiplying of identities diminishes the importance of birthplace as a precondition for the recognition of one's rights, cosmopolitanism, Benhabib writes, " is furthered by such multiple overlapping allegiances which are sustained across communities of language, ethnicity, religion, and nationality" (cited in Delanty 2009: 57–58). Benhabib's cosmopolitanism serves as a democratic element for mediation between total orientations, universal norms, local movements, and public discourse. For example, she translates Kant's claim for hospitality to a concrete demand from the citizens

---

behalf of a Kantian notion of cosmopolitanism as Katrin Flikschuh and Lea Ypi point out there is a developmental trajectory, though underdeveloped, in Kant's writings on cosmopolitanism in respect of European relations with the non-European that is often not included in literature critical of Kant's cosmopolitanism. What Flikschuh and Ypi explore is the question of *why* Kant wrote Perpetual peace. What they ably demonstrate is that Kant, in part, was motivated by the effects of exploitation and abuse on populations outside Europe that had recently entered into trading relations with European traders. He was also concerned with the effects of this exploitation on the morality and character of European societies. He recognized that a society cannot exploit the other without there being lasting effects on the self (Flikschuh and Lea Ypi (eds) 2014).

of the nation-state to be obligated to the rights of asylum seekers, as well as minorities and immigrants. One way of considering the impact of increased multiculturalism is that it has begun a process of ethical change within nation-states. Such a process underpins a way in which citizens of different national states live and act toward "others" regardless of national boundaries and also within the context of transnational encounters (Benhabib 2002).

Extending this project, Nash (2006) suggests that the international human rights system can only set the ground for the development of a more cosmopolitan world order if ordinary people are able to identify themselves with the values that constitute this system. Here Bonnie Honig's corrective concept of agonistic Cosmopolitics aims to rescue a program of ethical commitment to global others from the perception of a taint of elitism and Eurocentrism expansionism. Drawing on Arendt's idea of the right to have rights she argues that the process of agonistic Cosmopolitics is a process of continuous generation of new ideas and requires the continuous engagement of the citizen (Honig 1993, 2009). In pursuit of notions such as "vernacular cosmopolitanism" (Bhabha 1996; Nava 2002, 2007), "rooted cosmopolitanism" (Appiah 1998, 2006), and "actually-existing cosmopolitanism as a reality of multiple attachments" (Robbins 1998), have been put forward to articulate a lived understanding that transcends the tension between universalism and particularism.

Other scholarship has attempted to overcome the gendered, class, and ethnocentric biases that, it is claimed, has blighted the literature on cosmopolitanism. For example, Elizabeth Grosz (1994) is concerned with the ways in which a "universal" in the literature has in fact functioned as a veiled representation of a masculine that understands itself as the unquestioned norm. In her view, this representational positioning reduces the "other"—women, the "disabled," cultural and racial minorities, different classes, homosexuals. In response to this perception comes a call for "cosmopolitanism from below" which is not utopian, elitist, or Western-centered and which would have political implications of its own (Werbner 1999; Bhabha 1996; Nava 2007). This portrayal of the cosmopolitan as a typically privileged, male and upper-class citizen (Kanter 1995; Calhoun 2002; Hannerz 2004) has been challenged by research that points toward the existence of cosmopolitan attitudes among ordinary and working-class groups (Werbner 1999; Lamont and Aksartova 2002; Sassen 2006). As well as the interconnectivity of groups we see ideas, though not easily recognizable (Cohen 1992) of "rootedness" being concurrently expressed as in (Peterson 2011), upper-class cosmopolitan Cairene youth or working-class Pakistani cosmopolitan Indian families (Lamb 2010).

Anthropological engagement with "cosmopolitanism" has often entailed a critical, indigenizing, or localizing of the concept such that it becomes detached from a Western heritage and Enlightenment provenance. This is deemed insufficiently sensitive to its own cultural biases, also to radical difference, to history, to the masses, to realpolitik, and to the social logics of community solidarity (Hollinger 2000: 228). Scott Malcolmson (1998) has observed that "cosmopolitan" values and orientations characterize other cultural traditions. There is more than one way of being and doing the cosmopolitan, and non-anthropological literatures on cosmopolitanism have not taken enough account of this. This is the explicit intent of Arjun Appadurai's statement (cited in Robbins 1998: 1) that contemporary "cosmopolitan" experiences do not necessarily derive from Western models or authority, and James Clifford's claim (1998: 363–365) that there "plural discrepant cosmopolitanisms." Cosmopolitanism can be loosed from Eurocentric and universalist moorings to become a *travelling* signifier, in the company of other partial equivalents such as "exile," "immigration," "diaspora," "pilgrimage," and "tourism" (Rapport 2012b: 528). For Werbner (2006), the focus of cosmopolitanism, in anthropological terms, is not so much on the overcoming of particularisms but in the investigation of cultural plurality, democracy, and the existence of de facto cosmopolitan values in already existing communities. Additional types of anthropological cosmopolitanism such as the studies of Urry and others (Urry 2003; Szerszynski and Urry 2006; Thompson and Tambyah 1999; Molz 2006) regard the influences of mobility roots and interconnectivity on the identity of particular groups. At stake here is the attempt of a "counter-narrative" to "erase totalizing boundaries" to offer within the realm of the theoretical a position and a narrative authority for marginal voices or minority discourse. Attention is being focused on immigrants from the working classes who display cosmopolitan orientations "from below" (Lamont and Aksartova 2002; Sassen 2006) as well as local, emotional, and everyday expressions of cosmopolitanism.

However, this requirement is not a simple, value-free, and unproblematic transaction. As Benhabib (2002: 31) argues, reactions "can range from total bafflement in the face of another culture's rituals and practices to more mundane and frustrating encounters with others when we simply say, "I just don't get it. What do you really mean?" To ask what obligations one owes strangers seems to presuppose an audience that can afford the luxury of thinking about strangers. The political economy of the field of academic cosmopolitanism means that the question is usually posed by Western authors for privileged Western audiences, with a view to persuading them to treat outsiders with respect. This is a laudable objective, but one that does not engage with the subaltern outsider. Can s/he be expected to be cosmopolitan too? Liberal cosmopolitan thinkers identify individuality, universality, and generality as their fundamental philosophical premises: in other words, individuals are the ultimate units of concern, equally, for everyone. But if the "everybody" does not have an ontological understanding of the "individual" who chooses to engage with the world maybe, asks Rahul Rao, they may ask "what's in it for me?" (Rao 2012: 168).

In contrast to the cognate concepts of cosmopolitism, which places emphasis on the cultural identity of the pre-national "citizen of the world" other authors, particularly political scientists and IR scholars writing within the tradition of political cosmopolitanism, understand cosmopolitanism as an ethical-political ideal. Seeking to overcome the limitations of the nation-state to address global or humanitarian issues, cosmopolitanism in this sense operates as a political project. This new normative approach was signaled by David Held's *Democracy and the Global Order* (1995) which assumed Kant's vision in *Perpetual Peace* to argue for the apparently utopian possibility of cosmopolitan citizenship. At the root of these approaches lies the premise that globalization creates a new political context that necessitates a new political conceptualization in the form of transnational democracy.

Cosmopolitanism, as a democratic theory within this period of increased global interconnectedness aims to provide as our own, the results of collective decisions taken in a given polity affect parties outside the boundaries of that polity, such that the demand for the accommodation of the interests of those affected by such decisions risks rendering territorial boundaries morally arbitrary (Habermas 1999). This ideal is made tangible in the way aspirations for human rights conventions have evolved into international laws, and in the implementation of International Criminal Tribunals.[7] More moderate cosmopolitan approaches seek to establish a new constitutional global order, whose institutions will embody cosmopolitan values such as equality, solidarity, and human rights, grounded in an ever-expanding universal political consensus (Habermas 2001). Other moderate approaches seek to avoid changes in the national sphere and settle for change in the architecture and conduct of international institutions as a necessary means for establishing global justice (Pogge 2008). An early example of this approach is Karl Jaspers' plea for the creation of legal categories and judicial procedures with international validity (Jaspers 2001), such as "crimes against humanity." The aim of this is to foster new forms of supranational and transnational governance as well as developing a robust global civil society (Held 1995; Archibugi et al. 1998; Kaldor 2002; Rumford 2007).

The work of a cosmopolitan democrat offers an opportunity to reimagine the relationship between inside and outside. This represented a moment in

---

[7] It is important to note that within modern political theory there is a theme that is critical of the relationship between the pursuit of ideals and human rights. A good example is David Chandler's argument that at the heart of the discourse of human rights lies a paradox in that claims made on behalf of marginalised groups leads to the creation of new frameworks for the exercise of power (2013: 107–122; see also Lacroix and Pranchère 2018: 25–58).

which the creativity of my interconnectivity with humanity could be used to formulate a political and social perspective capable of destabilizing the legitimacy of the state as the sole arbiter of one's identity as a human being. In relying on the principle of autonomy as an axiomatic value, also prepares the ground for an instrumentalist justification of democracy. As Karlsson points out, the argument for cosmopolitan democracy goes further than general instrumentalist arguments for democracy. The cosmopolitan democratic account argues that a democratic structure can only meet the criteria of democracy if, and only if, they lead to the desired outcomes in terms of democratic public law (Karlsson 2004). While Simon Caney observes that in, "valuing autonomy not only does not commit one to valuing democracy: it may lead one to wish to circumscribe democratic government" (Caney 2005: 155). Though articulating an aspiration to move beyond the conceptual traps of modernity, the conceptions of democracy set out by the cosmopolitan still maintain the state as the arbiter of reasoning and rationality. Despite its radicalization of democracy, it still rests on an understanding of the nature of collectives as being closed and stable. This reliance on a statist political ontology informs the cosmopolitan democrat's formulation of agency. We can extend this to suggest that it would also exclude other available decision-making procedures, means of reasoning, forms of knowing and knowledge, and conceptions of what it is to be human and live with others. This reliance on a particular understanding of human agency, one that is based on a particular understanding of what it is to be human and to thrive, seems to restrict the debate on the future of democracy within the limits of its own social consciousness. Among its many manifestations, the concern of this book in developing a post-Western-centric, a post-universalistic social science understood as multidisciplinary and interdisciplinary (Fine and Boon 2007) allows us to visualize the growing interconnectivity that has been brought about by globalization and to link it to developments in social and political thought.

NON-EUROCENTRIC COSMOPOLITAN
SOCIAL THEORY

While Ulrich Beck does not provide any resources for, nor was interested in providing, a non-Eurocentric account of cosmopolitan social theory, in a path-breaking series of essays and books (1998a, 2000a, 2000b, 2002, 2002a, 2003, 2006), he and his wife, Elisabeth Beck-Gernsheim, did campaign persistently and urgently for the overcoming of the tradition of "methodological nationalism" within sociology. Their aim was the development of a "methodological cosmopolitanism" in its place. From such a position, one of our protagonists, Gerard Delanty, developed his own work.

For Beck, "Globalization" is a nonlinear, dialectic process in which the global and the local do not exist as cultural polarities but as combined and mutually implicating principles. Simply put, the global and the local are not distinct, hermetically sealed categories but are mutually constitutive (Beck 2002: 19). According to Beck, these processes involve not only interconnections across boundaries, but transform the quality of the social and the political inside nation-state societies (Beck 1992). Beck understands the present processes of globalization as a process of "cosmopolitanism" or of a "second modernity." This cosmopolitanism presupposes individualization as a process of global subjectivation (Beck-Gernsheim and Beck 2002). The conceptual instruments by which the cosmopolitan reality is analyzed by social scientists are still rooted within the narrow worldview of the nation-state (Beck 2002, 2004; Beck and Sznaider 2006; see also: Martins 1974; Chernilo 2006). The irrelevance of old social and political science, entails a reexamination of the fundamental concepts of "modern society." "Household, family, class, social inequality, democracy, power, state, commerce, public, community, justice, law, history, memory and politics must be released from the fetters of methodological nationalism, reconceptualized, and empirically established within the framework of a new cosmopolitan social and political science" (Beck and Sznaider 2006: 6). This is a transitional phase in which the world is connected beyond national frameworks through the rapid movement of capital, information, merchandise, and people around the globe (Beck 1992; Barber 1996, 2008; Bauman 1998).

These movements transcend barriers of distance, space, time, culture, and language and radically alter the nature of day-to-day social life and effects the most personal aspects of human experience (Giddens 1999; Bauman 2003; Beck 2007). At the same time, issues of global concern are becoming part of the everyday local experiences and the "moral life-worlds of the people." This transforms everyday consciousness and identities significantly. This process of "cosmopolitization" means internalized globalization, globalization from within the national societies. This, Beck claims, has produced a "dialogic imagination" in which the "internalized other" rejects the rupture of the particular from the universal and instead engages in critical transformation (Beck 2002). The encounter with alternative and competing worldviews requires individuals to adopt the perspective of the other in evaluating others' orientations toward the social facts faced by everyone in any society.

For Beck, cosmopolitanization as a grounded reality as opposed to philosophical cosmopolitanism is an ethical project, one opposed to the ideas of neoliberalism. The underlying political message is that through these processes that "individualized individuals" are given equal protection of the law which allows individuals to make life choices from a wider range of opportunities. This "freeing of agency from structure" and a multiplying process of "individuation" offers hope for a changed future "of alternative modernities." The shift in the sociological focus from the nation-state to globality is on the various facets of the cultural, social, economic, and political consequences of growing interdependencies, and so "it rejects the dominant opposition between cosmopolitans and locals as well: there is no cosmopolitanism without localism." As such cosmopolitanism "provides [a] promising approach to connect normative critique with empirically based analysis focused on exploring news ways of seeing the world" (Delanty 2009: 2–3).

CRITICAL COSMOPOLITANISM

Following Beck, Gerard Delanty offers a new, more precise theory that he calls "critical cosmopolitanism" (Delanty 2006, 2009, 2011, 2012, 2014). In his book *The Cosmopolitan Imagination—The Renewal of Critical Social Theory* (2009), he argues that the consensual pragmatism of Jürgen Habermas was capable of providing a significant influence and encouragement for new methods of cosmopolitan thinking. For Delanty, the critical aspects of cosmopolitanism emerge in the "gap" between the global and local in the open encounter between global social imaginaries. In that sense, cosmopolitanism is not a description of a local given state or an aspiration for a specific situation, but rather an imaginary situation that can put on or take off different forms according to the historic context and social circumstances. Cosmopolitanism exists, it could be argued, within all societies and is a transformative process of "transcendental immanence." That is cosmopolitanism, the creation of new forms of social and political experimentation, transcendence, is found in already existing circumstances, immanence.

The universalizing feature of modernity for Delanty "...is the drive to make all of culture translatable" (Delanty 2009). He is concerned with the way in which global cultures can reimagine their own agency through seemingly multidimensional social negotiations that overlap, confuse, and juxtapose one another. It is the interplay between Self, Other, and the World through which cosmopolitanism initiates the moment of Self and societal transformation (Delanty 2006: 41). This interaction of cultures "cultivates an attitude of critical deliberation and ways of *imagining new ways of living*" (Delanty 2011: 641). We allow ourselves to correct our own self-understanding considering those challenges. At the moment of this transformative dialogue, maintains Delanty, newness is created; a third culture of transcendence.

It is the dialectic between "structures of consciousness" which provides the heuristic processes within "global history." As an historical process, Delanty argues, though Western concepts have dominated these have lost their Western specificity due to their translation at the level of the local (Delanty

2009: 180–181). Echoing this Rovisco argues that the challenge "is to focus on processes of border shifting and crossing whereby foreign cultural elements (styles, artistic forms, codes, beliefs) travel from one alien local culture to another, being eventually accepted as familiar and no longer foreign, and to do so by tracing shifts in the meanings of historically rooted local memories, identities, and imaginaries" (Rovisco 2010). His means of translating this encounter is through the analysis of preconditions, social mechanisms, social processes, and trajectories of historical change (Delanty 2012). This trajectory of historical change, through the spread of cosmopolitanism, is accompanied by the spread of human rights and democracy (Delanty 2009).

To accomplish this Delanty draws on the idea of global history and the work of Benjamin Nelson (Delanty 2011). Nelson put forward the notion of "structures of consciousness" to capture the different kinds of outcomes arising from such encounters. However, Delanty acknowledges that problems could arise when concepts situated in the European experience are used to describe and evaluate non-Western communities. This difficulty only arises if, "one assumes that non-Western societies exist." From such a position, he argues that a case can be made that all societies have been influenced by Western concepts though these have now lost their Western specificity (Delanty 2009).[8]

MOVING BEYOND MODERNITY

According to Danilo Zolo (1997; Hardt and Negri 2000; also see Pagden 2000: 6), any cosmopolitan project must in practice be autocratic, hegemonic, and violent, for cosmopolitanism is an outgrowth and ideological reflection of global capitalism, which remains its enabling condition. Cosmopolitanism is the latest phase of capitalist modernity, operating on a global scale, with the term being used to disguise an old form of Western engagement with the other. In this context, some authors have attempted to show how past and present cosmopolitanisms shape distinct worldviews and identities in a variety of times and places (Mignolo 2000, 2010, 2011; Pollock 2000).

The work of Walter Mignolo crosses time and space to explore consciousness in an effort to understand how we have collectively arrived at this place and what possibilities are available to us for the future. He has attempted to

---

[8] It is important to note that throughout global history ideas have been exchanged or appropriated. See Brooks (2013) for an introduction to the emerging field of Global Philosophy. For an interesting and engaging introduction to the use of Eastern ideas in Western philosophy see Macfie (2003), and Bernasconi (1997), on the "paraxodical parochialism" of Western philosophy that reduces "proper" philosophy to the Greeks and the "standard narrative of philosophy."

provide space through which various anticolonial, postcolonial, and decolonial epistemologies can exist and connect in order to provide opportunities for new ways of seeing the world. The notion of decolonial cosmopolitanism is based on the claim that cosmopolitanism as "openness to the world" crucially also implies an "openness to the Other." This is motivated by the historical consciousness of how "Other" voices and peoples have continuously been subalternized, as well as by the political aim to challenge this subalternization.[9] Pollock (2000) offers a critical reading of triumphalism and neoliberal notions of Cosmopolitical coexistence. However, Pollock's point is broader than Mignolo's. To know that some people in the past have been able to be universal and particular, without making either their particularly ineluctable or their universalism compulsory, is to know that better cosmopolitan and vernacular practices are at least conceivable—and perhaps even, in a way those people themselves never fully achieved, eventually reconcilable (Pollock 2000).

Like Delanty, Mignolo too sees the creative possibilities incumbent in the cosmopolitan imagination. For theorists like Mignolo and his intellectual companion Enrique Dussel, ideas such as "Modernity" and "cosmopolitanism" were imagined as the house of epistemology (Mignolo 2006: 93). His concepts of border thinking and transmodernity provide the opportunity for the cosmopolitan imagination which occurs at the epistemic and ontic border between the marginalized and modernity. Decolonial cosmopolitanism thus "demands yielding generously (. . .) toward diversity as a universal and cosmopolitan project in which everyone participates instead of 'being participated'" (Mignolo 2000: 744). His project of critical cosmopolitanism is a critique of the Eurocentric presuppositions of cosmopolitan thought. Here a benign view of the march of progress and modernity containing the germ of cultural translation and transcendence omits an important aspect: its dark side or underside. While "a" European mind may like to reassure itself with its project of autonomy from the strictures of humanity's primitivism, Mignolo, among others, aims to remind us that someone paid the price for "a humanity's" strive for autonomy.

For Mignolo, it is only in the overcoming of the dichotomies of modernity by which we can transform the historical cultural and civilizational legacy of modernity. This would require the "self-restitution of barbarism as a theoretical locus," a learning from the "exteriority" of modernity. This epistemological critique links the epistemic location with the subject and challenges the myth about a truthful universal knowledge. In repositioning thought outside of the European projection of modernity, in rethinking critical thought or

---

[9] See Spivak (1988) Can the Subaltern Speak?

critical knowledge from other spaces and places as an account of relative universalism, is to represent a development of the emancipatory ethic that could not be achieved within the hegemonic practices of modernity. This holds the promise of thinking from different spaces through which to finally break away from Eurocentrism as the sole epistemological perspective. This demands not only a new sociology of knowledge but also a new normative epistemology that can correct and improve upon the modern/colonial world in which the logic of coloniality provides the point of departure for alternative projects that challenge this very logic (Mignolo 2010: 317–338; Alcoff 2007: 82–83).

For Mignolo, this epistemic call to "diversality as a universal project" would be a result of "critical border thinking" and understood as an epistemic intervention from the diverse subalterns (Mignolo 2000). "Border thinking" arises "at the intersection of local histories enacting global designs and local histories dealing with them," the former stemming from the "subaltern perspective," the latter launched by a "desire for homogeneity" and a "need of hegemony" (Mignolo 2000a: 310). This reveals the instances where the modern/colonial system has created spaces for new thinking and acting when dominant epistemologies met indigenous knowledges and cosmologies moments in which the imaginary of the modern world system cracks (2000: 23; Escobar 2004; Mignolo 2010c: 15–20). It also asserts that simultaneously, spaces for alternative thinking emerge from the places where indigenous and Eurocentric paradigms meet to create a particular consciousness stemming from the relative exteriority of the world system. The aim is not the creation of a universal ideological position. Rather, it instead emphasizes the acceptance of different ways of being, not by positing a "blueprint of a future and ideal society projected from a single point of view [that of abstract universals] that will return us [again] to the Greek paradigms and European legacies" (Mignolo 2000: 744), but by being reflexive about one's own, and more importantly, the "Other's" standpoint (Mendieta [2009] 2011: 252).

This concept of the border is meant to signify that the locality of subaltern knowing, far from simply being "the other side" of "Western" knowing, has a border-like quality. Though this may be reminiscent of some of postcolonial theory's concern with hybridity, mestizaje, and creolization (Venn 2006: 18–19; Bhabha 1994; Anzaldúa 1999), here Mignolo denotes a more radical stance toward transcending the mere celebration of postcolonial liminal, hybrid, and ambiguous consciousness. Opposed to "abstract universals," it is neither counterculture nor a Hegelian synthesis, but rather a "phagocytosis of civilization by the barbarian," implying a "barbarian" way of theorizing that has the "key configuration" of "thinking from dichotomous concepts rather than ordering the world in dichotomies" (Mignolo 2000a: 81–87, 110, 303, 327). The rationality of Eurocentrism is supplemented and enriched, signifying a radical human transformation of consciousness through its encounter with the Other. Through these processes, novel solutions, importantly local solutions, are devised to social and political problems. Border thinking then becomes a "tool" of the project of critical cosmopolitanism (Mignolo 2002a: 174) and a "future planetary epistemological and critical localism" (Mignolo 2000: 88, 157).

The human sentiment of cosmopolitanism is not a Western universal. Continuing from Pollock's argument, the most promising accounts of cosmopolitanism, opposed to the largely formalist moral and political accounts, come from cultural and anthropological theorists. As Nigel Rapport notes, there is more than one way of being cosmopolitan, and non-anthropological literature on cosmopolitanism have not taken enough account of this (2012a). We shall see that far from being a foreign concept, cosmopolitanism is already embedded in several non-Western traditions which would make the concept inherently global/universal. This desire has been shaped from a diverse legacy of epistemologies, ontologies, methodologies, and imaginaries other than those developed in the Western academy, but also through mutual phases of development. At the level of intercultural exchange, in recognizing the limits of a culture's "immanent critique" of itself holds out the potential to rejuvenate world philosophies through an engagement of mutual humility, of critique, and of cooperation. In this spirit, and in following the notion of a fusion of ideas, the following section will provide a brief summary of the main points of Buddhist and Confucian notions of cosmopolitanism.

ANOTHER PARADIGM

A non-Western cosmopolitan argument of interest comes from Siddhartha Gautama, The Buddha, as it informs the thought of Watsuji. While the Stoics gave a conditioned account of heterogeneity and otherness, based on contingency of birth, from the Buddhist perspective, the acceptance of difference and otherness, the impartial predistribution of assets and privileges, of the acknowledgment of other's freedoms, of community in multiplicity, is not conditional.[10] Whereas the Stoicism of Chrysippus limited citizenship in the cosmos to those who in fact live in agreement with the cosmos and its law, Buddhism begins with the idea that we all hold the capability for Buddha nature (humanity). It is this account of being human which informs Watsuji's work, which this book will argue offers the potential to provide an alternative

---

[10] Of course, the idea of Buddhism covers a wide and diverse range of traditions and perspectives. Therefore, this section can only give a representative survey.

and unique perspective to the debate concerning the development of a post-Western cosmopolitan social theory.

Buddhism represents a conceptual paradigm of holistic nondualism, the interdependence of subject and object, that asserts the nonduality of inner (personal) and external change. Importantly, it is this feature that differentiates it from other compatible forms of social activism (See Loy 2003; Hattam 2004; Arnold 2005; Ward 2013, for discussions of Buddhist social theory). The aim of this knowledge-wisdom is the temporal and ultimate cessation of suffering (Dukkha), which is a state that is referred to as enlightenment. Often, what could be understood as the essence of Buddhism is introduced in terms of the "Four Noble Truths." The first noble truth asserts that the human condition is by its very nature *dukkha* or suffering which can be understood to refer to the constantly repeated feeling that something is lacking, or incomplete in our lives. Somehow, there is something not quite right, therefore, we strive to continually fill the gap. It is in the examination of the cause for this profound dissatisfaction that leads to the second noble truth, the truth of the origin of suffering, understood as "desire," "craving," or "grasping." Such awareness then leads to an understanding of a " . . . sane, awake quality within us" that "manifests itself only in the absence of struggle" (Trungpa et al. 1987: 173), and so we discover the third noble truth: the truth of nonstriving or the cessation of suffering. Such a realization then leads us to examine the need to continue to practice "letting go," to practice some disciplined way of working on our minds, of practicing meditation: the fourth noble truth (Hattam 2004: 18; Loy 2002).[11]

Much of the contemporary debate concerning cosmopolitanism comes to us from the Stoics via Kant (Brown 2009; Nussbaum 1997). In the Buddhist perspectives, the stoical, Kantian and contemporary emphasis on individuation, that is first understood as a selecting self who determines principles by inventing them (Kristjansson 2010: 187) and then who "has to engage in some or other intellectual 'detour' to bridge the gap between what can be immediately experienced about the other person and that person's psychological states" (Asch 1952) is, in the context of the tensions between individuality and social power, delusional. Such an account can lead to the idea of assimilation of other by self. While the Stoics, and all who followed, emphasized

---

[11] Of course, in the popular imagination the Buddhist tradition is portrayed as a peaceful and non-violent movement. However, one could also point to the suffering of the Muslim community in Myanmar by the Buddhist community to engage that view. See Hayward (2014) for a discussion of the nascent nationalism within the dominant Buddhist tradition in Myanmar. As this chapter will make explicit below, I am not concerned with an argument for a Buddhist form of cosmopolitanism. That said, it would be remiss of me not to be clear that I do not hold that Buddhism presents an unchallengeable account of the human condition, for instance in respect of gender. See Sirimanne (2016), who puts forward the argument that Buddhism does not have a reformist agenda or an explicit feminist theory.

the rational nature of "Man" [*sic*], Buddhism's emphasis on the nonduality of being, and our interdependence, emphasizes the development of all aspects of being-in-the-world. This interdependence involves seeing oneself not as primarily separate from others, rather, as belonging in a network of relationships. However, importantly, one should not misunderstand this as a recognition of our communal identity. This is a much more nuanced approach from the staid dichotomy of self and community. In recognizing our interdependence offers us a unique approach to the hermeneutics of suspicion as it is in the "deconstruction and reconstruction of the sense of self is necessary to become aware of the most deceptive of metanarratives: the one we normally do not perceive because it is our ordinary, everyday reality—the 'real world' we take for granted but in fact is constructed" (Loy 2003: 4). Rather than an act of imperious cosmopolitan consensus the Buddhist argument plunges "us" into the hermeneutical depths of "what is?" to then ascend to "what is possible?"

CONFUCIUS AND COSMOPOLITANISM

The cosmopolitanism of Watsuji is not based on a teleology of nature, or an abstraction from structure of the rationality of Man. Rather, Watsuji is concerned with actual practical human relationships. While the Stoic and later accounts of cosmopolitanism emphasize the process of individuation, Ren, (仁, humanity, benevolence) from the tradition of Confucius, stresses the reciprocity in the meeting of persons which can only be developed through human contact. This is important to the development of the book's argument as Watsuji was deeply indebted to both Buddhist and Confucius thought. So rather than outline an account of Confucius thought, I want to take the opportunity to sketch out Watsuji's use of Confucius ideas for his development of a proto decolonial cosmopolitanism.

With the influence of Buddhism on Sino religious and philosophical development, from the tradition of Confucianism, we find a similar account of the connectedness of being human and of our responsibility to others. This acknowledgment of our interconnectedness with the recognition of a diversity of human cultures can be understood as having cosmopolitan themes. In Confucianism's concern for "all under Heaven" (tianxia) stands an ethical concern and responsibility for literally all that is under heaven. Following on from this is a distinctive principle of the "unity of Heaven and man" that refutes any opposition between man and nature. Lastly, there is the idea that if one has developed as a person one should contribute to society (See Young and Sang 2014). Both the Stoics and the Confucians emphasize the connection between ethical persons and the Heaven or Nature to create a harmonious political space.

To capture this relationality, Watsuji frames his ethical system in terms of the five cardinal relationships (roles/capacities) of Confucianism. As Odin notes (1996: 56), Watsuji wrote, "[I]n ancient China, the relationships between father and son, lord and vassal, husband and wife, older brother and younger brother, and friend and friend were known as 'the great relationships of man'" (1937: 4). Here Watsuji is drawing on the relational ethics manifested in the Confucian ideals of *li* and *Dao*. *Li* is usually translated as "ritual propriety" or "rites" due to its genesis in and close relationship with religious ceremonies in ancient China. *Dao* is the Way of Heaven (*tian*) that provides the guiding or prescriptive discourse for human beings (Hansen 1989). *Dao* is declared in and transmitted via various modes such as traditional texts, social institutions, and exemplary conduct of sage-kings who lived before Confucius' time (Tan and Tan 2016).

Odin continues:

> Like Confucian ethics, Watsuji understand the self as a center of human relationships, each of which is *governed* by a normative principle of *li* . . . or "ritual propriety." . . . Watsuji thus appropriates the Confucian view of the self as an ever-expanding we of social relationships which embodies increasingly larger social groups including the family, the community, the village, society, and the nation. (Odin 1996: 56)

Piovesana (1969: 141), therefore states that for Watsuji "ethics consisted essentially in the *aidagara* or the relationship aspect of contacts between man and man, man and his family, man and society." We will be discussing this concept in greater detail in later chapters, but for now, according to Watsuji, although the modern subjective turn often begins with an examination of the limits of individual existence, if a person is authentically a social animal, then things like our persistent relationships (*aidagara*) and society should not be separated from the person. Our lives begin in a relationship with our mothers; continue through childhood with our parents or guardians, in friendship, in employment, with lovers, and with our own children. Therefore, for him rather than reify the subject he aims to articulate an account of subjectivity as "withness," or as *aidagara*, and this transforms the lives of these actors in these relationships over time. Rather than present the individual as the homo economicus, or as the norm-following and role-playing actor of the homo sociologicus, Watsuji was instead concerned with exploring how ethical practice is enacted within concrete human relationships. For him any ethical system that "which abstracts away from the practical connections between person and person" is inadequate in that it overlooks the intercorporeal source of ethical agency (Watsuji 1996: 9). Opposed to such abstractions, Watsuji's account of socio-epistemology composed of his interconnected concepts of *fūdo* and *aidagara* emphasize the relational aspects of self and society and the intertwined nature of the natural phenomena and humanity.

Watsuji has been the target of considerable criticism. Charges leveled against him range from the construction of a static understanding of society, a conservativism, that subsumes the individual to the needs of society, to his supposed support for Japanese militarism during the first part of the twentieth century. While this book is concerned with about ideas, and this will be most reader's introduction to Watsuji's work, it is important to stress two facets of his work that carry with them significant importance for this book.

First, Watsuji's incorporation of the Confucius concepts of *li* and *Dao* which when interpreted as "Ritual proprieties" may suggest a static, unchanging, conservative understanding of social reality. However, as Confucius put it, "[T]he *ren* person is one who, wishing himself to be settled in position, sets up others; wishing himself to have access to the powerful, achieves access for others. To be able to proceed by analogy from what lies nearest by, that may be termed the formula for *ren*"[12] (Eno 2015: 6.30). As Tan (2017: 335) states, this means, understood through the idiom of Confucius thought, that within the network of social relationships one must perform one's roles in accordance with *li* (Hall and Ames 1998). Tan (2017) describes the pattern of *li* as the "internal structure" of *dao* (Hall and Ames 1987: 237), and that to broaden *dao* is to observe *li*. Such an effort requires critical thinking where individuals apply the cultural resources and shared ideals found in *dao* to situations in accord with *li*. Therefore, self-cultivation and articulation rather than rigid hierarchy define the lives of individuals living in a *li*-ordered community (Hall and Ames 1998). Broadening *dao* entails that the observance of *li* involves not just an adherence to but also a critique and revision of prevailing beliefs and practices (Tan 2015). The task of broadening *dao* needs the cultivation of both the self and others. The expectation is that our existing and taken-for-granted norms and presuppositions should be carefully examined and compared with the ideal standard that is embodied in *dao*. What this emphasizes is that within existing societal structures is contained not only the existing social forms but that this also includes moments of creativity.

In *Ethics III*, Watsuji applies this to the international realm through the application of emptiness to the history of nations. What we see here is a predecolonial account of relative universalism designed to show that various global ethical systems are grounded in and expressive of universal morality. Like history, nations only realize their climatic character and their respective

---

[12] In the Analects, Confucius never formally defined Ren. It has been translated as benevolence, love, altruism, kindness, charity, compassion, magnanimity, humaneness. See Fitz (2011) for a discussion of the relationship between Gandhi's and Confucius' understanding of the "good," as well as concerns about the translation of the term Ren.

fūdo in contrast to other nations. This represents the description of "self-realization of identity through difference." The self-awareness of finite totality is only possible through the consciousness of what one does not share with that exterior of one's own totality. As a precursor to decolonial theory, and in the context of early twentieth-century neo-imperialism and colonialism part of Watsuji's analysis is designed to show that morality is ontically and epistemic specific, and that the imposition of "outside" ethical systems amounts to violence. He argues that individual nations need to develop a heightened sense of individuality through which to contribute to a global ethic. This, of course, will be specific to the individual nation and would also highlight societal limitations. Through this process, in the contact between nations, it is possible for a nation to learn from another without one nation or community claiming to provide a privileged perspective. Watsuji stresses the importance of this:

> Thinking of it in this way, the realization of moral difference in each nation is indispensable for the fulfillment of the universal socio-ethical path. It saves each nation from conceit and spurs them to work to overcome their individual limitations. (*WTZ11*, 348, quoted in Sevilla 2015: 215)

Such an understanding of a global morality does not support the notion of an idealized other, or as an "empty-placeholder" of its own immanent values or norms, but looks toward the enunciation of concrete experiences, that is at the intersection of proclaimed ideals and the practices of life.

COSMOPOLITAN SOCIAL THEORY: SHATTERING REALITY

To begin the process of developing a conceptually post-Western form of critical cosmopolitan social theory this chapter has set out four different accounts of cosmopolitanism. These have been presented to give the reader some scope of how human cultures have articulated its need to answer the perceived contradictions of being human: inside and outside, space and time, and unity and diversity. Though cosmopolitanism possesses a capability to provide a means of a more humanistic account of global social theory, although the accounts set out above differ in the nature of the ultimate unit of analysis, the individual or relational, they all fail to provide an explicit means for societal and self-transformation. The projection onto the world of internalized ideals as a cosmopolitan project has the dual result of the reification of the internal structures of a society and results in epistemic and ontic violence in the interstate realm. The approach that has been suggested here is that cosmopolitanism's premise of incompleteness offers the opportunity to consider the encounter of self, other, and world as a mutual phase of development. This methodology we have described as critique and cooperation.

Incompleteness interconnects our three tasks of critical cosmopolitan social theory. These are the tasks of intercultural heuristic exchange, intracultural analysis, and the role of the self. However, cosmopolitanism cannot be reduced to a text, tradition, or discipline, unless there is an explicit advocacy of reflexive negation, as this would reduce the concept to reification. Instead, cosmopolitanism begins and ends with people, as understood through the tension between individuality and society, the opportunities for change that they encounter, and the lives that they lead. Though cosmopolitanisms may profess to "everything under Heaven" or "everything within the cosmos," such perspectives rely on temporal notions of completeness: cosmopolitanisms are done to people. By temporality I mean how these notions provide a stabilizing narrative to collective and individual identities. This allows the audience as a whole, through society's material and symbolic imaginary, to be carried along with the narrative landscape as the story unfolds. But as with all genres of temporality, it asks from its audience the suspension of disbelief of obvious untruths or hurtful and fantastic elements. In failing to recognize that the interaction between self and other, or one culture with another is a reciprocal process of societal/self-development, which links the outside with the inside, ironically has the consequence of obliterating difference and prohibits the overcoming of self and societal limitations.

Cosmopolitanism maintains its critical edge when it is in genuine and revealing conversation with the other and the other's other. I have described this process as that of critique and cooperation. This process begins by returning to the question of how does a cosmopolitan think? As I commented earlier, this must appear as a naive question. However, the answer to it is only assumed in the literature and lies at the heart of the problem of cosmopolitanism. In the accounts of cosmopolitanisms set out above the critical potential of the concept is betrayed as they understand the world as being constructed of diametric dualities; us versus them, West versus the rest of the world, modernity versus tradition. While expressing a curiosity for the diversity of humanity in its unity, they do so through a claim of the closure of fundamental questions concerning the human condition.

In the work of both Delanty and Mignolo, and in the non-Western accounts of cosmopolitanism that have been set out, we find a recognition of the practical nature of the co-cognitive, the cognitive cocreativity, interconnectedness of self, other, and the world. But this "immanent transcendence" or "border," or in "everything under heaven" that they seek is prejudiced through a reliance on temporal moments of clarity, of beginnings, of uniqueness. Though non-Western forms of cosmopolitanism provide us with a relational form of humanity, in their insistence on *being* as a foregrounding of identity represents a self-imposed separation of self, other, and the world. Identity is only ever implied through my relationship with another. To foreground identity fails to recognize thought's own incompleteness and sociohistorical interconnectedness and mutual influence across and between multiple sources of creativity. It fails to return thought from "out-there" to "in-here," through which to provide for internal transformation-being cosmopolitan.

Cosmopolitanisms are not concerned with the articulation of an ideal located in a specific time and place. It is not a mantra of "we have found an ideal, and if only you were like us, . . ." Such a projection from "inside" to "out-there" leads to assimilation and allows for the reification of "in-here" in which identity is foregrounded or essentialized. Though there is the recognition of a connection, humanity, both spaces, the inside and the outside, are basically detached. This essentialization of identity recognizes human diversity as a mirror image and against the background of human history, of relative closure; fundamental truths have been answered.

It needs to be stressed that an object of this project is not the undermining of tradition, religious, or philosophical perspective. The intent is quite the contrary. The developments in human understanding that we have encountered in this chapter originated in different locales, under different conditions and are rooted in the lives and experiences of people. But they are partial and conditional. By setting aside notions of exceptionalism or the foregrounding of identity(s) enables the linking of immanent sociopsychological structures of society with its encounter with the world to extend theoretical horizons. In accepting the partial, conditional, and entangled nature of the human condition and bring different practices of life together, we may, if we choose, gain a glimpse of other ways of doing things to consider own limitations.

However, to engage in the process of imagining other than thought, our specific localized form of objectivity, we need a neutral "place," an unbiased universal medium in which various cultures can meet, converse, and consider our interdependence and the effects on our own sense of reality. A post-foundationalist, or positionless account, characterized in such a way proposes an ecology of knowledges and intercultural translation as an alternative to a general theory that cannot grasp the infinite diversity of the world. This book, itself, is an example of an alternative project in bringing together in humble conversation different forms of global consciousness into dialog for the purpose of self, societal, and intercommunal critical heuristics. This has two effects. First, the destabilization the relationship between "I" and the local arbiter of rationality, of inside and outside, which shifts otherness to an implied rather than foregrounded assumption of the world. On matters of common concern, this provides a space to link and intertwine endogenous and exogenous sociohistorical experiences to provide a point of critique from outside the dominant modes of social, economic, and political conventions.

That is, openings for social and political experimentation are created through the negation of present affirmations through which new affirmations are, in turn, created. Though it would be possible to apply this methodology to the encounter with other global traditions of relational sociology, Chinese and African examples for instance, in this book, we will be concerned with bringing together the ideals of critical theory, decolonial theory, and the work of Watsuji.

This recognition allows us to suggest that if critical thought, in our case cosmopolitan thought, is to maintain its criticality, then it needs to begin with the assumption of a pluralistic account of agency. As may be apparent, while the gaze of much of contemporary political and social theory is on the nature and revitalization of distinct and sovereign autonomy, cosmopolitan criticality must step-outside of its own birthplace through which to find a pivotal point to articulate a locus of enunciation capable of overcoming these abstractions. Cosmopolitanism's spatial perspective allows us to step-outside of, momentarily, these terms. While temporal-spatial modalities enunciate ideals as objective and necessary, we are concerned with actual existing lives and their reciprocal relationships with existing forms of social praxis. Instead, through a spatial evacuation of the temporal-modalities of our time, we are concerned with the continuous tension within the space "in-between" modernities answers to our human contradictions.

In the model of post-Western cosmopolitanism that will be set out in this book, we are concerned with how you, the self, engages with the world and how we can bring change into being. The temporal-spatial modalities that shape our lives and the institutions of modernity provide an answer to the contradictions of the human condition, inside and outside, space and time, and unity and diversity. Cosmopolitanism, as a spatial critique of the temporal, existing human conditions, provides another set of resources through which to answer these contradictions. Specifically, through posing such a critique it recognizes that rather than being isolated and autonomous beings, with the sole legitimate site of rationality being the state, that we are in fact immersed within the material and symbolic structures of our societies, which frame the cognitive, the subjective and the objective. Such units of analysis, the individual or societally structured identity, fail to capture the rich tapestry of human existence.

The cosmopolitan space for societal analysis, as presented here, draws in and integrates the manifold loci of enunciation, including the body, social practices, time, and physical space, beyond singularities such as the individual, democracy, globalization, or the social. Its constructive criticality begins with a human being's constant enactive with the social forms of their time that either provide blockages for human self and communal realization or a means of mutual self-development. We are embedded within the norms, values, and standards of objectivity of our societies. However, the account that follows appreciates agency through our notion of incompleteness, then the tension between individuality and totality allows us to understand agency as a constant enactive and generative process between self, other, and the world. This recognizes the immanence of the everyday but draws the real from out of the realm of temporality's perceptual and conceptual reification to enunciate what has been silent and confined within the objectivity of the limitations of one's societies ideals. Cultural reproduction and production are brought about *between* the self and its polymodal interaction with totality. The moment of change is elicited with the silent suggestion, the silent thought as negation, that is already present in the affirmations of say modernity, and which emerges from the individual through their engagement with the greater whole. This reaches inside of self and requires it to contribute to the greater whole. This allows us to recognize not only the infinity with other but also the infinite within ourselves. The point here to stress is that though the self is centered, it is at the same time part of an enactive interaction with other and the world through which new ways of being and acting in the world come to light. Transformation occurs through this space. Beginning in the deconstruction of temporal claims of objectivity, the movement of cosmopolitanism then proceeds to find new affirmations of the human journey unceasingly.

Chapter 2

Global Critical Theories

INTRODUCTION

This chapter begins the process of the deconstruction of critical cosmopolitan social theory to then transcend its limitations through drawing on the resources of post-Western critical cosmopolitan social theory. This will be carried out through bringing together two moments in social thought: the critical theorist and the decolonialist. While claims of temporality, modernity for instance, shape how we conceive of the cognitive, the intersubjective, and the objective, incompleteness asks us to understand these claims as partial, provisional, and conditional. What we do as societies and individuals is adopt or choose certain objects that are convenient fictions. The perspective of incompleteness, in its deconstructive phase, is not at odds with these conventional standpoints, only with a particular philosophical understanding of it that takes the conventional to be more than merely conventional. Recognizing that the cognitive, the intersubjective, and the objective are intimately linked to specific localized conditions allows the critical cosmopolitan perspective to transcend our internal approaches. Constructively, undermining the temporal-modalities of our time through a spatial critique of the practices of everyday life provides a moment to move away from perpetual, conceptual, and linguistic reification to reimagine new truths of the human condition.

Contrary to Allen (2016), who similarly aims to overcome the Eurocentric perspective of the critical theorist through an encounter between critical theory with the decolonial perspective, the book will not turn to "Western" resources only through which to provide a solution. However, this is not simply as a rejection of "Western" ideas. Rather, we aim to explore the theoretical-historical opportunities provided when we understand critical cosmopolitan social theory as a process of critique and cooperation. Instead of rehearsing a staid antinomy encounter between Mignolo and Delanty, their work is brought together as critique and cooperation, to offer a creative destructive moment that shatters the totalities of both authors' conceits of reality through which to identify positive theoretical opportunities. The proto-cosmopolitan conceptual forms that will emerge consist of Mignolo's understanding of relative universalism, and Delanty's relational ontology and Mignolo's aesthesis. This reconciles Mignolo's plunge into hermeneutics with Delanty's ascent into the critique of ideology. This then provides a position for the book to outline an alternative perspective on critical cosmopolitan social theory as a post-Western endeavor. However, as will become clear as the chapter progresses, such a synthesis is not capable of fully addressing the criticisms of cosmopolitanism.

This chapter will develop as follows. The first section is concerned with setting out the theoretical landscape of critical theory for the general reader. This is important as it will give you a broad introduction to the development of critical theory through which to situation the proposed synthesis of Delanty's and Mignolo's work. The second section outlines Delanty's account of a globalized critical theory. The next section moves onto the decolonial project of Mignolo. The decolonial critique represents a significant challenge to critical theory, but also in respect of the future of democracy, the international order, environmental studies, and capitalism. The concluding section begins the process of developing a new affirmation of critical theory. This section provides the basis for the reconstructive phase that will be developed in the second part of this book.

The dangers of considering one's own way in the world as exceptional are provided by the European example of critical theory. The West has become accustomed to setting out "standard narratives" of development or progress in respect of its intellectual monuments. This is carried out through a meta-narrative of history, with *a* West, an excluding section of Western societies, representing a messianic saviour for humanity and is mirrored through the material and symbolic structures of our societies and beyond our geo-territorial horizons. These meta-narratives are found in the stories that we, the West, tell ourselves about who we are, in our buildings, in our literature, in our educational curriculums and in our institutions. Cosmopolitanism has played its role in this emancipating narrative containing "mystical" elements such as Kant's notion of the teleological guidance of nature in human affairs. Unfortunately, critical or otherwise, it has failed to draw on the heuristic capability of the concept to develop intercultural exchange beyond assimilation. Neither has it provided a means to overcome one's own limitation beyond the globalization of self. It has completely disregarded the existence of non-Western accounts of cosmopolitanism as critical collaborators and interlocutors as they are viewed as primitive, traditional, or premodern.

In a similar way, the "standard narrative" of the history of critical theory generally begins with Kant's introduction of critical thought accompanying modernity and leads us up to the present day. In this narrative critical thought and the competences required to navigate the demands of modernity were given birth in *a* West, a West of self-excluding privilege. Pristine and self-seeking, this West is isolated from the trauma within its own *being* and, drawn toward its own teleology of consciousness, regards itself separated from the other. From the Age of European "Discovery" and "Enlightenment," this West recognizes the encounter between itself and the other, of the poor, of colour, of gender, or vernacular, or cultures alien to itself as the meeting with an inferior. Even in the work of those considered most radical, Mouffe, Castoriadis, and Žižek, is present an idealized articulation of being through a West's self-perception of natural entitlement. This view of the West understands itself, within the flow of history as exceptional, self-radicalizing, and commensurable with the needs of humanity, with the Other incommensurable with the teleology of human progress.

Much of the criticism of the effects of modernity does not reject modernity, but points to the dissonance between the projection of the ideals and the effects on populations around the world. The hope of such projects is the emergence from such a practical critique is a more humane and positive way of understanding being human and acting in the world. Of course, we are concerned in this book with the critical potential of the decolonialism of Walter Mignolo. His project elegantly and profoundly undermines the image of the West as the harbinger of human progress. It would not be unreasonable to argue that the majority of the world's population have been dealing with the underside of interconnectivity for over 400 years. That behind the stage furniture of ideals and principles of radicalized consciousness, the age of "Discovery" and of "Enlightenment" is concealed the crooked timber of humanity. While the French Revolution proclaimed the Rights of Man, French women were oppressed at home and slavery continued in Saint-Domingue. While the Enlightenment declared the arrival of humanity's maturity, whole populations in what has become known as the Americas were about to have their lives destroyed.

For many, the emancipatory effects of the Enlightenment and modernity were, and still are missing. Freedom, the ability for human creativity through the protection of positive and negative rights, however rational the public space may imagine itself to be, is the privilege of a few. So for Mignolo, the idea that the psycho-emotional and intellectual life of the West has be partitioned from the rest, that "the West" have been disengaged from the practices lives and worldviews of others is an inanity at best and disingenuous at worst. While "a" European mind may like to reassure itself with the idea of the emancipating tendency of thought from the strictures of humanity's primitivism, these thinkers aim to remind us that someone paid the price for what was deemed to be "Humanity's" freedom. Mignolo's model does reveal the socially embedded ethnic identity(s) traumatized through colonialism and offers an opportunity to move beyond claims of absolute universalism, to relative universalism capable of a cosmopolitanism which connects multiple autochthonous epistemic and ontic locations. However, offering an account of decolonialism as a mirror image of European exceptionalism, runs the risk of descending into the preclusion of internal heterogeneity. Furthermore, in totalizing Otherness through ethnicity implicitly excludes those within "Western" societies who are marginalized and who live an existence of a limited experience of emancipation but are condemned by lottery of birth to a life of self-alienation.

How can we provide space for the individual within this matrix of individuality and social forces? What this involves is engaging in a theoretical *en passant* move: the mutual passing through of the decolonial imagination through that of critical theory's but to move beyond both accounts. The theoretical movement, predicated on our notion of reflexive negation, brings the social dynamics of the decolonial unit of analysis, the sociohistorically, informed identity of the colonized, together with the exclusive abstraction of the individual. Though maintaining the positive protection of the individual, this shatters the ideal of subjectivity of critical theory to overcome the imposition of an account of the decontextualized individual as an ultimate unit of concern. At the same moment, the introduction of the imagination of critical theorist to that of the decolonial theorist provides a space for the protection of the individual. This allows for social power to be articulated against though not at the expense of individuality as it de-essentializes identity to nurture internal heterogeneity. The normative commitment of such a model is the articulation of injustice.

INTRODUCTION TO CRITICAL THEORY

Critical theory, as a radicalized consciousness, attempts to unearth the real from the reality of the modern world.[1] The critical theorist, "insists on the necessity to address the central, urgent and disturbing questions of a society and a culture in the most rigorous intellectual way we have available" (Hall

---

[1] It is important for the reader to appreciate that the account of critical theory that will be set out here comes from the work of Gerard Delanty and his desire to overcome the limitations of critical theory, its Eurocentrism, through the incorporation of cosmopolitan theory. Such a development, he hopes, would revitalize critical theory's ability to confront the problems that have arisen during the recent period of increased globalization.

1992: 11). This forces theorists to wrestle with the recognition of the limits of consciousness as maps of reality. That is, how can theorists overcome the patterns that one understands as reality when we are deeply embedded within the norms, customs, material, and symbolic signifiers that give us a sense of reality? However, critical theory's aim is to posit hope within the present, which is not unavoidable, but pregnant with the hope of a more socially just future. It attempts to move through claims about ideals and principles of a society, to unravel the contradictions, the injustices that lay within the shadows, the silences of any society. But it can only ever be a provisional claim as new features of the world emerge.

This means that from the outset critical theory as *a sole paradigm* was never adequate to its task. It is always unfinished. Not only is it not possible for any extant social theory to account for the sheer complexity of the present but also such a theory must be open to ongoing revision when considered in the context of changing social, economic, technological, cultural, and political conditions. Never being up to its task as a philosophy of a complex and changing present means that critical theory is deeply imbued with an anti-dogmatic impulse. Such an impulse is captured by Horkheimer (1972):

> Yet there is no fixed method for doing this; the only universal prescription is that one must have insights into one's own responsibility. Thoughtless and dogmatic application of the Critical Theory to practice in changed historical circumstances can only accelerate the very process which the theory aimed at denouncing. (v)

Therefore, being an accompanying voice to the narrative to modernity, critical theory may only be a provisional and partial social theory. It is in critical theory's attempt to unearth the real from reality of the contemporary, and in its provisionality, that the critical theorist wrestles with the recognition of the limits of consciousness as maps of reality. As Adorno (1977) argues, we must reject the illusion that "...thought is sufficient to grasp the totality of the real" (p. 120). And as Ricoeur reminds us, critical theory itself has traditional roots that frame the power of its emancipating mission:

> Critique is also a tradition. I would even say that it plunges into the most impressive tradition that of liberating acts, of the Exodus and the Resurrection. Perhaps there would be no more interest in emancipation, no more anticipation of freedom, if the Exodus and the Resurrection were effaced from the memory of mankind. (1981: 99–100).

For Ricoeur, the liberating mission of the Enlightenment and of modernity still nevertheless draws from principles of authority and from a "tradition" that were sustained by means of its own "prejudices." As Marianna Papastephanou points out, the origins of this understanding of being, a being freed through modernity from the shackles of tradition, in fact lapses back into its onto-theological roots which are now presented as universal claims to truth (Papastephanou 2002). This tradition is rooted in a scientific ontology explicitly supported by a philosophical ontology embedded in a teleological framework of universal history that is part of a moral universe whose identities are socially, culturally, militarily, and politically constructed (Anderson 1983). But I would suggest that it is in the very recognition of thought's closure that one may find an opportunity to go beyond thought to "*construct keys*, before which reality springs open" (1977: 130. My emphasis Adorno).

Mignolo's critique emphasizes the maintenance of the location in the production and use of knowledge and holds the potential to broadening the lens of social theory to provide exciting opportunities for social and political experimentation. While critical theorists wait for reality to spring forward, reality is already present in the lives of communities that have suffered the trauma of colonialism. The decolonial critique emerged out of the need to offer a counterposition to a history of philosophy in which conquest established an order of center and periphery through which the identity of the decolonial self emerged. Through the underside of modernity, the legacy and legitimizing of real and epistemic violence, and of how knowledge is produced and used, the decolonial project offers us the opportunity to construct keys to spring open realities. To achieve this, it needed to address the ontic and epistemic suppression that has been internalized through colonialism. From this view, the universality of modernity's *social imaginary* stands for a period of subjugation and asks if we are correct to base cosmopolitanism on "Western" assumptions. The decolonial negation of the affirmation of modernity, the existences of real and existential injustices alongside the ideals of the Enlightenment, provides the opportunity to open up space for all. However, the decolonial theorists create theory that negates the irrationality of self and plural ways of agency which threatens, much like the project of modernity, to become a new totality.

Both Mignolo and Delanty offer triadic models of what they describe, respectively, as critical cosmopolitanism.[2] Delanty's rests on the individual as the ultimate unit of analysis, that this is universal, and that bringing these two-components together in the intercultural encounter creates a space for the cosmopolitan imagination. Delanty, in maintaining the transformation and translational effects of modernity, argues that conjoining critical

---

[2] In later works, Mignolo changed the title of his project from critical theory to decolonial theory. For ease of exegesis, I will retain the use of critical cosmopolitanism, though use decolonial cosmopolitanism when Mignolo or others use that term.

theory with cosmopolitanism provides for a non-universalizing account of global dialogue that overcomes the intellectual and normative residues of Eurocentrism. However, though important his project fails as it remains tied to fundamental assumptions of Western thought. The claim that the cognitive order of modernity, as a context-transcendent principle, that all hold corresponding cognitive states, divides the world into diametric dualities of tradition versus modernity, self versus other. This assumption of the nature of social space restricts his project's ability to engage with a more conceptually confident post (de) colonialized world. However, Mignolo and Delanty understand the aims and methods of their endeavours in different ways.

Mignolo's model provides an ultimate unit of analysis through the recognition of a socially embedded ethnic identity traumatized through colonialism. As this trauma was experienced in different ways across multiple locations such an identity is not universal but as a form of relative universalism that draws on multiple autochthonous epistemic and ontic locations. It is through the connection between these communities that the cosmopolitan imagination emerges through which social and political experimentation can develop. Like Delanty, Mignolo, even more powerfully and compassionately, draws our attention to the fallibility of claims to certainty which highlights incompleteness. However, Mignolo's totalization of reality either spatially or temporally, which is in many ways Manichaean, causes ambivalence in his account of difference and identity (Pappas 2017). His reliance on the ethnic as the unit of analysis indicates a totality that lacks the internal dynamics to provide a vocabulary through which to enunciate societal tensions beyond abstraction. This also forces us to question Mignolo's professed rejection of Eurocentric universalism as he himself sets up a singular universal perspective as a parallelism to Eurocentrism: the ethnic.

GLOBAL CRITICAL THEORY: MODERNITY, RATIONALITY, TOTALITY

The "Western" tradition of critical theory seeks "...to liberate human beings from the circumstances that enslave them" (Horkheimer 1982: 244), and begins with the premise that "men and women are essentially unfree and inhabit a world rife with contradictions and asymmetries of power and privilege" (McLaren 1989: 166). The re-emergence of cosmopolitanism in the European mind has largely been associated with Kant's argument within *Perpetual Peace*. Similarly, the idea of critical theory begins in Kant's famous essay, "What is Enlightenment," in which he dared us *to be wise* and that "[E]nlightenment is man's emergence from his self-incurred immaturity which is self-inflicted not from a lack of understanding, but from the lack of belief in one's own intellectual resources." It was Man's [*sic*] entry into modernity, which prompted Habermas to proclaim the emergence of "...a radicalized consciousness [detaching] itself from all previous historical connections and [understanding] itself solely in abstract opposition to tradition and history as a whole" (Habermas 2007 [1980]: 363–364). Critical theory demonstrated this radicalized consciousness through the exploration and denunciation of the inequalities that arise through the class structure of capitalist industrial society and its modes of cultural production and consumption. Together these provided the ground for the systematic investigation of the causes of inequalities and injustices within emerging capitalist societies to carry through on the promise of rationality, democratization, and legitimacy of the "Enlightenment Project."

For many the mention of critical theory immediately brings to mind an instinctive retort to the work carried by the interdisciplinary group of anthropologists, cultural studies, psychologists, psychoanalysts, political and social theorists that have gathered in 1923 at the Institute for Social Research, the Frankfurt School (Institut für Sozialforschung) in Germany. By critical theory, I am referring, in broad terms, to "the attempt to construct a systematic, comprehensive social theory that can confront the key social and political problems of the day" (Kellner 1989: 2). The institute provided the first institutional environment for the interdisciplinary study of capitalist societies and to provide the means for their transformation. Drawing on the dialectical formulations of Hegelian and Marxist thought, the musings of Nietzsche, Freud, Max Weber, and other fashions in contemporary thought it has generated profound theories of social and political domination, power and legitimacy that have filled University library bookshelves and student's reading lists. Of course, there is not, nor was there ever one critical theory. As Agger (1998: 4) notes critical theory is best to be understood as a "theory cluster." Kellner's (1989) provides a periodization of critical theory into three generations.

The first generation is assigned to the early Frankfurt School, especially Horkheimer and Adorno, and their retheorizing of Marx considering the changing nature of capitalism, the emergence of mass culture and the bureaucratic state, the ascendancy of positivism in the human sciences, and the rise of fascism in Germany. The second generation is defined in terms of the "linguistic turn" of Jürgen Habermas, whose critiques of modernity have aimed to overcome the pessimism of the early Frankfurt School. Demonstrating a commitment to a philosophy of intersubjectivity, his work on critical theory also aims to counter the increasingly commodification of knowledge through an ongoing commitment to the critique of the public sphere. Writing in 1989, "Critical Theory now" can be thought of in terms of a third generation, involving a rejuvenation from theoretical sources outside of it, including poststructuralism (Poster 1989), postmodernism (Flax 1990; Best and Kellner

1991), feminist theory (Benhabib 1992; Benhabib et al. 1995), postcolonial theory (Spivak 1988), new social movement theory (Touraine 1985). More recently, a fourth generation of critical theorists have emerged who have attempted to rescue critical theory from its exclusionary focus on economism and to adjust its analytical focus on a relational account of sociology within an increasingly interconnected world. Marinopoulou (2017), Milstein (2015), Allen (2016), and Jaeggi (2014) have sought to rectify critical theory's omission of racist theories and an appreciation of the social dynamics of alienation. They have also introduced in the canon of Western critical theory approaches that incorporated discourses on the resistance to colonialism and empire in colonized countries. The lack of these perspectives in Western critical theory has had a profound effect on its ability to either recognize reality or transcend it. As Said noted in his *Culture and Imperialism*, (1993: 278), this was not a lamentable mistake by the critical theorists but was a motivated silence (see also Allen 2016: 1):

> Frankfurt School critical theory, despite its seminal insights into the relationships between domination, modern society, and the opportunities for redemption through art as critique, is stunningly silent on racist theory, antiimperialist resistance, and oppositional practice in the empire. (Said 1993: 278)

Relying on a spirit, a Geist, of what Said described as an invidious and false universalism which is central to European thought represents a "blithe universalism" that "assume[s] and incorporate[s] the inequality of races, the subordination of inferior cultures, the acquiescence of those who, in Marx's words, cannot represent themselves and therefore must be represented by others" (Said 1993: 335). According to this view, the Indians have their traditions, while the West has analytical and methodological rigor. The "Chinese" have ancient protocols to draw on, and the West has objective analysis. Where the "African" mind languishes in the poverty of superstition, the Western mind provides clinical guidance. And while "Islam" constantly longs for the past of religion, the Western mind resonates with the emancipation of secularism. It is from this perspective, in this era of global conceptual interconnectivity that the ultimate responsibility for the emergence of a reflective and critical social theory lays with the nursemaid of the epistemic and ontic lucidity, the West or the Westophile.

The history of social theory is brief in terms of the history of humanity and has, up until now, been largely tied to its European roots. Sociological theorists of modernity (and of multiple modernities), put forward ideas of the modern world emerging out of the twin processes of economic and political revolution located in Europe. This conflates Europe with modernity and renders the process of becoming modern, at least in the first instance, one of endogenous European development. The history of modernity, then, comes to rest on "the writing out of the colonial and postcolonial moment" (Bhabha 1994: 250). The radicalized consciousness of modernity, and of social theory, have found a self-certainty and prospered alongside war, violence, and poverty. This has left the neglected questions of not only how colonization and empire effected the colonized but also the effects of colonization on the population of colonizing countries waiting in the common room. Or, is the assumption that a people can conduct such acts and psychically get away scot-free?[3]

However, the world has changed once more with old certainties flagging. New social logics and ideologies are emerging which will require new ways of seeing the world beyond the certainty of either/or, of absolute abstractions from reality. This must be in a way that can identify sources of critical dialogue, to draw from and to not assimilate, and the cultivation of critical thought from multiple spaces. If the tradition of critical thought is to engage with this new world, cosmopolitanism, the key factor is the development of critical powers that moves beyond "blithe universalism" to offer a way in which the recognition of our incompleteness in our encounter with other and the world, can be reciprocally beneficial.

GLOBALIZING CRITICAL THEORY

The question is what is modernity? The answer is not just "instrumental rationality" (Max Weber), "optimal use of capital" (Karl Marx), or "functional differentiation" (Talcott Parsons, Niklas Luhmann), but supplementing and conflicting with these, it is *political freedom*, citizenship and civil society . . . meaning morality with these and justice are not pre-ordained . . . Quite the reverse is true. Modernity has an independent, living and simultaneously ancient and highly up-to-date wellspring of meaning in its midst: political freedom . . . Modernity accordingly means that a world of traditional certainty is perishing and being replaced, if we are fortunate, by legally sanctioned individualism for everyone. (Beck 2002: 157)

The term "individualization" refers to the dis-embedding and re-embedding of individuals that is not voluntary or historical but which occurred all at once through the conditions of the welfare states in the advanced Western societies since the 1960s. Individualization means the transformation of

---

[3] As I mentioned in the last chapter, even Kant was aware of these effects. Also see Aimé Césaire's Discourse on Colonialism (2000: 35–36). May thanks to Aurélia Mouzet, University of Arizona for reminding me of Césaire's essay.

the certainties of industrial society to a compulsion to invent certainties for oneself and others. In outlining the relationship between politics and sub-politics, Beck suggests that this individualization does not remain private but becomes political in a new sense as individuals shift into becoming "individualized individuals." For Beck, the everydayness experiences of the individual are transformed through the ideation of the transnational connection. Individualization, in Beck's work, is conceptually different from that associated with neoclassical economics and neoliberal governance (individualism). Rather than the atomizing reductionism associated with the latter, Beck's conceptualization concerns a reformatting of the relationship between society and individuals where individualization is celebrated as representing a shift toward a "legally binding world society of individuals" (Scott 1990: 4), where institutions "are no longer seen as *managers* of risk, but also as *sources* of risk" (Beck 2009: 54).

Beck recognizes a "double world" of complex interplays between symbolically rich political institutions (industrial modernity) and everyday life political practices that remain largely concealed (reflexive modernity). "On the one hand, a political vacuity of the institutions is evolving and, on the other hand, a non-institutional renaissance of politics. The individual is returning to society" (1997: 98). The neoliberal view of the individual understands the human being as a totally self-sufficient entity with a capacity for action that comes from within. In contrast to this, Beck deploys a specifically sociological understanding of individualization that recognizes civil, political, and social rights as well as paid employment focused upon individuals rather than the group. It can be understood as a dis-embedding of the practices of industrial society (nation, class, family, and gender) without any form of re-embedding.

In other words, traditional society was first supplanted by the industrial revolution which may be described as simple modernity which saw the development of class structures and the arrival of industrial and capitalist society. For Beck, we are now in the grip of a shift from the simple form of modernity to a third phase, which is for Beck, is the period of reflexive modernity.[4] The cognitive order of modernity consists of the whole range of second-order, reflexive or synthetic rules which emerged from the social orientations and activities of the different social groups and collective

---

[4] "Western" thought has shown itself to have developed a propensity to think in stages of development, which are usually accompanied by an underlying teleology of progress. Adam Smith (1723–1790) is a prominent example of such a tendency. During his lectures, Smith tells his students "there are four distinct stages which mankind passes thro: 1st, the Age of Hunters, 2dly, the Age of Shepherds; 3dly, the Age of Agriculture; and 4thly, the Age of Commerce" (LJA, 14), that have been driven by the, "...natural progress which men make in society" (LJA 207: see Smith 1978). Another prominent example is Auguste Comte (1798-1857), a founding figure of modern sociology, who in his *Cours de Philosophie Positive*, explained how societies evolved in accordance with a natural law. These stages are the theological-military, the metaphysical-transitional, and the

actors. These have had an input into the processes of formation of the state, capitalist economy, civil society, modern law, and corresponding cultural forms. Since then, these rules have been sustained and modified in keeping with changing circumstances with succeeding generations having continued to participate in the reproduction of these various societal forms. This new modernity has to solve the human-constructed problems which arise from the development of industrial society; to tackle how the risks produced as a consequence of modernity can be "prevented, minimized, dramatized, or channeled" (1992: 19). This notion of reflexive modernization as exemplified by Beck can certainly be seen as expressing a more optimistic alternative to the postmodern theses, with the importance of human agency figuring strongly.

Immersed within the confines of a reflexive or second modernity, of an enlarged world, this would lead to the emergence of a growing consciousness and what Beck and his associates describe as "cosmopolitization." Cosmopolitanism, for Beck, is an inherently ethical project as it raises the individual awareness of global human rights against a common back-drop of local abuses "human rights are no longer associated with citizenship status, and inequalities in life opportunities are not experienced solely within national contexts" (Beck 2005: 31). "Cosmopolitization" disrupts the relationships between the individual and local institutions, with, "my life, my body, my 'individual existence' become part of another world, or foreign cultures, religions, histories and global interdependencies, without my realizing it or expressly wishing it" (2006: 19).

SELF, OTHER, AND THE WORLD

Beck's dual thesis accounts of the "individualized individual" and the process of cosmopolitization leads Delanty to state that as such, "[I]t also offers a route out of the critique of domination and a general notion of emancipation that has so far constrained critical theory. It provides a promising approach to connect normative critique with empirically based analysis focused on exploring news ways of seeing the world" (Delanty 2012: 41). Like Beck, Delanty sees cosmopolitan theory as offering an alternative to liberal and republican theory (2011: 634). However, unlike Beck, Delanty is keen to avoid the perceived residues of conceptual Eurocentrism, the idea

---

scientific-industrial. See Comte and Andreski (2015). Of course, as the reader will appreciate this development trajectory of humanity is undermined by the existence of anomalies as suggested by the decolonial perspective.

that concepts generated in the West are universal. He also wishes to draw on the critical aspects of cosmopolitanism. This incorporation of cosmopolitanism to the perspective of critical theory, Delanty hopes, offers the opportunity for critical social theory to meet the new challenges in the era of globalization.

In terms of developing a cosmopolitan social science, the research objective becomes one of identifying the relevant mechanisms and processes of such forms as developmental processes that provide the basic diachronic level of analysis (Delanty 2012: 348–349). This would seek to identify those features of all civilizations that display internal logics of learning and is characterized by a new role for the imagination in social life (Delanty 2009: 180). Delanty's argument is that "...modernity offers an overarching framework for the world is also a way in which to see how commonality is possible" (2014: 10). Such a "cognitive universalism" indicates universalistic concerns that are not specific to any single culture. This does not commit oneself to a perspective on the other but, as modernity problematizes identity, meaning and memory, it would problematize one's own assumptions and those of the other. Therefore, in ontologizing social relations, the moment of immanent transcendence, of finding the means to overcome societal problems within the resources of the everyday, provided through cosmopolitanism "provides [a] promising approach to connect normative critique with empirically based analysis focused on exploring news ways of seeing the world" (Delanty 2009: 2–3).

The idea of critical cosmopolitanism is relevant to the renewal of critical social theory in its traditional concern with the critique of social reality and "...the transformative potential *within the present*" (Delanty 2013: 336). Though Delanty concedes that historically, critical theory has neglected the implications of cosmopolitanism in respect of the development of theoretical perspectives, he argues that cosmopolitanism is relevant to both the renewal of critical social theory and in the need to address new challenges. To develop this argument, he draws on key defining features of the critical theory as developed through its Hegelian/Marxist heritage (Delanty 2012: 38).

For Delanty, it is Honneth's notion of a disclosing critique, the encounter of different viewpoints that provides for the basis for the cosmopolitan analytical perspective. For Honneth (2000), the conception of critique is a "disclosing critique" that exposes the social world to new interpretations and existential perspectives. Here critique is understood as being immanent in social relations and the self-understanding of social actors conducted through a process of self-problematizing and reflexivity. This is the core-defining tenet of the epistemological framework of cosmopolitanism and will require some unpacking as it provides one of the steppingstones to developing the account of critical cosmopolitanism set out in this book.

Critical theory undertakes to understand social phenomena through the dialectical interpretative process of articulating contradictions. What does this
mean? It means that critical theorist, through a process of self-problematizing
and reflexivity, is looking for the contradictions within societal structures,
economic, political cultural, and that the means of overcoming these can be
found in the practicality of the real-world. As Piet Strydom notes, "[T]he
sense of the concept of immanent transcendence which distinguishes Critical
Theory's form of critique from the rest, resides in the basic conceptual and
methodological requirement that the adoption and exercise of the critical perspective must have an objective foothold in social reality" (2010: 5). Such a
notion of immanent transcendence constitutes, as argued by Strydom (2011):

> ...the core of the cosmopolitan imagination in so far as this is a way of viewing
> the social world in terms of its immanent possibilities for self-transformation
> and which can be realized only by taking the cosmopolitan perspective of Other.
> (Strydom 2011: Cited Delanty 2012: 41)

This immanent transcendence, the overcoming of contradictions within
present social relations and "that a critical analysis of society needs to be
tied to an innerworldly instance of transcendence" (Honneth 2003: 204).
Immanent transcendence operates like a double critique in that it first signifies
a process of reflective practice. Second, it also suggests a capacity within that
process that makes the process possible in the first place (Sandbeck 2011).[5]
It is in the recognition of this moment of transformative dialectic, maintains
Delanty, that newness is created. This has the potential to "cultivate an
attitude of critical deliberation and ways of *imagining new ways of living*"
(Delanty 2009, 2011: 641, 2014: 9. My emphasis). What Delanty is seeking
to find are sources of critical dialogue for the cultivation of critical thought.
To theoretically enable this attitude, Delanty draws, but transforms Axel
Honneth's notion of disclosing critique.

For Honneth (2000), the conception of critique is a "disclosing critique"
that exposes the social world, the tension between its ideals and their anomalies, to new interpretations and existential perspectives. Delanty's incorporation of the cosmopolitan imagination into critical theory, allows him
to transform Honneth's notion through the encounter with alternative and
competing worldviews, or "civilizational encounters" (Nelson 1976: 1981).
To pursue the cosmopolitan potential of a disclosing critique his point of
departure begins with the idea of multiple modernities (See for examples
Taylor 1999; Eisenstadt 2003). However, to deprive this universality of any

---

[5] Far from the radicalisation of consciousness, this has its roots in Christian theology, and has at its
core two aspects. See Sandbeck (2011).

determinate historical content or analytical function, Delanty approaches the problem of modernity from the perspective of global history (Delanty 2009: 186–192). Here he draws on Arnason (2003) who extends the perspective of the "civilizational encounter" of Nelson (1976, 1981) and Eisenstadt (1986, 2001, 2003). Delanty puts forward the thesis that "modernity" should be theorized in terms of "self-transformation" which takes different forms against the background of widening networks and communication. If one argues that the universalizing feature of modernity, its cognitive universalism, "is the drive to make all of culture translatable" (Delanty 2009: 194), then the difficulty of epistemic and historical privilege no longer arises as we can no longer "assume[s] that non-Western societies exist" (Delanty 2009: 181).

Delanty is arguing that such an approach would serve as a corrective not only to the "tradition" versus "modernity" debate, but equally in respect of the perception that modernity represents the latest stage of European civilizational progress. In drawing on an underdeveloped implication of Arnason's work (2006), he argues that rather than relying on external or internal factors for explaining the rise of the West, the emphasis must be on the dynamics and modes of cultural interaction.[6] Here distinct parts of the world become linked through the expansion and diffusion of systems of exchange, networks of communication, and various forms of third culture. Theorizing modernity in such a way provides Delanty with the means to modify the analytical stress from the idea of *plurality* toward *means of interaction*, such as cross-cultural encounters and interactions, rather than by arrogation and assimilation by the West. For Delanty, the argument that modernity offers an overarching framework for the translatability of the world, also provides a way in which to see how commonality is possible in terms of developing a post-universal critical dialogue (Delanty 2014: 10). Culture, like cosmopolitanism, is both discursive and an arena of claim-making which entails the imagination, and which raises the possibility of critique of the status quo (Delanty 2011: 641).

DECOLONIAL THEORY: HETEROGENEITY AND NEGOTIATION

Rather than the "patented" claim to originality of the critical theorist as a companion to modernity, for Mignolo, cosmopolitanism is *critical* when it

---

[6] Johan Arnason (2006) argued that in the study of nation-building that comparative approaches had remained remarkably limited and underdeveloped. Delanty takes the logic of Arnason's observation further by arguing that nation-building, cultural development should be understood through the dynamics and modes of social, political, economic, and cultural interaction. I expressed this idea of a phase of mutual development.

acts as a critique of the Eurocentric presuppositions of cosmopolitan thought. Acting as a curator,[7] it is only in the overcoming of the dichotomies of modernity, when viewed from the exterior of modernity, joined with but at the edges of Western political, economic, social, and cultural structures, that we can transform its historical, cultural, and civilizational legacies.[8] A claim central to the decolonial project is that European cosmologies, epistemologies, and practices of knowledge production have come to be taken as universally valid and "objective." This is motivated by the historical awareness of how "Other" voices and peoples have continuously been subalternized and articulates the political aim to challenge this subalternization. In rethinking critical thought or critical knowledges from other spaces and places represents a development of the emancipatory ethic that could not be achieved within the hegemonic practices of modernity (Wals 2007; Caney 2001; Connolly 1995).

To counter the totalizing effects of Eurocentrism, rather than viewing indigenous epistemic practices as parochial and "cultural" simply due to their differences, the decolonial project aims to develop an account of self-realization where these different forms of consciousness meet (Smith 2005; Quijano 2000; Mignolo 2008). Importantly, rather than accept the "neutrality" of principles of the "Enlightenment project," it aims to uncover the reality *today* caused by historical patterns of power that have been based on exploitation and domination. Through linking the cosmopolitan premise of openness to the world motivated with the historical consciousness of how "Other" voices and peoples have been continuously subalternized and allows for the transcendence of the exceptionalism of European thought and to rethink reality through the prism of addressing the effects of domination and exploitation (Mignolo 2006: 323). As Caruth argues, it is "[T]hrough the notion of trauma . . . we can understand that a rethinking of reference is aimed not at eliminating history but at resituating it in our understanding, that is, at precisely permitting *history* to rise where *immediate understanding* may not" (2015 [1996]: 11). It is in confronting the consciousness of European modernity with the trauma of colonialism that announces the political aim

---

[7] I would not to give the impression that I wish to detract from the intellectual and practical accomplishments of Mignolo. This would be far from the case. From my perspective, Mignolo acts as a curator, in the sense of a precise technical term, in bringing together substantial ideas to protect and develop them as a unified a vision. It is in this role, that is in the bringing together of diverse ideas, that is the interest of this paper. Also, see Wood (2017: n.53) in which he argues that in respect of epistemic decolonial projects Mignolo's work could be described as providing a metanarrative account.

[8] The choice of Mignolo should not be understood as a detraction from the substantive work other decolonial thinkers and activists. For a nonexhaustive set of examples, see Wood (2017); Morgensen (2011); Dhanda and Parashar (2009); Gordon (2010) Diversi and Moreira (2009); Wiredu (1995); Apffel-Marglin (1996); Santos et al. (2008); Mohanty (2003); Allen (2016); Smith (1999); Kangas and Salmenniemi (2016); Thiongó (1981); Ndlovu-Gatsheni and Zondi (2016); Hoppe and Nicholls (2010); Pieterse and Parekh (1995); Santos (2014).

of "Critical consciousness and decolonization," to facilitate a vision of the right of a people *to be*, *positive liberty*, through which capacities within the individual subject and peoples must be allowed to emerge.[9]

For Mignolo, his concern is not "to tell the truth over lies, but to think otherwise, to move toward 'an other logic'" (Mignolo 2000: 67–70). Such a nonuniversalizing kind of research, a "paradigma otro" (Other Paradigm) (Escobar 2004: 31) stems from the borderlands of the world-system and acts, as postmodernism once claimed, as a "disruptive counterforce to the social practices which says, 'do not tamper with me for I am good, and eternal'" (Poster 1989: 3). Rather than draw on the reactions of the postmodern or the postcolonialist with their emphasis on "reason as a reason of terror" (Dussel 1995: 66), Mignolo argues that the decolonial project must aim to,

> rethink and reconceptualise the stories that have been told and the conceptualization that has been put into place to divide the world between Christians and pagans, civilized and barbarians, modern and pre-modern, and developed and undeveloped regions and people. (Mignolo 2000b: 98)

Foregrounding Mignolo's approach, philosophy, for Dussel, is supposed to be a thinking about reality. As an intellectual traveller with Mignolo, Dussel's method of "analectic" or "anadialectic," comes about through the "revelation" of the other, and goes beyond the self-enclosure, the completeness, that Dussel asserts typifies the dialectic in "Western" ontology. If philosophy is supposed to be the activity of thinking about reality, Dussel asks, then it is,

> ...distant thinkers, those who had a perspective of the center from the periphery, those who had to define themselves in the presence of an already established image of the human person and in the presence of uncivilized fellow humans, the newcomers, the ones who hope because they are always outside, these are the ones who have a clear mind for pondering reality. (Dussel 1985 [1980]: 4)

It is the "clarity" of thinkers at the periphery that has the same revolutionary potential as the proletariat had for Marx. "Philosophical intelligence is never so truthful, clean, and precise as when it starts from oppression and does not have to defend any privileges, because it has none" (Dussel 1985 [1980]: 4). Like this, he takes his position to have gone beyond ontology: it

---

[9] In Africa, concern has been expressed at the use of Western models of self in the field of trauma counselling. Gilbert reminds us of the fact that each culture provides its members with a conceptual framework for making sense of illness and emotional distress (Gilbert 2006). However, the theoretical assumptions that underpin counselling interventions are based on models of human nature and emotional distress that stem directly from the implicit cultural assumptions about the "Self" within North American/European cultures.

is a trans-ontology, a genuine metaphysics. The philosophical problem is not to describe "in reality" both sides of the border. The problem is to do it from its exteriority. It is from those that are marginalized beneath the ideals of emancipatory and radicalized consciousness of modernity that a philosophy of liberation can materialize (Dussel 1985 [1980]: 15).

Eduardo Mendieta describes Enrique Dussel's use of the term "transmodernity" as "underscore[ing] that Liberation Philosophy is not about either negating modernity or blithely accepting it, but about transcending it anadialectically; that is, to think the couplet modernity and postmodernity not just from within, but also and especially, from the perspective of its reverso, its underside, its occluded other" (Mendieta xxii). If modernity is linked to Eurocentrism, the notion of "transmodernity" is meant to indicate an alternative account of the interconnection of peoples. This does not rely on divisions that are based on a putative cognitive capacity, Eurocentrism, and promises a way out of the impasses of postliberalism and postmodernity. This also promises to provide an alternative to the narrative inevitability of the neoliberal order.

Transmodernity operates to displace the teleological and linear progression of modernity and postmodernity, rendering even the most anti-Western postmodernists still complicit with the temporal concepts of colonialism that erased the colonial difference.[10] While "postmodernists criticize modern reason as a reason of terror," Dussel writes, "we criticize modern reason because of the irrational myth that it conceals" (1995: 66). From the decolonial perspective, the postmodern denunciation of the totalizing spirit of European modernity merely poses an alternative "universe" of different "Western" world of white, male, and professional upper classes. Rather than construct an alternative universe, Dussel states that the concept of transmodernity seeks to subsume "the best of globalized European and North American modernity" from the perspective of liberating reason (not European emancipation), and

---

[10] Marita Rainsborough (2016: 487, n. 38) describes Mignolo's account of critical cosmopolitanism as postcolonial. Mignolo is critical of the postcolonial approach and distances himself from it. However, see Mignolo (2007: 452) "Coloniality and de-coloniality introduces a fracture with both, the Eurocentered project of post-modernity and a project of post-coloniality heavily dependent on post-structuralism as far as Michel Foucault, Jacques Lacan and Jacques Derrida have been acknowledged as the grounding of the post-colonial canon: Edward Said, Gayatri Spivak and Hommi Bhabha. De-coloniality starts from other sources . . . The de-colonial shift, in other words, is a project of de-linking while post-colonial criticism and theory is a project of scholarly transformation within the academy." Mignolo argues that postmodern thought attempts to be a liberating discourse, but still maintains the myth of a progress of human liberation with its roots in the European tradition and which reduces the located and embedded human condition to an abstraction. Though the rationality of the centre may make claims to universality these need to be accounted for by the reason and understanding of the periphery. But more than this, "subaltern reason," as for Mignolo Postcoloniality should examine how these experiences of liminality can be used to create political agency based on the concrete experiences of postcolonial subjects, a stance that some parts of postcolonial scholarship refuse for being overly "antagonistic" (Lazarus 2005: 423).

on the other the critical affirmation of the liberating aspects of the cultures and knowledge excluded from or occluded by modernity" (Dussel 2002: 223). While theorists of modernity may embrace the benevolent belief in modernity's power of translatability, the project of decolonial cosmopolitanism aims to demonstrate how colonialism was constitutive in the making of modernity and the capitalist world-system. This can be understood as both a call for moving beyond modernity and its effects and, most importantly, as critically engaging and supporting non-Western knowledges. This is followed by the claim that subjugated or local knowledges always tend to do less violence to the local particulars or to impose hierarchical structures of credibility that foreclose the contributions of many unconventional or lower-status knowers (Alcoff 2007: 80).

This underlines the importance of constructing theoretical approaches that instigate research from the perspective of the marginalized through which to shatter the complacency of reality. Such research intends to show how the underlying logics of epistemic, social, political, and economic coloniality can be traced in the very distinct situations of the modern, "wretched of the earth" (Fanon 2008 [1952]), but which indicate new forms of social being. The focus here is on creating a border thinking where epistemic traditions may *intersect in novel and more democratic ways* (Mignolo 2000b). Reminding one of disclosing critique, border thinking arises "at the intersection of local histories enacting global designs and local histories dealing with them." Here the former launched by a "desire for homogeneity" and a "need of hegemony" (Mignolo 2000a: 310), confronts the latter, the "subaltern perspective," in which the imaginary of the modern world system cracks. This reveals the instances where the modern/colonial system has created spaces for new thinking and acting (Mignolo 2000: 23; Escobar 2004; Mignolo 2010c: 15–20). Simultaneously, this carries with it the assertion that, "border" spaces in which new forms of consciousness relationship to the world emerge from the places where indigenous and Eurocentric paradigms meet.

Opposed to "abstract universals," this concept of the border is meant to signify that the locality of subaltern knowing, far from simply being "the other side" of "Western" knowing, has a border-like quality. Border thinking then becomes a "tool of the project of Critical cosmopolitanism" (Mignolo 2002: 174), and a "future planetary epistemological and critical localism" (Mignolo 2000a: 88, 157). To advocate such an approach is not to aim at the creation of a universal ideological position, but instead emphasizes the acceptance of different ways of being. The point is not the positing of a "blueprint of a future and ideal society projected from a single point of view [that of abstract universals] that will return us [again] to the Greek paradigms and European legacies" (Mignolo 2000a: 744). But it is to advocate being reflexive about one's own, and more importantly, the "Other's" standpoint (Mendieta 2009:

252). Therefore, "border thinking is the epistemology of the exteriority; that is, of the outside created from the inside" (Mignolo and Tlostanova 2006: 206). Such a shift is important for what it helps reveal, including the subjects left out or marginalized by much of critical theory and their sociopolitical and epistemic agency but also the association between thought and social and political intervention. This points toward the formulation of counterhegemonic research and political programs that reflect the lived experiences of the other.

RECONSIDERING THE LANGUAGE OF CRITICAL COSMOPOLITANISM

Delanty and Mignolo do contribute to the development of the family of cosmopolitan social theories. The task of this family of theories is one of undermining homogenous claims of finality or closure. However, though both make a promissory claim to emancipatory fidelity, a promissory claim to creating newness in the encounter of self, other, and the world, through a setting down of a stake of closure, of finality, the debate is over. In the case of Delanty, it is his pledge to the extension of human rights and democracy, and in the case of Mignolo, is the exclusivity of ethnic origins that provide the means of exceptionalism. So what does this mean for either of our protagonists and for the development of this book?

Delanty is keenly aware of the problems that arise if we assume that global social theory is centered on the supposed unique and splendid isolation of the European historico-socio-theoretical experience. The decolonial project is premised on the statement that the rise of modernity was accompanied by the domination and exploitation of foreign peoples and resources. Though we have come to understand the Enlightenment and modernity as purely European/Western experiences, the truth is that it was global encounters, in respect of knowledge or conquest, which allowed for the particularity of these moments in human history. Thus, the knowledge which provided for those temporal moments did not arise from purely European sources.

Delanty does embrace the notion of cosmopolitanism. He recognizes that the concepts that he wishes to develop in a global context cannot be assumed to be purely European but must recognize that these concepts have changed as they have travelled. However, he does so while maintaining modernity's fundamental claim to provide a singular cognitive-temporal moment. It is through this moment that critical theorists augments reality as modernity through the projection of ideals and competences. The objectivity produced by this moment saturates the social environment and the body as a "deep structure" through which the life-form of the West and agency-individual and societal is justified and stabilized.

However, the stability of this view of self, whether in respect of the identity-formation of the individual and the formation of Western society's identity is not justified in the light of the decolonial critique. Mignolo, and the wider decolonial project provide an assessment of the shallowness of the ideals and competences of modernity. It has rightly reacted to the temporal proclamations of modernity's ideals with a call for the enunciation of injustices of the global economic, legal, and political system from "other spaces." The decolonial rejection of decontextualized ideals represents a radical account of transmodernity that undercuts elite discourse to instead focus on the re-appropriation of self, social, cultural, economic, and political projects. However, though it does enunciate what was glaringly silent it fails to move through its own geo-theoretical horizon to nurture difference and to provide a means of global transformation. This is a missed opportunity, one that misses Dussel's own project of epistemology, the global overcoming of the underside of modernity. Here a conceptual post-Western critical cosmopolitan social would look to provide resources across borders not as another account of absolute universalism that claims to be attractive as a distillation of common universal experience, through which to explain modern global history as a teleological or hierarchical order. Rather, the aim would be to provide an account of critical cosmopolitanism which accepts existing, multiple imagined and existent ideas of progress, or "modernities." This opens modernity to form a transmodernity and destabilizes modernity's subjectivity, inside (as in its internal self-image) and outside (as it experiences this with the other). Furthermore, rather than provide an "superior" alternative account, following Ashis Nandy's call for a cross-cultural cosmopolitanism (Nandy 1998), such a project would look to enunciate beyond borders and elites discourses, to offer an account capable of serving as a critical resource of exchange for global relational sociologies.

The richness of borders only comes through the nourishing of self-appropriation. The decolonial project provides an unparalleled critique of modernity and critical theory from the exterior. It demonstrates how the ideals of a society carry with them an underside. Such ideals are maintained through the interlinking of political, social, economic, judicial, and cultural material and symbolic signifiers. These signifiers maintain the agent's sense of reality, rationality, the irrational, inside and outside, and mediate human agency. However, despite this critical perspective, because of its totalizing of reality into diametric dualities, West versus the rest, it fails to provide a space for internal heterogeneity. To allow the richness of the border to flourish, to provide a means for social and political experimentation to take place, requires the provision of social structures and signifiers that facilitate enactive and pluralistic forms of agency to emerge.

THE BORDERS OF THE IMMANENT
AND TRANSCENDENT

Both Delanty and Mignolo do recognize the practical nature of the co-cognitive interconnectedness of self, other, and the world. Knowledge of things is achieved by sharing mental resources, attitudes, and contents of thought, and this application of knowledge transforms "I" into "we." Delanty demonstrates this through his notions of a relational sociology and immanent transcendence and Mignolo through the idea of border thinking.

However, these notions are prejudiced through assumptions based on a supposed temporal moments of clarity, of beginnings, of uniqueness. Through the closure of fundamental questions concerning the human condition this fails to recognize thought's own incompleteness. We can describe this through the application of our heuristic device of diametric dualities. The decolonial critique makes us aware of how the material and symbolic structures of society that enunciate its ideals disguise injustices to personhood and peoples. Mignolo aims to set out a sociohistorical informed account that bridges the gap between theory and practice to provide loci of enunciation for claims of injustice. In terms of our account of the creation of societal diametric dualities, this establishes space "within" of normality, of rationality, that is totalizing in effect and which generates an "outside" of otherness to signify difference and reification between my ethnic identity-formation and a wider source of humanity out-there. In turn, the articulation of this identity, and thereof reason, is placed within the hands of an authority which fails to acknowledge the multiple composition of identity. Lastly, such a totalizing account of social space focuses attention of the whole rather than the direct and immediate needs of the parts of a community. This sets up a tension between an authority and the individual. As identity-formation is reduced to reification, this does not provide imaginative resources for self and societal change that would come through the individual's enactment with, through the enunciation of injustices, the space of the social.

The idea of immanent transcendence of the critical theorist which Delanty draws on, evokes the possibility of things to come, of a teleology of reason in the mastery of the relationship between self, other and the world. Not utopian, it looks for the contradictions in the present, in what is given as rational within modernity. However, the problem for critical theory's account of immanent transcendence is that it is neither immanent nor transcendent. It is not immanent as it fails to account for the reality of the societal and individual dynamics that were introduced to the social spaces of both colonizing and colonizer countries during the processes of empire building and colonization. Because of this, it is not transcendent as it is not an authentic account of immanence as it fails to capture the means of negation, change, that is present though silenced in the European mind. It would appear to be a problematic proposition to sustain, that in the critical analysis of modern societies, one can make a claim to immanence, when its theoretical horizon stops at the shores of the Atlantic and Mediterranean seas. In failing to account for the question of race and colonialism within its own theoretical horizon, it cannot provide a description of immanent effects of the enactment of these phases of societal development on the sociopsychological structures of society. This failure to do so means, specifically, that it cannot engage with critical dialogue beyond the supposed competences of modernity.

While it is correct to state that the traditions of European and Latin American critical theory do advocate notions of emancipation, what emerges through the analysis of both thinkers is that they do so through maintaining a diametric dualistic understanding of social ontology. Both accounts have created a world of identity and non-identity, good versus bad. This results in a balbative world, in which a complex world is reduced to monochronal shades, that fails to capture the experiences of life and spaces in which these take place, in all their vivid variations. Because both social ontologies' see the world through self-reliant diametric dualities, both fail to accommodate the ability of cosmopolitanism to provide a means of internal critique and the ability for internal change. Both miss the space in-between. That is, both consciously miss that we *share consciousness*.

But despite their limitations, both authors have made through their triadic models, significant contributions to the evolution of critical cosmopolitanism. Drawing from Mignolo's and Delanty's strengths and weaknesses, and if we follow the cosmopolitan principle of critique and cooperation, it is possible to begin to formulate an account that safeguards the individual while drawing our attention to the importance on the practical implications of co-cognitive creativity, aesthesis, through which to articulate abuses of economic, social, and political over-positioning and injustices that are hidden through discourse. Understanding the encounter between Mignolo's decolonial project and Delanty's critical cosmopolitanism as reciprocal phases in societal development, as originary though nonbinary moments, allows us to begin a movement of cosmopolitan creativity. In bringing Delanty and Mignolo together in such a space shatters critical theory's commitment to an inherently Eurocentric idea of historical progress and opens it to up to the prospect of relative universalism. Introducing Delanty to Mignolo equally shatters the totalities through which the decolonial theorist represents the world and allows for internal heterogeneity. Though this initial synthesis is promising, we would be still left with the vestiges of both thinker's totalizing accounts of social theory which constructs the social world into diametric dualities.

What is required then is an account of social ontology capable of providing the grounds for radical thought beyond the confines of the abstract or as an essentialized identity. This must be capable of replicating the creative tension between individuality and sociality, Delanty and Mignolo, and of providing a critical perspective, diametric duality, and of offering the opportunity for critical learning, concentric duality.[11] That is, we need a social ontology into which we can "dock" the positive contributions, their critical perspective, of both Mignolo and Delanty but which is grounded in existing social practices. Watsuji's socio-epistemology of *fūdo* and *aidagara* provides a space that is capable of accommodating these processes with Delanty and Mignolo offering the critical perspective. But before we can begin this descent into human understanding to then ascend to critique, as most readers will not have encountered Watsuji before, the next chapter turns to his work.

---

[11] Again, to be clear, these notions of concentric and diametric dualities are heuristic devices to allow us to spatially uncover structural blockages to individual and societal openness, enactive agency, and the articulation of injustices.

Chapter 3

Watsuji, Modernity, and the Existential Explanation of the Phenomenon of Life

INTRODUCTION

The world of social science that Watsuji Tetsurō bequeaths to us is the study of the space that we inhabit, "our" institutions, "our" values, the planet that we share with other beings, and how these can be undermined or allow human well-being to flourish. It is a world of science that recognizes and nourishes its incompleteness and uncertainty. Of course, for many acquainted with the work of Watsuji, this will give some measure of discomfit. Watsuji, and his colleagues within the Kyoto School of philosophy,[1] for a significant period after the end of World War II, have been presented as archetypal characters of resistance to modernity. However, what will be argued in this chapter is that Watsuji's work represents an account which can address the fear which has haunted modernity since its birth pangs: the recognition of our incompleteness itself provides the means to move beyond our own limitations. Furthermore, I will argue that his thought represents an engagement with the effects of modernity globally and provides a non-Eurocentric account of social theory for the decolonial cosmopolitan project.

Watsuji was a remarkable thinker. He managed to escape, momentarily, the confines of his own social consciousness. But let us be clear about this claim. Watsuji is firmly rooted in the world-forms of Japanese culture. This was informed by Shinto, Confucius, and Buddhist thought. Equally, he lived during a period immediately after the formal reentry into the realm of interstate relations and during the expansion of Western imperial power. However, the remarkable aspect of Watsuji's thinking and that of the broader

---

[1] Though Watsuji had a relationship with the Kyoto School, he was really on the fringes of their work.

Kyoto School was their recognition that any system of thought was temporal-spatial located and, as such, was only a partial account of being human. Watsuji did this through presenting a theoretical account that drew not only on his Shinto, Confucius, and Buddhist heritage, but one that could appreciate the benefits of phenomenological studies. Watsuji was a cosmopolitan thinker first and foremost in his recognition of the limitations of all systems of thought.[2] As we shall see, not because he drew on "exotic" forms of consciousness, but because he looked for the synergies between different ways of understanding the world through which to provide new ways of seeing and being in the world.

Of course, one can find roots for his presentation of a relational sociology in the Confucist concepts of *Li* and *dao,* but to claim these as solely Chinese phenomenon, as concepts that are descriptive of social practices, would be to enact a claim of exceptionalism. While the importance of Watsuji's intellectual heritage for his work is undeniable, one should not consider it is an alternative or competing view of seeing the world. As I shall demonstrate, the model of social analysis that Watsuji presents is capable of exchanging ideas with other examples of relational social theory generated by global cultures. I will argue that his work represents a form of proto-decolonial thought that has the capacity to illuminate and address our societal limitations through intercultural exchange. Here Watsuji shares an affinity with the decolonial movement in that he rejects absolute universalism and instead posits the multi-spatial transmodernity that challenges singular accounts of being human. While the chapter will demonstrate the importance of Watsuji's intellectual heritage for his work it will not do so to suggest that it is an alternative or competing view of seeing the world. The more modest and humbler proposition that this chapter will offer, one that the evidence suggests that Watsuji would support, is that the model of social analysis he presents is capable of exchanging ideas with other examples of relational social theory generated by global cultures.

To begin, I will introduce the reader to the philosophical anthropology that Watsuji derived from his study of East-Asian cultural traditions and which he used to his ethical system. Watsuji and the Kyoto School of Japanese

---

[2] Of course, although the chapter makes the claim that Watsuji provides a form of cosmopolitan social theory that draws on East- Asian as well as "Western" disciplines, this is not to suggest that he is alone in articulating a "cosmopolitan" framework from Japan. The Japanese concept of Kyōsei (Kyō meaning together and sei meaning living), articulates the view of the individual and society as "living together, coexistence, and conviviality" (Mayaram 2009; See also Sugimoto 2012: 452–462). As Sugimoto notes, the demographic changes that have occurred in Japan since the end of the World War II have had a significant impact on the image of Japan as a supposedly mono-ethnic culture. Therefore, though cosmopolitanism has some currency in popular parlance the term Kyōsei has since the 1990s been effective in challenging notions of Japanese uniqueness as well as promoting practices of cultural coexistence domestically and internationally.

Philosophy have been subject to significant criticism in respect of their alleged involvement with the promulgation of Japanese Fascist ideology in the period surrounding the Pacific War during the twentieth century. Though on the fringes of my concerns on this book, not to explore and respond to these concerns could be viewed as a significant omission in a book that is emphasizing the importance of Watsuji for global social theory. The argument that will be developed is that Watsuji is a decolonial thinker who challenges cosmopolitanism's emphasis on institutional change or as an analytical accompaniment to globalization, to one predicated on personal/social transcendence.[3] In applying Watsuji's work as a challenge of hegemonic norms entails that modernity, and its accompanying institutions, and the experience of the colonized are originary but not binary traits, and that both beginnings and endings are revealing. To begin to locate Watsuji's work within his intellectual milieu, we shall now turn to an account of his philosophical anthropology.

COSMOPOLITAN ROOTS

From the confines of being an isolated, distinct, and autonomous group of islands in Eastern Asia, Japan "entered modernity" during a period described as the Meiji Restoration.[4] Concomitant with this was the emergence of what we now understand as modern Japanese philosophy through which their intellectuals negotiated Japan's relationship to European intellectual trends. However, one needs to be mindful that in introducing the term "modernity" into the commentary that one may be taking sides in the debate concerning Japanese or decolonialist thinkers supposed rejection of modernity and its so-called "values." As the discussion on decolonial theory's conception of the underside of modernity and its proposition of epistemic and ontic knowledge from a borderline demonstrated, it may not necessarily be analytically useful to construct boundaries, such as modernity, for the spatial capturing of time. Watsuji and the Kyoto School of philosophers attempted to transcend the gulf between "Eastern" and "Western" "traditions" of philosophy to produce a school of thought capable of addressing the problems of modernity. This was not an understanding of multiple modernities as hybridity with an explicit teleology, but as existent, multiple imagined, and lived ideas of progress, or

---

[3] To preempt any premature criticism, in part two, I argue that this process of self-realisation needs to have structural support.

[4] See Swale (2009), for an accessible introduction and analysis of the Meiji Restoration. Swale's work is useful as he positions the Restoration in terms of other important global social and political events as well as reflecting on the historiography of the Restoration and its implications for Japan.

"modernities." And, it was into this intellectual, ontological, and ontic period of change of Japanese society that Watsuji began to develop as an intellectual.

While early in his philosophical career, Watsuji had been attracted to the work of Nietzsche (Parkes 1991), he was also a thinker that was attracted to the cultural and intellectual life of Eastern Asian and Japan as his publication record demonstrates: *Nietzsche Studies* (1913),[5] in his reminiscence of Natsume Sōseki in *Revival of Idols* (1918), and his interest in Buddhism in Dōgen (1926) and *The Practical Philosophy of Primitive Buddhism (1927)*. However, it was while on an academic visit to Europe in which he encountered Martin Heidegger's *Sein und Zeit* (Being and Time 1927) that began the development of his account of a relational ethics. This combined his Confucius and Buddhist heritage with his appreciation of European phenomenological thought. This synthesis of global practices of thought would result in his production of his systematic account of *Ethics*.[6] This point cannot be stressed sufficiently. In the context of the transformation of Japan, its entry into the global system and geo-socio-political circumstances, Watsuji produced an extraordinary synthesis from his training in European thought and in East-Asian philosophical and religious traditions. This synthesis stepped outside of modernity's temporal frame to provide a means of revealing the social practices of Japan's entry into modernity and of the dynamics of global modernity. Not dependent on the construction of antagonistic polarities, his work demonstrated that nation-identity formation and cultural development should be understood through the dynamics of interaction.

Much is made of Watsuji's disagreement with Heidegger. However, as Liederbach notes (2012), there is much that the two philosophers did have in common. First, Watsuji and Heidegger were dissatisfied with the prevalent philosophical currents of the time, Neo-Kantianism, with both striving to articulate a method for either ontology or ethics that could overcome the subjectivity prevalent since Descartes. In this respect, they were concerned with exploring the everyday world through engaging with philosophical hermeneutic and phenomenology methodologies. Lastly, both thinkers were profoundly concerned with providing an account of being-the-world that emphasized the notion of authenticity or authentic self-understanding. Whether either thinker was successful in their attempts is a matter of significant and ongoing debate.

---

[5] As Parkes (1996: 192), notes in the preface of Watsuji's work on Nietzsche he writes, "The Nietzsche who appears in this study is strictly my Nietzsche. I have tried to express myself through Nietzsche."

[6] The first English language translation of the first volume of Watsuji's Ethics, was published as, Rinrigaku: Ethics in Japan—Yamamoto and Carter (1996).

Nevertheless, it was under the influence of Heidegger's hermeneutics, though drawing on his Confucianism and Buddhist heritage, that Watsuji explored the question of ethics through his etymological investigations. According to Watsuji, Heidegger had emphasized the individuality of *Dasein* (Being-there) to the extent of neglecting the sociality of *Mitsein* (Being-with).[7] He further points out that while Heidegger focused on an existential-phenomenological description of "temporality" in order to underscore the individuality of *Dasein* as the basis for authentic existence, he neglected the aspect of spatiality, which is precisely the surrounding context of social relationships from which selfhood emerges (Odin, Jul. 1993: 480). It was Watsuji's argument that Heidegger's account was only a one-sided privileging of the temporal over the spatial and of the individual over the social.

Watsuji begins his *Study of Ethics*:

The primary significance of the attempt to define ethics as the study of "human beings" (*ningen*) is its getting away from the misunderstanding of the modern world, which takes ethics as simply a problem of the individual consciousness. This misunderstanding is founded on the modern individualistic view of humanity. Our grasp of the individual, itself a product of the spirit of modernity, holds a great significance that we must never forget, but individualism tried to take the individual, which is one moment in human existence, and substitute it for the human totality. Its abstractness became the root of every kind of misunderstanding. The standpoint of the isolated ego taken as a starting point in modern philosophy is just one example of this. (WTZ 10: 11)

Watsuji developed an etymological analysis of the Sino-Japanese concepts of *sonzai* (existence), *ningen* (man, person, human), *rinri* (ethics), *fūdo* (milieu), and *aidagara* (relationship, betweenness) to support a relational view of concrete human existence. Watsuji's etymological analysis of East-Asian ethical concepts was concerned with the effects of radical individualism on the isolated social self and its consequent effects on communities. Specifically, he could see that the two answers available to the ethicist or social theorist, the individual and the social, set up a contradiction in that

---

[7] Heidegger's thought is famously difficult to explain. However, for the general reader, one way of appreciating *Dasein* and *Mitsein* is through their relationship and not as dichotomous concepts. Heidegger was concerned with the fundamental question of: What is Being? *Dasein*, being-there, his answer refers to the paradox peculiar to the human condition of being aware of our relationship to other beings but being ultimately alone. *Mitsein*, being-with, postulates that the human condition only takes shape in relation to the other, the world. Specifically, when we are born, we emerge into preexisting social and natural fields that give structure to who we are. However, it is important to stress are both elements of an interconnected structure of the world.*Dasein* and *Mitsein* are both elements in the circular construction of worldliness. James M. Shields (2009) provides an excellent introduction and discussion of the relationship between the work of Heidegger and Watsuji.

both resulted in anomalies that could not be resolved through internal conceptual resources. To overcome these contradictions, he looked to, like Sōseki Natsume before him, the notion of the "betweenness of person of person" (Odin 1996: 52; Carter 2001: 125). In contrast to Heidegger, Watsuji makes the embodiment of lived space the point of departure for his own existential-phenomenological description of authentic selfhood to highlight the contextual, social, and relational dimensions of the person.

From such a perspective, the study of ethics becomes the study of the "countless possibilities of social interaction and interconnection" of the patterns of human relations (Carter 2012: 125). To challenge the radical isolation of individualism, one cannot think of human beings as first isolated individuals who then somehow become entangled in relationships with one another. On the other hand, we should not think of society as a kind of super-organism, an account of absolute collectivism, of which the individual forms a mere part. Instead, Watsuji claimed that we must think of these relationships as having equal priority to our individuality. Our relationships are just an authentic part of us as our individuality. For him, both the individual and the whole exist within a larger field of possible relationships, and or individuality is part of the greater whole with "Neither [is] able to be 'prior'" (WTZ 10: 107). This analysis was not predicated on a theoretical or a priori perspective, or through the claimed objectivity of the individual or be reliant on the notion of a homogenous cultural whole. The English word "human being" is translated into Japanese using the word *ningen* 人間. It is written with two characters. The first, *nin* 人, can also be read as *hito* and means "person" or "someone." The second, *gen* 間, can also be read as *aida*, *ma*, or *ken* and means a "betweenness" or "relatedness," that indicates a spatial or temporal interval. Consequently, the term *ningen* designates a "relatedness between persons," whereupon the human self now becomes defined as both an individual and a part of society. As linguistic expressions it was the multiple usages of *ningen* that revealed a fundamental truth of the human condition: we are both particular and discrete and relational and continuous.

Of course, caution needs to be displayed here and raises a point that I am keen to stress throughout this work. As Shields has argued (2009), in a rush to condemn "Western" individualism, Watsuji missed some possible allies. In Shields' work such an ally is found in the work of Georg Simmel (1858–1918). In *The Sociology of Sociability* (Simmel and Hughes 1949), Simmel describes sociability as the social counterpart, beyond utility, in which individuals cooperate with their material interests and desires held in abeyance for the sake of the common pleasure of each other's company. A similar resource that could have been available to Watsuji would have been the work of Pierre Leroux (1797–1871). Leroux is an intriguing figure in the history of the Western social theory in that he pointedly rejected any attempt to provide social analysis based on absolute individualism or absolute collectivism. Leroux, described as "the most philosophical of proletarians and the most proletarian of philosophers" (Breckman 2016 [2013]: 58), offers a fascinating counterexample to nineteenth-century left/Marxist thought that relied on an account of the social in the alleged anterior material reality. Rather, Leroux turned to symbolic sensibility to attempt to construct a democratic politics based on the "opening" that results from the nonidentity of the symbolic and the real, and the relationship between transcendence and immanence (Breckman 2016 [2013]: 59]). This present work should not be viewed as a claim to a new or better way. Other relational sociologies exist (Comte, Tarde, Marx, Mead, Elias, Bourdieu, Castells, Latour, Jaeggi, to name just a few), and entering into conversation with each other would provide a means to reexamine old problems through new eyes.

With his interest in ameliorating the excesses of individualism and fresh from his excursions into European and American philosophy, Watsuji required a method of enquiry that recognized the codetermination of the individual and society. He found an ontological grounding in his attempt to reexamine the question of the patterns of human activity and the interconnections that we experience through his studies of East-Asian traditions, that is the term *sonzai*. Composed of the Chinese characters *son* and *zai*, he defines sonzai as follows:

The original meaning of the Chinese character *son*, of *son-zai*, is "subjective self-subsistence." It means maintenance or subsistence over against loss. [. . .] The original meaning of *zai* of *son-zai* lies in the fact that the subject stays in some place. [. . .] Now the place where the subject stays is a social place such as an inn, home, homeland, or the world. In other words, it consists in such human relations as that of the family, village, town, or the general public. (WTZ 10: 24; Watsuji 1996: 20–21)

Sonzai can be translated as existence. However, Watsuji goes to great lengths to distinguish *sonzai* from *Sein* (being), pointing out how *sonzai* emphasizes being in relationships in both spatially and temporally. In this idea, and in respect of comparing Watsuji's work with that of Heidegger, one recognizes a decisive difference between the notion of *sonzai* and the notion of existence as Sorge (concern, care) (See Liederbach 2012). It is Watsuji's claim that the true meaning of "concern" must be expounded in relation with the phenomenon of being with others (Mitsein), whereas for Heidegger, the meaning of human existence has to be found in *Daseins's* radical individuation of "anticipatory resoluteness" and "Being-towards-death." The source of human authenticity, for Watsuji, and the vitality of life is this dynamic process of interplay between the self as individual and the self as communal

(WTZ 10: 195). Watsuji is attempting to go beyond the ontic description of the fact of a self in relation and to radically reconsider existence (*sonzai*) as fundamentally linked to relational *Ningen* (human). Put another way, he is looking for a way, a description of human existence, to describe how "out-there," "the practical interconnectedness of acts . . . in its concrete structure" (WTZ 10: 28; Watsuji 1996: 24), is linked to "in-here" (as in one's self), that "give expression to a wide variety of relations between human beings" that is "between/amongst people" (WTZ 10: 169; Watsuji 1996: 161).

To provide an alternative to "modernity's" fixation with the individual, the relational ontological structure provides a means for social analysis capable of illuminating the space "in-between" person and person, as the "subjec-tive, practical, and dynamic structure of human being." To do so, he points out that the Japanese word for ethics, *rinri*, is itself composed of the two characters *rin* "compassionate association," and *ri* or "principle,": "Fellows" means both the group as the relational system of specified persons and the individual persons who are prescribed by the group. [. . .] It follows that *rin* means "fellows" and also a specified form of linkages of conduct. As a result, *rin* comes to mean a "pattern," "form," or "order" in human existence. (WTZ 10: 12–13). Acting through our process of critique and cooperation, while engaging with the phenomenological studies of Heidegger, Watsuji is draw-ing on his appreciation of the Confucius ethical system. But caution needs to be exercised here, as a conclusion could be reached that he is basing his ethi-cal system of on a sense of communal ethics. There is a relationality at work here. However, and remembering his engagement with phenomenological as well as East-Asian philosophies, he is looking for a deeper, a more immediate sense of relationality that is located and embodied.

To develop this notion of human relationality, Watsuji examines various classical styles of art and literature, especially the Japanese tea ceremony and linked verse, because of the unique way in which they express the interdepen-dence of individual and society LaFleur (1978). Watsuji writes:

> But at the same time, in the figurative space of a reading (between the author and the reader), in a School (between teacher and student), or amongst friends. *Ningen* is asking about *ningen*—and in ethics, *ningen* in a sense *comes home to itself.* And we seek ourselves in our shared expressions—*words, literature, paintings, religious practices, political life, and so on.* (1937: 4–5) (parenthesis added)

In drawing our attention to the nonduality of individuality and totality reveals a "hermeneutic" approach that considers the social dimension. This is not merely subjective but objective as well and expresses reality as inter-subjectively meaningful. This shift from "experiences" to "expressions," to the realm of symbolic, indicates a shift from Heidegger's "phenomenology," which is largely individual.[8] As Yuasa Yasuo notes, "[W]atsuji argues that man's life can exist only in the 'betweenness' (aidagara) that is its foundation ... This view of man ... inherits the East Asian tradition of Confucian ethics. Insofar as his mode of behaviour is concerned, a person (*ningen*) is determined *a priori by his position within a social hierarchy*" (1987: 170; emphasis and parenthesis added).[9] However, this shift in emphasis to expressions also carries with it an acknowledgment of the interpersonal nature of expressions and how they illuminate the relational existence of *ningen* (WTZ9: 143–145). The resulting definition of human existence, *Ningen Sonzai*,[10] as inextricably both individual and social in which life unfolds through the relational web of *fūdo*.

Drawing on the Sino-Japanese linguistic tradition, *fūdo* literally means wind and earth and was introduced by Watsuji to counter the characterization of Asian art as a whole to be unsophisticated and barbarous.[11] However, Watsuji did not treat *fūdo* as solely the natural environment, but as a concept in which biological, physical, and geographical features exert forces on human living and through human beings in turn transform the environment.[12] In *fūdo* he aimed to "uncover" the fundamentally social and intersubjective nature of human existence (contextualized human beings). All expressions that indicate the interconnection of the acts of human beings, for example, intercourse, fellowship, transportation, communication, the aesthetic, can be understood only with a subjective spatiality of this sort. The structures we employ to manage the flow of information and communication comprise the "nervous system of society" (1996: 160). Yet these are not mere things. Rather, they carry human intentions and dynamically organize the relationships of those who create and use them. They are infused with meaning. In

---

[8] However, it is important to stress that though it is correct that Heidegger does not provide significant analysis of the intersubjective dimension of spatiality, it would also be correct to state that Heidegger's analysis into the "things being at hand" does have a systematic function within Heidegger's fundamental ontology. As Liederbach notes (2012), though Watsuji's point of Heidegger's one-sidedness of "care" is well made, Heidegger's account of "things being at hand" would never be consistent with Watsuji's theory of ethics. In Liederbach paper, what is important is the bringing together of these two thinkers, with the recognition of their respective aims and limitations that Liederbach endeavours to develop an engagement with the two thinkers.

[9] Therefore, unlike in Heidegger, the fundamental question for Watsuji, of a first philosophy, is not ontology but ethics.

[10] Relational existence

[11] For example "from the East, we are inundated by elemental, formless literature, music, and painting-half barbaric but filled with vital emotional energy of peoples who still fight the battles of spirit in novels and twenty-foot-wide paintings" Dilthey (1985 [1887]: 31). See Watsuji (1961: 171–175).

[12] The manner of thinking in which the human being and nature are treated as two separate entities misses the more fundamental bond between being human and climatic phenomena. To be clear, Watsuji is challenging the division between nature and culture, to argue for a transdisciplinary approach that aims at an understanding of the fluid interconnectivity between the two realms (See UNESCO 2013).

this way, *fūdo*, they scaffold the material space of intersubjectivity. In other words, they extend into what we might call the "meaning spaces" of social relationships, the aesthetical nature through which the artist explores and exhibit their own sort of "subjective extendedness" (1996: 165). Therefore, it is the case that no full social analysis can succeed if (1) it does not include aesthetic appreciation and (2) that it relies on an understanding the human condition as an abstract reduction. This "subjective extendedness" also defines interpersonal dynamics on a more immediate face-to-face level.

The second stage of Watsuji's socioepistemological framework, *aidagara*, stresses the nondual nature of the relationship between individuality and social relationships.[13] It highlights the "practical interconnections through acts," in which we inhabit the social arena. However, this is not a merely cognitive account. In Watsuji, his concepts of selfhood, body, rather than beginning from the isolated individual, the ethical subject is in relation. Therefore, according to Watsuji, although the modern subjective turn often begins with an examination of the limits of individual existence, if a person is authentically a social animal, then things like our persistent relationships (*aidagara*) and society should not be separated from the person as these transform the lives of the actors in these relationships over time. *Aidagara* is written using the same character, 間, as the *gen* in *ningen*, which, as mentioned above indicates a spatial or temporal interval, plus *gara*, which means a recurring pattern. This "betweenness" (aidagara) or lived social space, as the space of action, thus has an intrinsic qualitative character and interactive dynamic that differentiates it from geometrical space. *Aidagara* does not mean simply the relations between one atomistic self and another but refers directly to the structure of the self. *Aidagara*, then, is a kind of field or space in which our persistent relationships with others repeatedly occur, as described in the five Confucius Cardinal relationships such as familial bonds, and which cannot be severed merely through a change of attitude or circumstance.

Applying this at the level of ethics, Watsuji finds the "fundamental law of human existence" is that individuals must negate the totality to which they belong to individuate themselves, but they must negate that negation to return to the totality. To stress this point in less abstract terms, we have the individual rebelling against, enacting and generative, within the limitations of their society but then returns to contribute to the greater common good through their experiences. This is a space that provides a means for the individual to question the silence of ultimate meaning, effectively countering narrow

---

[13] It is important for the reader to be aware the fūdo and aidagara form of a whole and should not be isolated. Equally important, is that the socioepistemology is dependent, for its coherence and effectiveness, on Watsuji's use of the Buddhist concept of emptiness, to which we will explore in the next chapter.

and single-minded insistence that faith must be expressed only in terms of its accompanying ideological framework. Such an understanding, to draw on Castoriadisian terminology, views the "social imaginary" as having the characteristic of openness and creativity which would allow for continual alteration of the given meanings and the innovation and change of significations. This is not to set aside ontic and epistemic location and its importance for subjectivity, but only to weaken their claims, to identify cultural limitations.

This account of social space provides not only for a philosophic hermeneutic of the doctrinal stances of the various religious traditions, but that it also recognizes that traditions and practices are enmeshed in a complex of cultural ideas and assumptions. Far from the abstract individual within the context of neutral societal norms Watsuji stresses how *aidagara* involves not merely reason, but the body, feelings, the will, and consciousness. These are mediated, they are contextualized, and we come to understand these, through the mediation of the concrete structures of our societies. Through our gestures, our expressions, our languages, our social, political, and cultural institutions. It is from this two-stage socio-epistemological perspective that provides our understanding of intracultural and intercultural space. Anticipating later relational sociologists, and contra Jürgen Habermas as well as deflecting Walter Benjamin's classical modernist worries about the aestheticization of politics, Watsuji offers an account that insists that the social, properly understood, inevitably contains an aesthetic dimension. Significantly, the perspective of the entanglement of the "human" with natural, material, and technological worlds that Watsuji described, decades before Bruno Latour for example, asks us to consider what social forms can become imaginable?

However, the key to understanding the account of space provided through Watsuji's concepts of *aidagara* and *fūdo*, and to further understand the account of critical cosmopolitanism that will be developed in this book, is the concept of emptiness. Through the dialectics of emptiness, he attempted to overcome what he saw as the one-sidedness of other ethical systems, to consider key dual-structures of human existence: subject versus object, individual versus totality, and other dualities that arise from these (private versus public, space versus time, climate versus history, universal versus particular, ideal versus material, and so forth). Derived from the contribution of thinkers such as the second-century (CE) Nāgārjuna, the concept of emptiness appears in Watsuji's scheme as a double negation that characterizes the structure of being human: "On the one hand, the standpoint of the acting 'individual' comes to be established only in some way as a negation of the totality of *ningen* . . . On the other hand, the totality of ningen comes to be established as the negation of individuality . . . .These two negations constitute the dual character of a human being" (Watsuji 1996: 22). However, emptiness should not be confused with the nothingness of "Western" thought. Whereas the

Western tradition has tended to understand the ultimate universal or the absolute in terms of "being," Eastern traditions have tended to understand it in terms of "nothingness" or "emptiness" (Davis 2014). This emptiness can be understood as holding the created as well as the creative aspects of existence: the possibility of change. It is this respect that we are transposing cosmopolitanism's concept of incompleteness, as a manifestation of reflexive negation, through Watsuji's account of emptiness.[14]

JAPAN AND MODERNITY

"The entry of Japan into modernity" was accompanied with the concomitant emergence of Japanese philosophy which became a site in which Japanese society and their intellectuals negotiated their relationship to the "Other": the West. What came to be identified as "philosophy" within Japanese society moved through stages as opposition to the supposed traditional, the "conservative" religio-aestheticism of Confucianism and Buddhism which were increasingly regarded as feudalistic. At first Japanese thinkers and Watsuji made a significant contribution to this process in his substantial work on Nietzsche, concentrated on exegesis and commentary of Western philosophers. However, as the intellectual interest in Western philosophy among Japanese philosophers broadened, there began to emerge a theme of "reconciliation" between the thought provided by the "West" and that provided by the "fusion" of Japanese thought; Shintoism, Confucius, and Buddhism.

Any analysis of Japanese international policy during that period that only concentrated on the Japan's competition with the European colonial powers in Asia was insufficient since it would fail to acknowledge the role of "unconscious assumptions and values which in a fragmentary way reveal themselves in the activities of everyday life" (Maruyama 1966: xiii), and the view of the role of the individual within Japanese society. Since the end of the War World II, the role of Japanese intellectuals in the legitimatization of Japanese militarism and expansionist ideology has been a subject of debate both within and outside Japanese society. Commenters such as Robert Bellah, Gino Piovesana, and Peter Dale have argued that the form of communitarianism set forth by Watsuji and other members of the Kyoto School, despite its profound moral and religio-aesthetic dimensions, had the tendency to slide into an impossible totalitarianism that ultimately fails to preserve the integrity of the

---

[14] We shall discuss this further in the next chapter. For the moment, the problem arises as Watsuji, though drawing on his Buddhist heritage to develop his work, appears to conflate the concept of emptiness, derived from Mahāyāna Buddhism with the Zen Buddhist concept of Nothingness. This later concept is derived from Daoism though heavily influenced by Hegelian dialectics.

individual in relation to the state. However, this fails to acknowledge the role that "Western" imperialism, economic colonialism, and extension of power had played in the development of Japanese foreign policy in the region.

This type of criticism has been especially prevalent since the 1990s, when it became even more difficult to rescue Watsuji's thoughts from mounting contemporary theoretical criticism of culture, notably from a postcolonial and cultural studies perspectives. Characteristic of this approach to the study of Watsuji is *Translation and Subjectivity*. In this important work Naoki Sakai criticizes Watsuji's invocation of emptiness, as, claimed Sakai, by introducing such a conceptual framework was to present a "reductionist" account of personhood. On Sakai's reading, Watsuji's person is no more than the social construction, that is, as a construction of a closed social structure that defines their capability, subjectivity, and agency. However, he writes:

> Not only am I an other to myself but I am also other to the dual structure of subjectivity; that is, my relation to myself always bears a surplus value that is irreducible to the dual structure of the whole and the individual. Thus, I am never reduced to an identity, an individual who identifies with the whole. I am not a unity fashioned after the unicity of the whole. In short, I am not an *individuum*. (1993: 98)

Therefore, on this reading, the Confucian values that Watsuji brought to his work at the political level of discourse lead to the perceived dangers of communitarian ethics with the accompanying dangers of "totalitarian state ethics" and even a "fascist ideology." Bellah (1965) sought to expose that a pathological ideology of "emperor-system fascism," lay behind Watsuji's *ningen* model (pp. 593–594). Piovesana (1968), critiqued Watsuji's ethical system, describing the dialectic of mutual emptying, between the individual and society into an absolute negativity as symbolizing the emperor and nation-family:

> The individual only through the negation of the self can join the whole of the nation. This absolute negation ends in the *ku* (the emptiness of the self), to reach the "absolute totality," not dissimilar in purport to Nishida's nothingness. (1968: 142)

Piovesana concludes that when we honestly confront the political implications of Watsuji's social relationism, it amounts to a "totalitarian state ethics," adding that this aspect of his thought was corrected in the revised edition of postwar times (1968: 143). Peter Dale echoes the views of Bellah and Piovesana, asserting that "[L]ittle wonder that even sympathetic readings concede that in this form Watsuji's aidagara theory amounts to little more than a 'totalitarian state ethics'" (1986: 218). According to Dale, the result is that "Watsuji moves to a position which denies autonomy to private, individual consciousness itself" (217). For Dale, Watsuji's theory of *aidagara* reinforces the social relationism of Japanese group-consciousness, which, he argues, has the consequence of the complete submergence of the individual into society. In this reading of Watsuji, his dialectic between the individual and the collective is the tyranny of the collective over the individual. This leads to the charge of cultural nationalism and the idea of a seamless cultural totality, and second (and directly correlative of that) is the lack of embodied singularity. As the argument goes, Watsuji's desire to posit the harmonious, seamless "imaginary" character of the Japanese nation, he effectively argued for a system of society wherein individuals are completely subsumed into various roles.

On a similar theme, Harry Harootunian argued in his work *Overcome by Modernity: History, Culture, and Community in Interwar Japan* (2000) that Watsuji's work was part of the unsuccessful effort on the part of Japanese intellectuals to overcome Western modernity. In an earlier work, Harootunian and Tetsuo Najita (1993), commented on the proceedings of a symposium held in 1941 titled "The World Historical Position and Japan." In their article, they state that "members of the Kyoto faction openly acknowledged their admiration of European fascism and its own struggle with the forces of modernity," and by a characterization of "some of the members of the Kyoto faction" as "Japanese-style fascists" (cited in Parkes 1997). For Harootunian and Tetsuo Najita, in drawing on the ontological concept of "space" of Nishida to describe the "world stage," a space in which Japanese leadership would create the conditions for the solving of global cultural, political, and social problems would be solved. This involved the Kyoto philosophers unashamedly speaking out on behalf of Japanese imperial expansion as the creative moment of a vast historical movement to a new level of human excellence (Najita and Harootunian 1993: 742; Parkes 1997). As Christopher Ives notes, from the viewpoint of Arima Tatsuo, "[T]he primary sin of a Nishida or a Watsuji was not that their ideal of harmony in the individual might be untenable, but that they confused the realities of politics with personal longings for serenity and harmony" (Tatsuo 1969: 12–13; cited Ives 1994: 36–37). Arima further asserts that "[T]he philosophical category of pure experience, with all its logical embellishments, was used to preach social resignation as a means of achieving individual enlightenment . . . When the idea of pure experience is realized within the individual, it encourages a kind of religious submission to reality. This being the ultimate reality, there is no need for the self to remould its social surroundings."

These are significant criticisms and would have an impact on the desire to explore the potential for Watsuji's work to be utilized within a conceptually post-Western critical cosmopolitan social theory. Specifically, the criticism that emptiness represents the construction of the totality as both immanent in and anterior to individual consciousness would be antipathy to my stated aims. The theoretical/ideological and historiographical perspectives and self-interest that have shaped the debate since the end of World War II and up to today casts a shadow on the exploration of possible socially useful ideas (Masayuki 1999: 159; Parkes 1997, 2009; Williams 2014). What this debate amounts to is a cause of friction between Eastern and Western thought. This is regrettable, but there is an irony when one reflects on the debate concerning *nihonjinron*[15] is that the objective that Watsuji and the Kyoto school had set themselves, and they were not alone in this endeavor (Bose 2006: 267–271), was to challenge the notion of an absolutist understanding of modernity (Cestari 2010; See also Konishi 2013: 7–13).

Rather than provide a new universalism, there is clear textual evidence that Watsuji and the Kyoto School in general were experimenting with *both* Western-style philosophy *and* Japanese thinking. The idea was that Japan, as a non-Western nation, could provide something "universal" of its own, the truth of which the West could recognize (Nishida 1965: 404–405). Their aim, despite the persistence of claims of incommensurability, was to bring East and West closer together, regardless of the obscurities that this unaccustomed blend might give rise to (Cestari 2010). What can be seen is the development, arguably the first, of a global philosophy. In the work of Watsuji and others, we see a path of philosophy that tried to blend and learn from different philosophical positions. This concentration on the *nihonjinron* as the principal representative of cultural debates within Japan has suppressed other internal voices of protest, analysis, and rival readings of postwar Japanese society. What is significant about Japanese *philosophy* in this context is its self-positioning vis-à-vis Western universalism. The dialectic of self and society that Watsuji proposed, in which self and society "empties each other" offer a means to overcome the absolutism of modernity and its accompanying competences, political structures, and settlements. In this respect, one could understand why such a radical undermining of modern thought has been so disquieting for advocates of the global liberal settlement. The persistent tension between individuality and society ensures that neither absolute individuality nor absolute totalities are possible. Absolute totality and absolute individuality are "nothing but a product of the imagination," and it is in the constant flux of existence totality is never fixed. All such vantage points are temporary, no one gaze able to encompass society as a static whole abstracted from its fundamental transience. What these thinkers, and Watsuji, were

---

[15] To remind the reader, these are theories that focus on the "uniqueness" of Japanese national and cultural identity and how Japan and the Japanese should be understood.

trying to articulate was a "novel" identity of modernity, of relation and difference, but also a post-individualistic identity of self.

As Sho Konishi (2013: 9–12) has forcibly argued, the view of Japan, and the non-West in general, is that it was Western modernity that provided the starting point from which we have arrived at much of our scholarship on modern Japan and for the non-West. What is significant about Japanese *philosophy* in this context is its self-positioning vis-à-vis Western universalism. The idea was that Japan, as a non-Western nation, could provide something "universal" of its own, the truth of which the West could recognize. The work of Watsuji, in its appeal to overcome the universalizing tendencies of modernity, is representative of the decolonial cosmopolitan project. In recognizing the limitations of localized thought, Watsuji set out a developmental agenda that aimed to use the resources available globally through which to engage in intercultural learning. A principle point of Watsuji's view was the use of these resources to overcome one's own communal limitations. Furthermore, Watsuji's work, and that of this book, was not a comparative agenda. In effect, he brought into question the inherent parochialism in Western "universal" ideas, and did so by alternatively adopting, criticizing, complementing, and thinking otherwise beyond the hegemony of received categories of thought. Here Watsuji, as a cosmopolitan thinker recognized that all hegemonic, ontological, systems of thought, were broken and that the intertwining of the ontological and the ontic provided the perspective to acknowledge and challenge the limitations of our social consciousness. In doing so Watsuji pursued the goal of an account of global social theory that may allow for the development of new forms of positive and humanistic thinking.

THE DECOLONIAL PHENOMENOLOGICAL
EXPLANATION OF LIFE, PART ONE

The contemporary decolonial theory reveals the underside of the hegemony of modernity. While the fable of modernity, with its dreams and aspirations, continues to seek ideals, the decolonial project forces upon us the recognition that modernity is happily capable of existing alongside violence, war, inequality, and poverty. Modernity is intellectually tied to the same roots of "emancipation", "liberty," and "equality" stemming from the Enlightenment whose values of abstraction and the separation of culture and nature that thinkers like Mignolo and Watsuji criticize for its denaturalizing of humanity. In the work of Watsuji, we see the emergence of an account of social science that synthesizes knowledge as an originary but nonbinary development. One finds in Watsuji's work a similar account of cultural, social, intellectual exchange, and social movements expressing a notion of progress beyond liberal, utilitarian, or instrumental understandings. Such an account of global history does not rely on a vocabulary of hybridity or hierarchy to describe the diverse trajectories of alternative modernity's.

Just like the decolonial and cosmopolitan projects, Watsuji is concerned with the effects of modernity on colonized nations. However, rather than proposing an ontic and epistemic account aimed at grounding thought on a new, Japanese account, Watsuji, was looking for connections between East and West focused on intercultural learning and the identification of limitations. Such a reading suggests that for Watsuji communities are, far from being hermitically sealed designators, fluid, and interconnected. Furthermore, it is this interconnectedness that is necessary for intracommunal transformation. This suggests that Watsuji is positing a relative universalism as opposed to an absolute universalism of modernity; an account of multiple modernities, though an account that does not set out ideals, such as European modernity. In doing so, Watsuji would recognize Dussel (2002), call for a pluriversal world. And it is into such an understanding of a decolonial pluriversal world that Watsuji's cosmopolitan embracing of various cultural and intellectual practices and methods offers further resources for the decolonial project.

The decolonial movements' concept of border thinking and Watsuji's account of intercultural socio-epistemology, offers a glimpse of a "border," a transcendence, that emerges where indigenous and Eurocentric paradigms meet. This offers the opportunity to create a consciousness stemming from the *relative* exteriority of the world system. It is into such an understanding of a decolonial pluriversal world that Watsuji's cosmopolitan embracing of various cultural and intellectual practices and methods offers further resources for the decolonial project. However, where theorists and historians have defined the exploration of alternative forms of modernity in the non-West they have been inclined to speak of a "hybridity" between what are two ultimately foreign ontic and epistemic experiences. Bringing Watsuji into the conversation offers the creation of a space for the inclusion of the historical trajectories, epistemic and ontic perspectives of East and West, North, and South.[16] This would also allow for terms such as capitalism, globalization, and democratic institutions, to be reconsidered. Here his project anticipates the work of Sho Konishi's (2013), account of an anarchist history.[17]

For Konishi, the term "anarchist history" refers to a view of modern global history that is absent of teleological or hierarchical ordering, but which accepts "existing, multiple imagined and lived ideas of progress, or 'modernities'"

---

[16] Though not as totalities. See chapter 4.
[17] It needs to be stressed that this is not a claim that Watsuji was an anarchist, at least not as understood in terms of "Western" political theory.

(Konishi 2013: 6). One finds in Watsuji's work a similar account of cultural, social, intellectual exchange, and social movements expressing a notion of progress beyond liberal, utilitarian, or instrumental understandings in the work of Watsuji. Such an account of global history does not rely on a vocabulary of hybridity or hierarchy to describe the diverse trajectories of alternative modernities. Watsuji's notions of *aidagara* and *fūdo* suggest the rejection of the closure of objective, subjective, and intersubjective identities and political and social commitments. Instead, it proposes the exploration of pluralistic individual and collective agency and posits the multi-spatial transmodernity that challenges singular accounts of being human. Similarly, in respect of the decolonial movements concept of border thinking, Watsuji's account of socio-epistemology offers a glimpse of a "border," a transcendence that emerges where forms of consciousness meet.

Mignolo's concepts of the loci of enunciation and *fūdo* are an attempt to move away from absolute notions of universalism for cross-cultural transformation and communication. Where for the decolonialist, the concept of a border signifies the knowledge of the subaltern, Watsuji's account of socio-epistemology, when imbued with criticality, suggests a critical tool being available to challenge orthodoxies and social conventions. Bringing the critical edge of decolonial thought with *fūdo* provides the opportunity to incorporate both singularity, relationality, and difference as a phenomenological analysis and the articulation of injustices beyond modernity, rationality, and totality. In exploring the connection of ideals and the practices of life and valuing the face-to-face encounter with self, other, and the world as less distinct and relational, entangled, and conditional, allows us to step outside the temporal-modalities of time to rethink who we are. This, of course, must be at the level of localized, spatial, and suggests the moment of relative immanent transcendence.

Aidagara is both objective, as in existing practices of social power, and subjective. Immanent transcendence/border thinking springs from the individual through their engagement and exchange with the liminality and potentially dangerous space of *aidagara* as a concentric duality. This permits one to dismantle our self-conceptions as it allows us to reach some understanding of our circumstances. Though temporal, as an event, its importance lies in the interlinking of the temporal with spatial change. In positioning these encounters within the heuristic spatial devices of diametric and concentric dualities embraces internal (self and societal) heterogeneity and alienation, allowing us to explore the potential for self and societal experimentation. Alienation, understood within dividing diametric dualities, becomes the means of domination and control, out of which arises the need for the reappropriation of self and which becomes a social, cultural, and political question through construction social institutions that support openness and self-realization. However, when we view the structures of society through the heuristic lenses of concentric duality, capable of accommodating both positive and negative rights as a point of critique, we find an account of the enunciation of alienation that can undermine claims of closure. Specifically, it allows a loci of enunciation from outside of the dominant social and political discourses. This holds the potential, when politically, socially, and culturally harnessed, for the redefining of existing social, political, and cultural practices.

Watsuji was a global thinker who drew on Western intellectual resources, but who then transformed these through his cultural indebtedness to Buddhist and Confucian traditions. These latter traditions, with their epistemological emphasis on practical interconnections, provide a unique and bold vision of the potentiality of social analysis. In acknowledging the limitations of our social consciousness, the work of Watsuji would allow for the inclusion within the speculations of social theorist's work of several interesting avenues of thought that present a significant critique of modernity. The crucial point to keep in mind here is that I, following Watsuji, am not suggesting that a "Asian" vision of social analysis is more suitable than the cluster of traditions generated in the "West" or the "South". Rather, our aim is to set out a cluster of ideas that provide a hermeneutical point in which all traditions are capable of communication. Introducing the diametrically opposed premises of critical theory and of decolonial theory to the concentric space of *aidagara* provides a theoretical space to overcome the impasse of either/ or of social theory. The point is to find a means of intercultural critique that acknowledges the ontic reality of our shared life.

As Clammer (2018: 293) argues, the dominant feature of Western social and political thought focuses on the transformation of society through the structural change of its institutions. However, in Buddhism, Hinduism, and Confucianism, the emphasis is on the transformation of the self as the basis for any long-lasting social change. In presenting a relational theory of the relationship between self and society, these traditions argue that it is the transformation or transcendence of the self that is a precondition for systematic social transformation. Far from Confucius thought representing a static ontology of tradition, the analysis that has been presented argues that in broadening the *Dao* provides a precondition that requires social justice to provides the conditions for self-cultivation. This aligns with our argument that the principle of emptiness, as a reflexive negation provides for an account of liberty as critique and that self-transformation can only be achieved with the sustenance of institutions fashioned in a way that supports the relational model of personhood.

Watsuji's twofold account of socioepistemology also provides a novel perspective on the relationship between human and nonhumans, and the environment. Until recently such relationships have simply been ignored. However, the recent announcement of the arrival of the Anthropocene geological age (See Delanty 2017), has sparked considerable interest in human beings' relationship with the environment. In the following chapters, the reader will see that Watsuji's account of *fūdo*, with its emphasis on the relational aspects of self and society, stresses the need not to understand nature as being opposed to culture, but as the intertwined state between physical natural phenomena and humanity. Following through with our rejection of abstract or essentializing notions, this suggests that climatic warming could be tackled if we were to focus our attention on the localization of sentiment to improve local environments.

Third, Watsuji anticipates Mignolo's exploration of aesthesis. This call for the aestheticization of social theory, or to "see it whole," has been present from Simmel and more recently in the work of Toscano and de la Fuente (Simmel 1949; Toscano 2012; de la Fuente 2013). Up until now these calls have fallen on fallow ground. There are a number of reasons for this which includes the professionalization of social sciences, standardization, the technocratic control of governance, and the lack of sociological imagination in social science departments and research funders. While, on the whole, it would not occur to the average academic working within fields such as sociology or cultural studies to do away with considerations of power or the material interests served by specific forms of human conduct, it is interesting that art has been considered much more dispensable (de la Fuente 2013: 2). However, given the decolonial project's concern with ability of aesthesis to challenge the universalizing features of modernity then Watsuji's account of *aidagara* can provide new resources.

Where Watsuji investigated the potential for the development of novel and innovative forms of social thinking, it would follow that this process continues through a conceptually post-Western centric project of critical social theory. This is theoretically enabled through the shifting of analytical attention from a homogenous and ideal understanding of culture or the exclusivity of the individual, to the meeting point of the imaginary axis of ideals and the practices of life. Introducing the diametrically opposed premises of critical theory and decolonial theory to the socio-epistemology provided by Watsuji offers a theoretical space in which the contradiction contained within the either/or of social theory can be resolved. To pursue this task, in the next chapter, I will explore the potential of developing Watsuji's concept of emptiness as an epistemic principle of reflexive negation to move beyond the problems identified in both the critical and decolonial approaches to critical cosmopolitanism.

Part II

Cosmopolitanism has the triple objectives of setting out a means of intercultural communication and conversation that draws on a method of intracultural study grounded in an account of personhood which is not diminished to abstraction. These tasks intend to overcome the conflict between unity and diversity, between the inside and the outside, and between space and time. Chapter 4 begins the process of reconstruction through presenting the concept of emptiness as the epistemic basis for a post-Western critical cosmopolitan social theory. Over the last thirty years, there have been repeated calls for what have been variously described as cosmo-logic or the logic of pluriverses. In this chapter, I will argue that Watsuji's account of emptiness provides an ideal resource for critical cosmopolitanism. Drawing on this epistemic source chapter 5 looks to develop an account of immanent relative universalism. Importantly, this is not as an abstraction but is embodied and attached to local communities. As such, I will argue that it provides an understanding of social dynamics capable of offering a site of constructive resistance to the dominant social, political, and economic discourses, which become practical and *familiar* when explored through the socio-spatial dynamics of nullification by jury. The final chapter introduces personhood into critical cosmopolitanism. Rather than present an ideal type identity, the individual or a socially constructed identity, the model of pluralistic agency sees an enactive, pluralistic, and generative agent engaging with the world. This allows us to understand creativity of the infinity of otherness and self as the outcome of the collision between the cultural, social, political, and economic world with our multitudinous and interconnected ways of being.

Chapter 4

The Emptiness of Cosmopolitanism

The Epistemic Basis for Post-Western Critical Cosmopolitan Social Theory

INTRODUCTION

This is a book about a conceptually post-Western account of cosmopolitan social theory. However, before we plough into the theoretical abyss that awaits us, we need to first find the answer to the question of how one think's as a cosmopolitan. Of course, we could have a simple triadic model of cosmopolitanism beginning with an ultimate unit of analysis, say, humanity, that this is an absolute claim, that is it impartially applied, and from this we have the possibility of the cosmopolitan imagination. This imagination, it is claimed by many cosmopolitan thinkers and activists, gives us a platform to see beyond parochial concerns to instead focus on wider worldly issues. However, the moral history of cosmopolitanism gives rise to the concern of its proclivity to assimilation. Therefore, rather than set out a conjunctive conceptual format that draws on global resources, though itself an honourable tradition of reflecting and nurturing the diversity of being human, one needs to be aware about what thinking like a cosmopolitan is really like. That is, in being in the self, cosmopolitanism allows us to escape the limitations of our own horizons to then return to contribute to the greater good.

Of course, over the past two decades there has been an interest in the "West" for exploring the implications of the cosmopolitan imagination. Most famous of these formulations has been the call for a cosmo-logic, a logical form capable of escaping the myopic conceptual enclave of the nation-state set out by the late Ulrich Beck. However, within the Beckian worldview, the assumption remains, despite his cosmopolitanism, of a hierarchical nature of the international: between a Euro/American "us" and the rest of the world. Here the model of development, sociologically, economically, and political, is the "West" which with the cosmopolitan turn needs to emulate. As

Gurminder K. Bhambra notes, Beck states that "the West should listen to non-Western countries when they have something to say about the following experiences" (Beck 2000: 89 cited in Bhambra 2010: 39). What this amounts to is a de-sensitizing toward the "Other" and a mere toleration of their experience with little regard for the context of people's lives. Rather than rejecting the either-or principle Beck's cosmopolitanism merely provides a refashioned simplistic, homogenous, and monolithic understanding of global and local societies that, "betrays the very ideal the concept (cosmopolitanism) expresses" (Bhambra 2010: 41). This is an assumption about the nature of reality and of how we can observe it that was provided through the European Enlightenment's answer to the contradictions of the human condition. This totalization of reality populates the world with the application of diametric dualities, a world of self and other, us and them. Sadly, the Beckian view was 500 years too late and is a view that maintains a paradoxical parochialism beyond philosophy to extend into matters of existential threats for billions of people around the world. Therefore, in terms of providing an insight into formulating a non-Euro-centric social theory, Ulrich Beck can provide no basis.

Of course, these diametric dualities have the dual purpose of cosmopolitanizing internal power externally, but they also function to bolster existing social, economic, and political power internally through the creation of frameworks of belief. The Beckian worldview misses that the development of what we can understand as the accomplishments of modernity, the rise of the nation-state, the development of liberal democracy, took place during a period of massive intercultural exchange and interconnection. In terms of structures of knowledge and their effects on the practices of everyday life during and after the Enlightenment, there was no principal vein for development located in the heart of Western Europe. Rather, it was in the development of trade with the Americas, Asia, and Africa that allowed Europe to act as a curator for global knowledge. Unfortunately, though global development may have begun in a benign way, subsequent global history displays the malignant effects of prestidigitation masquerading as beneficence (See Hobson 2004; Araújo and Maeso 2015). Therefore, Beck's call for the shifting of the sociological categories from a "methodological nationalism" to "methodological cosmopolitanism" to meet the challenges of the postnational world (Beck 2012: 7) fails to acknowledge that the categories of modernity were inadequate in the first place.

However, despite the regrettable failure to grasp the potential for a global philosophy, as a process of critique and cooperation, there are signs that global history and global philosophy are beginning to broaden the horizon of the theoretical tools available (See Brooks 2013 for an excellent introduction to the idea of global philosophy). As part of this movement, this chapter is concerned with providing a means of thinking for such an approach. If critical cosmopolitanism's claim to evidence of incompleteness, that is, an acknowledgment of epistemic humility, is to be supported, then any account needs to offer a method of thought that can support this aim. Furthermore, such an approach will need to acknowledge that one's consciousness is not fixed with an accompanying stable conceptual system within a changing perceptual world.

Rather than begin in abstraction, we are concerned with the practical activities of everyday life. As a movable site of ideas, the aim of our model is to provide resources at the level of the local for individuals and communities to reimagine themselves. Concerned with *becoming* what is important to stress is that the instant of enunciation is not in an abstract or essentialized *to be*, but through the enactive and generative nature of the subject. For now, what this implies is moving away from the stativity of transitive, *to be*, or intransitive states, reified social relations, to understanding agency as an active inference and generative language of change within the *familiar*, localized and real-world. Though within the chaos of existence *to be* may provide the appearance of security and certainty, in defining *to be* one automatically defines nonbeing. Rather, in *becoming,* this enacting agent, liminal, uncertain, and potentially dangerous, springs up from between the tension of individuality and the world—immanent and transcendent. Created and creative, this third space contains the creative nature of being human and the potential to change and transform the world through providing the means to enunciate the multitudinous encounters of self and the world. To expose the potential of this lived betweenness, a guiding heuristic principle must be available that can transcend the historical conditions to which all human understanding is subsumed but which can ascend to a critique of ideology.

I will argue that a source of critical thought, a nontemporal source of critique can be found in the Buddhist concept of *emptiness*. However, this is not to suggest that cosmopolitanism then rests on some new transcendental notion. I am concerned with deriving an account of the concept as an example of a reflexive negation. Recognizing the created and creative elements of reality, as a principle of socio-epistemology, reflexive negations endlessly shatter the meaning of reality. This addresses the tendency of the human mind to find or impose patterns on input, *to be*, "apophenia" (Dietrich and Fields 2015). That is the human propensity to project meaning onto social formations that are either meaningless or which can be clearly understood as something else. In recognizing the necessary contingence of life, reflexive negations allow us to move away from abstract or essentialized universalisms, to instead provide a means of the complex analysis and enunciation of common concerns. Specifically, the account of emptiness as an example of reflexive negation presented in this chapter, will allow us to posit post-Western critical cosmopolitan social theory, when applied to matters of common concern, capable of increasing complexity through the enunciation of added variables that allow us to transcend obstinate oppositions of subjectivist or holistic accounts of social reality.

I shall first introduce the concept of emptiness as developed by the first- and second-century CE Indian philosopher Nāgārjuna. I will then outline Watsuji's application of emptiness in his work. This will allow us to gauge whether the idea of emptiness, which is understood to frame Watsuji's work, can provide a cosmopolitanism as critical reflexive practice or whether Watsuji's account needs to be accordingly reconsidered. I will then show why and how Watsuji introduces nothingness into his work. To develop such a research project, they introduced into their own work what they considered was a corresponding concept to emptiness from the Daoist tradition, a concept heavily influenced by Hegelianism. It is in vacillating between ontology(nothingness) and nonfoundationalism(emptiness) that creates the issues surrounding Watsuji's construction of what may appear as static finite totalities. However, we shall see through textual analysis that Watsuji's account of emptiness, when set aside from his inclusion of nothingness, does demonstrate the ability to act as a heuristic intercultural and intracultural heuristic device. Finally, I will demonstrate to what extent/how an understanding of emptiness as a reflexive heuristic tool for critical cosmopolitanism. I will argue that the account of emptiness outlined in this chapter provides the epistemic basis for a post-foundational account of critical cosmopolitan social theory not as a metaphysical account but as a basis for a nondualistic heterogeneous method of social analysis.

However, before the chapter develops further, it may be an opportune moment to offer what could be described as a reader's guide to emptiness. It offers such a reading being mindful that most readers, outside of Asia, will not have encountered the concept before. And, admittedly, when it is first encountered, it can appear to be a metaphysically deep and ponderous concept.

A READER'S GUIDE TO EMPTINESS

A useful analogy through which to begin a conversation about emptiness is that of a good teacher with a student. Imagine that during a tutorial session that the student has come up with an answer to a particularly divisive social question. The question that was put to the student was in the form of "What causal factors could be said to contribute to outcome a?" The student's response is that factor x is the answer. The role of the teacher, in developing the critical skills of the student, is to take the student from their initial position of certainty to then explore not only the causal factors but also the interconnections that led up to *a*. It is also to let the student discover what other factors and interconnections through which the outcome *a* is dependent on. That is, for the student to discover through examination that outcome *a* and the causal factors are empty, as in lacking independent existence but are dependently co-arisen. That is all that emptiness is. It is not an account of the nature of reality. All emptiness represents is a way to move beyond everyday language games and the prejudice of necessity, pattern-forming, through which to apprehend the contingence of complexity and the incompleteness of ourselves and human societies but also the interconnectedness of self-other-world.

A reasonable interpretation of Watsuji that is often put forward tie's emptiness to history and tradition. Sakai's is one such interpretation and which I do have some sympathy with. However, I will argue that such an interpretation misses a key argument contained within the work of Watsuji. Namely, that for Watsuji, emptiness is a heuristic device. Admittedly, Watsuji does not make it easy on the reader to engage with such an account. However, in his defense, he was operating with a complex concept and applying it to complex problems: society and the global. One feasible way for the reader to appreciate the point here is to understand that the accounts that "capture" Watsuji's totalizing concept are just that; they are the capturing of moments within a movement.

WHAT IS EMPTINESS?

One is reminded, in terms of the "outside" interpretation of emptiness, of Umberto Eco's discussion of Marco Polo's cultural translation in respect of Unicorns and Rhinoceros, being determined by his cognitive model (Eco 1999: 72). Emptiness is a complex and difficult idea to experience. This is not only due to its technicalities and subtleties but also because it has been interpreted, and misinterpreted, in many ways throughout the long history of Buddhism (Cestari: 326; Priest 2013: 129).[1] These complexities and alternative conceptual structures have also been misinterpreted by those from outside the tradition.[2] For instance, as early as 1896, Kern described (1896: 126) emptiness

---

[1] As James Mark Shields pointed out in private correspondence on Emptiness and Nāgārjuna, there are as many accounts of emptiness as there are historical Nāgārjunas. Cestari (2010: 326–327) notes, most traditions within Buddhism have developed their own interpretation of emptiness. Surveying the literature, it seems unlikely that any formulation of the idea of emptiness can be singled out as the most representative. Equally it is important to note that it, the concept of emptiness, has come under considerable criticism as being contradictory. See Burton, 1999.

[2] As I shall discuss later in the chapter, the distinction, as Conze has noted, is equivalent to the Madhyamika distinction between "Absolute truth" (paramārthasatya), "the knowledge of the real as it is without any distortion," and "Truth so-called" (saṃvṛti satya), "truth as conventionally believed in common parlance." (Conze, 1959:140-141, 244). See also Beckwith, (2015).

as "complete and pure nihilism," with Keith (1923: 237, 239, 247, 267) understands Mādhyamika as a doctrine of reality as "absolute nothingness." Following on from this, in more recent work, Žižek has continued the tradition of what has been described as misreading emptiness equating it with quietism and fascism, and modern consumer capitalism.[3] As Žižek understands the distance between the Buddhist notion of emptiness "far from being the same as [Buddhism's] nirvana principle (the striving toward the dissolution of all tension, the longing for a return to original nothingness), the death drive is the tension which persists and insists beyond and against the nirvana principle"(Žižek 2005). However, in key respects, Žižek does acknowledge that Buddhism and his account of Lacanianism are philosophical kindred spirits. Both posit an emptiness or a gap at the center of us humans, which we are always striving to fill with whatever is available. In other words, far from being opposed to the pleasure principle [which Žižek had earlier critiqued], the nirvana principle is its highest and most radical expression (Žižek 2012: 132).

In the following section of this chapter, I intend to draw out the socio-epistemological implications for the critical cosmopolitan project. However, the core of the argument put forward by Nāgārjuna, the relationship between the relative and the absolute, goes to the principal of an account of critical cosmopolitanism: that every proposition of a relative reality can be deconstructed to reveal its emptiness, and/or its dependent origination. In confronting the apophenia of relative reality enables infinite multiplicities through destabilizing limitations. In other words, the epistemic principle of emptiness, as a reflexive negation, allows us to refocus the cosmopolitan imagination to the level of the local and not as an assimilatory project of abstractions and essentialization.

NĀGĀRJUNA

Nāgārjuna, considered by many to be the founder of the *Mādhyamika*, or Middle Path, Schools of Mahāyāna Buddhism, lived in South India in approximately the second century CE. He was the first to conceptualize the idea of emptiness which, he argued, was present within the teachings of the Buddha. The most important of his texts is the Mūlamadhyamakākarikā[4] (Santina 2002; Garfield 1995; Priest 2009; Priest and Garfield 2002) and is considered to represent the foundation of the highly skeptical and dialectical analytic philosophical School. As Huntingdon notes (1989: 18), Nāgārjuna's work was in part concerned with moving away from the more abstract work

---

[3] See Boon, 2015.
[4] Nāgārjuna, 1999. Literally Fundamental Verses on the Middle Way.

of Hīnayāna Buddhism.[5] The central topic of the Mūlamadhyamakākarikā is emptiness.[6] Emptiness is the Buddhist technical term for the lack of independent existence, inherent existence, or essence in things. It refers to the fundamental Buddhist teaching that phenomena, including the self, are devoid or "empty" of intrinsic existence (Nhat Hanh 1999). Buddhism adopted a distinctive approach to the concept of the self (Kelly 2008). Buddhism holds that personal identity is delusional and that each of us is a self that turns out to not actually exist (Giles 1993; See also Siderits 2003). This is one of the Buddha's key insights and is what distinguishes Buddhist views from other views of the human condition. From the Buddhist perspective, it is through gaining an understanding of how the "illusion of self is constituted and how it functions" (Loy 1996: 85), that is essential if we are to develop a view of the possibility of nirvana (Lama 2005).

Despite its numerous definitions of what emptiness is or is not, the concept does not, due to its diverse meaning throughout the Buddhist traditions, have a clear or definitive conceptualization.[7] As Cestari notes (2010: 333), while the concept is often discussed in terms of its relationship to the early Buddhist conception of anatta, or to Nāgārjuna, or in terms of ""void," open," "without," "nothing," "nonexistent," it also indicates a practical view on reality that supersedes language games (Shonin et al. 2015). Within the *Mahāyāna* literature not only is the individual "I" reduced to a reified concept, but all aspects of everyday experience, both subjective and objective, are emptied of any ontological content, whether defined as "self" or as "intrinsic being" or "essence" (Daye 1975). Here the three aspects of the cognitive, the subjective, the objective, as well as the act of knowing are destabilized.

Much of Nāgārjuna's text is dedicated to undermining the notion that entities exist according to their own inherent existence. He takes it as a fundamental philosophical task to offer an understanding of what Buddhist philosophy, refers to as *pratityasamutptida*, dependent co-origination. As Eilís Ward argues, the principle of dependent origination, or interdependency, refers to the law of mutual causality (Ward 2013: 142). This denotes the "nexus between phenomena in virtue of which events depend on other events, composites depend on their parts, and so forth" (Garfield 1995: 95). Therefore, all phenomena ascend from multifaceted sets of sources and

---

[5] The ontological position of Mahayana texts is most clearly viewed as a reaction to or critique of the Hinayana ontology (Huntington 1989: 17). Hinayana texts are those which accept a sort of radical pluralism, analyzing all mundane experience into a precisely determined number of ultimately real, discrete atomic constituents, called dharmas.

[6] Pāli: suññatā, Sanskrit: śūnyatā.

[7] As this discussion should illustrate, I feel that it would be misguided to suggest that there is something like a generally definable meaning for Buddhist *śūnyatā*, or at least a descriptive indication of its range of meanings.

circumstances and exist as interacting processes in a relational world of inter-penetrating nonduality (Ward 2013: 142).[8]

For the reader to gain some traction on this concept, and its radical nature, Garfield suggests that when a Madhyamika philosopher suggests that a table is empty, is to invite the question "Empty of what?" (2005: 25). The answer is that the table is empty of inherent existence, that it lacks an essence. Importantly, it must be remembered that the Madhyamika philosopher rather than claiming that the table does not exist is only suggesting that it does not exist from its own side. In destabilizing the cognitive, the subjective, the objective, and the act of knowing, Nāgārjuna is arguing that the table's existence as the object depends not on itself, nor on any purely nonrelational characteristics, but depends on us as well (Garfield 2004). The point is to illuminate, show, and undermine the human tendency to pattern-forming from external stimuli that lead to closure, and not to show that the table is completely nonexistent.

Therefore, to say that the table lacks essence is to argue that if our culture had not advanced this custom of furniture, what seems to be an obviously unitary object, might instead be correctly described as a collection of pieces of wood. It is also to suggest that the table depends for its existence on its parts, on its causes, on its material, and so forth. Apart from these, there is no table. The table is a purely arbitrary slice of space-time chosen by us as the referent of a single name and not an entity demanding, on its own, rec-ognition and a philosophical analysis to reveal its essence. That independent character is precisely what it lacks on this view. The point to take away from the analysis of the table is the view that entities do not bear their own essence within themselves. Rather, it is their relationship with and interdependence with other entities through which we give them meaning of which we need to be mindful (Garfield 2002: 26).

TWO TRUTHS

Though the doctrine of emptiness has been understood differently across the many Schools of Buddhist thought, it was Candrakirti's[9] presenta-tion of the idea of two truths that can be understood as the most radical. According to his exposition of the doctrine, all means of knowledge are

---

[8] As Garfield notes, (1995: xxxvi), how this dependency is defined, and its ontological status, is, as was noted above, still a matter of considerable debate.

[9] Once again, very little is known at Candrakirti's life. He is unanimously attributed with only one work, a commentary of Nāgārjuna's Mūlamadhyamakakarikā. See Saito 1984, for a partial transla-tion; cited Huntington (1989: 33, n.38).

only "conventionally veridical," for in all cases, the act of knowing is contingent on the interdependence between knower and known (Huntington 1989: 18). Such an account of the interdependence between subject and object under normal circumstances vitiates the cognitive act and therefore to know is unreliable (Huntington 1989: 18). Therefore, the truth of a higher meaning, an ultimate truth (*paramarthasatya*), must be realized through a means of knowledge not grounded in the rigid dichotomy set up between reified concepts of subject and object. As Huntington describes the process, "knower and known are experienced as interdependent events within a larger matrix of other such impermanent, unceasingly unstable movements, through a way of understanding referred to as *prajna* (wisdom), resulting in *advayajnana* (nondualistic knowledge)" (Huntington 1989: 18). Therefore, the perspective of emptiness is not at odds with the conventional standpoint, only with a particular philosophical understanding of it which takes the conventional to be more than merely conventional (Garfield 1995: 314).[10] Nevertheless, to assert that all things are empty of any intrinsic reality, for Nāgārjuna, is not to undermine the existential status of things as simply *nothing*. On the contrary, Nāgārjuna argues, to assert that the things are empty of any intrinsic reality is to explain the way things really are as causally conditioned phenomena.

THE EMPTINESS OF EMPTINESS

To better approach the idea of the emptiness of emptiness, and its relevance for socio-epistemic inquiry, let us now consider what it is one means when we say that emptiness itself is empty. As Garfield admits (1995: 314), even in the context of Buddhist thought such a claim as the emptiness of emptiness does have an air of paradox about it. For emptiness is, in Mahāyāna philosophical thought, the ultimate nature of all phenomena. And the distinction between the merely conventional nature of things and their ultimate nature would seem to mark the distinction between the apparent and the real. This may lead to the view that among phenomena, emptiness has a metaphysical quality beyond the conventional nature of reality. On this view, the argument for the two truths would seem to suggest that, on an ontological basis, as a basis for claims about the grounds of reality, that the two truths are radically distinct from each other. However, to see a conventional phenomenon as empty is not to see a beyond of the conventional. While it is plausible to say that what is merely apparent is empty of reality, it seems nihilistic to say

---

[10] Daye (1975: 84) has suggested that "emptiness" is a "nonreferring term," a "third-order capstone reflexive concept" (See also Huntington, 1989: 202 n4).

that what is ultimately real is empty of reality. Contrary to Žižek's analysis, the Madhyamika are quite consciously antinihilistic. However, if we say that phenomenon is empty, that they are dependent upon convention, are we not also forced to concede that emptiness itself is also is dependent in convention?

When we say that a phenomenon is empty, we mean that when we try to specify its essence, we come up with nothing. When we look for the substance that underlies the properties, we find none. In a case, such as a table, the emptiness of the table is dependent, as in lacking essence, on the table itself. Nāgārjuna's central argument to support his radical nonfoundationalist theory of the two truths draws upon an understanding of conventional truth as tied to dependently arisen phenomena, and ultimate truth as tied to emptiness. Since the former and the latter are co-constitutive of each other, in that each entails the other, ultimate reality is tied to being conventionally reality.

However, as Huntingdon (1989: 56) points out, this is a relative and not an absolute assertion, which is tailored to the demands of a particular concern. At a deeper level, the Mādhyamika thinkers want to draw our attention to the presuppositions about the conceptual and perceptual foundations of the world. They argue that to view the world as being comprised of independent, self-sufficient entities is a tacit, preconscious, pretheoretical failure to engage with the contextualized nature of reality. Here the concept of emptiness is at odds with the conventional view of reality which takes the conventional view of reality to be more than merely conventional As Nāgārjuna stated, someone would be incurably insane if they took the teaching of emptiness as a belief system:

> I call incurable whomever holds emptiness as a philosophical view. Kasyapa, it is as if a physician were to give medicine to a sick man, and when the medicine had cured all the original problems it remained in the stomach and was not itself expelled. What do you think, Kasyapa, would this man be cured of his disease? No indeed, Blessed One, if the medicine cured all the original problems and yet remained in the stomach, unexpelled, the man's disease would be much worse. The Blessed One said: Thus, it is, Kasyapa, that emptiness is the exhaustion of all philosophical views. I call incurable whoever holds emptiness as a philosophical view.[11]

What I wish to highlight at this stage is that what Nāgārjuna is proposing is not a belief system about the metaphysical nature of reality, but a heuristic deconstructive method for conventional reality that does not rely on a metaphysical account to substantiate its claims. In plainer terms, what this method will allow for is an understanding the relationship between self-other-world

---

[11] See also Loy 2002: 84).

through the logic of reflexive negation, and not one that is predetermined by "self-evident" axiomatic principles.

To develop an interpretation of cosmopolitanism that functions through the socioepistemic principle of emptiness, the following section now turns to Watsuji's account of the concept. While the centrality of emptiness to Watsuji's work cannot be disputed, what is not so clear is what emptiness means for Watsuji. Is the notion of emptiness that he is working with consistent with the interpretation of Nāgārjuna's concept offered here or do we need to look to another source through which to explain the difficulties that become apparent in his work? While others have focused on the functional aspect of emptiness for Watsuji, that is, whether it is to be equated with community or cultural awakening, here the chapter is concerned with whether Watsuji's understanding was consistent with our reading of emptiness as a critical heuristic tool.[12] Does a textual analysis of Watsuji's work provide a means to position thought in way that allows it to go beyond itself; the social reality that we encounter.

WATSUJI AND EMPTINESS

At the heart of Watsuji's exploration of a relational ethics lies the concept of emptiness. He writes:

> Now, that ningen's sonzai [human existence] is, fundamentally speaking, a movement of negation makes it clear that the basis of ningen's sonzai is negation as such, that it is absolute negation. The true reality of an individual, as well as totality, is "emptiness," and this emptiness is the absolute totality. Out of this ground, from the fact that this emptiness is emptied, emerges ningen's sonzai as a movement of negation. (Watsuji 1996 [1938]: 19)

However, the clarity and precision of the concept is clouded through Watsuji's introduction of apparently interchangeable synonyms for emptiness such as nothingness, absolute totality, absolute negativity (Sevilla 2015: 235).[13] Sevilla argues that Watsuji's understanding of emptiness gradually developed through several publications and that this was aimed at accomplishing three objectives. First, in *fūdo*, though Watsuji makes no mention of "emptiness," he does introduce the term "absolute negativity" to identity the relationship of individuality and totality as being dual structured,

---

[12] See Sevilla 2014 and 2017 for an excellent coverage of these questions

[13] Watsuji was not alone in introducing such conceptual synonyms and as such potentially obfuscating conceptual clarity. However, and I agree with Cestari's assessment in this respect (2010: 324), the aim that Watsuji and many of the Kyoto school had set themselves, an overcoming of the dualism of West and East, and the development of a new logic, meant that they were attracted to Kantian and most importantly Hegelian categories.

and in so doing the nonduality of subject and object. In *Ethics as the Study of Ningen* (WTZ9), Watsuji recasts the term as absolute emptiness that lay at the *foundation* of subject and object, with the double negation of individual and totality. However, this is further developed in its dialectical form in *Ethics I*:

> Now, that *ningen's sonzai* is, fundamentally speaking, a movement of negation makes it clear that the basis of *ningen's sonzai* is negation as such, that is, absolute negation. The true reality of an individual, as well as of totality, is "emptiness," and this emptiness is the absolute totality. Out of this ground, from the fact that this emptiness is emptied, emerges *ningen's sonzai* as a movement of negation. The negation of negation is the self-returning and self-realizing movement of the absolute totality that is precisely social ethics. Therefore, the basic principle of social ethics is the realization of totality (as the negation of negation) through the individual, (that is, the negation of totality). (Watsuji 1996 [1937, 1942, 1949]: 23)

As Sevilla notes, Watsuji, in setting the contradictory moments of human existence, individuality and sociality, as the basis of human existence, is rejecting any ethical accounts that rest on either as substantive moments. He rejects the inherent essence of either and points instead toward their interdependence. However, Sevilla rightly points out that if we were to ask the question, "What comes first, individuality or totality?" Then within *Ethics I*, Watsuji gives two separate accounts of the same theoretical model (Sevilla 2015: 126). This first model Sevilla describes as a "model of continuous negation." In this model, we see that this movement of negation is continuous and constant. Watsuji writes:

> We cannot first presuppose individuals, and then explain the establishment of social relationships among them. Nor can we presuppose society and from there explain the occurrence of individuals. Neither the one nor the other has "precedence." (Watsuji 1996 [1938]: 102).

The other model present in *Ethics I is* described as "a three-stage model." Here Watsuji defines "emptiness" as the negativity originating in the mutual negation between individuality and community. Here one travels from fundamental emptiness (the unnegated totality), to individual existence, and then to social existence (WTZ10, 123-124; 116-117. Cited Sevilla 2015: 11). Individuality can only be understood by negating the submergence of the individual in community, and community can only be understood by negating the separateness of individuals. Therefore, both poles exist only by negating each other, and this activity of negation itself is captured in the word "emptiness" (Sevilla 2015: 125–126).

In *Ethics II*, Watsuji developed an account of emptiness as the principle of finite relation. Here Watsuji presents the concept in a developed form with the aim of proving that human existence has a dual structure of both individuality and totality. As in the previous formulation, his aim is the refutation of any claim that ethics can be based on the individual or the community solely (Sevilla 2015: 269). Therefore, for Watsuji, while human existence is always relational, with the individual always determined by relationships, totalities cannot occur deprived of the existence, contribution, and commitment of individuals. What we see here is that both sides of the dual structure are "empty," *lacking in self-existence and dependent on its "other."*

In *Ethics III*, Watsuji applies this account of emptiness to the international realm through the application of emptiness to the history of nations. As a precursor to decolonial theory, this analysis is designed to show that morality is ontically and epistemically specific, and that the imposition of "outside" ethical systems amounts to violence. However, his study is also designed to show that various global ethical systems are grounded in, and expressive of, auniversal morality. Like history, nations only realize their climatic character in contrast to other nations. This represents the description of "self-realization of identity through difference," or nondialectical heterogeneity, of the process of mutual phases of self-development. This self-awareness of finite totalities is only made possible through the realization of what one doesn't share with those outside of one's own totality.

Such an account radically relativizes all forms of singularities in the face of absolute relationality. However, Watsuji's account of cosmopolitanism is not as a cosmopolitan morality based on "self-evident" principles governing all individuals equally as autonomous agents, but as a morality of selflessness through truthful response to trust relationships. In doing so, Watsuji distances himself from abstractions such as "rationality," "humanity," or of a "world government." Instead, he argues that individual nations need to develop a heightened sense of individuality through which to contribute to a global ethic. This, of course, will be specific to the individual nation and would also highlight societal limitations. Through this process, in the contact between nations, it is possible for a nation to learn from another without one nation or community claiming to provide a privileged perspective. Watsuji stresses the importance of this:

> Thinking of it in this way, the realization of moral difference in each nation is indispensable for the fulfillment of the universal socio-ethical path. It saves each nation from conceit and spurs them to work to overcome their individual limitations. (*WTZ11*, 348, quoted in Sevilla 2015: 215)

Given such an exposition, it may appear difficult to sustain an argument that Watsuji's model supports the justification for totalitarianism. However, Sakai Naoki among others have provided such a critique. This needs to be addressed at a deeper theoretical level than in chapter 3 if the book is to maintain that emptiness, as a model of thought, provides the basis for critical cosmopolitanism through which to move beyond what Bauman appropriately designated as the "sedentary imagination" (2003: 12) of Western modernity.

WATSUJI: EMPTINESS AND NOTHINGNESS

Negation is the focus of Watsuji's philosophical anthropology, but what exactly is negation? As Liederbach (2012) notes, Watsuji clearly means for "negation" to be understood in the context of Nishida Kitarō's "self-identity of absolute contradiction" and the Buddhist doctrine of emptiness. Watsuji writes, for instance, that

> in the extremity in which we seek the individual independence of the physical body, we break through to *the disappearance of individual independence*. In another field, this has also been expressed with the phrase "the dropping off of body-mind." (WTZ 10: 71)

Here Watsuji is referring to the work of the Sōtō Zen monk Dōgen Kigen (1200–1253), which Watsuji published in his book *Monk Dōgen* (1926). In Buddhism, emptiness means that things lack the substantiality that we seek in them, and as a result, life is unsatisfactory. In Zen Buddhism, one's "authentic countenance" is the true self apart from the conceptual discriminations that obscure it. That is the discriminations of, say, gender, place of birth, sexuality, and color should not be the foreground of our experience of ourselves, but must only be implied.

Absolute totality involves the nondiscrimination among self and other. Here nondiscrimination means on the one hand, the achievement of the individual through dedicated practice, and on the other, nondiscrimination represents a return for the individual to what it is authentic and original. That is the milieu of relations out of which one emerges as an individual. Rather than treating, in real terms, self and other as autonomous and distinct, the claim being made here is that relationships are one of nonduality. Therefore, when Watsuji writes, "...the individual is one who becomes an individual as the negation of *emptiness from which the self originates* (that is, authentic emptiness)" (WTZ 10: 124), he means that the supposed duality of self and other is only the middle phase of a larger process that begins and ends with nondifferentiation. That is, that the fundamental law of human beings is ultimately the negation of emptiness itself. In the process of double negation, emptiness is our source and our destination.

To solve the problem of the "subjective, practical, and dynamic structure of human being" (WTZ 10: 25; Watsuji 1996: 21), Watsuji turned to the method of dialectics:

> On the one hand, the standpoint of an acting individual comes to be established only in some way as a negation of the totality of ningen. An individual that does not imply the meaning of negation, that is, an essentially self-sufficient individual, is nothing but an imaginative construction. On the other hand, the totality of ningen comes to be established as the negation of individuality. A totality that does not include the individual negatively is also nothing but the product of the imagination. These two negations constitute the dual character of human being. And what is more, they constitute a single movement. On the very ground that it is the negation of totality, the individual is, fundamentally speaking, none other than that totality. If this is true, then this negation is also the self-awareness of that totality. Hence, when an individual realizes herself through negation, a door is opened to the realization of totality through the negation of the individual. The individual's acting is a movement of the restoration of totality itself. [. . .] Now, that ningen's sonzai is, fundamentally speaking, a movement of negation makes clear that the basis of ningen's sonzai is negation as such, that is, absolute negation. (WTZ 10: 26; Watsuji 1996: 22–23)

However, as Liederbach argues (2012: 126), the problem that now arises, the central issue that has concerned many of Watsuji's critics, is how are the two aspects of *ningen*, that is individuality and sociality, related to each other? Furthermore, it is important to remember that even though Watsuji's dialectics is intended principally to elucidate the ontological structure of *ningen*, the movement of dual negation must have some reference in concrete reality. Of that "factuality" Watsuji writes about his concept of *aidagara* that

> That is, already existing persistent relationships are ultimately the absolute totality of self-other nonduality. They are the *authentic countenance* before your mother and father were born. They are *authenticity* as the origin out of which we ultimately come. (WTZ 10: 195)

How are we to make sense of this motion in the context of everyday life? One might put it this way: At the heart of Watsuji's *aidagara* is not simply an obligation to community, but the "double negation," of both the individual and society. In the first movement, the individual sees herself as an individual by rebelling against the group. The second movement is the individual's negation of herself by returning to the whole and incessantly situating the individual, the family, or the nation within greater and greater unities.[14] However, while an understanding of the relationship between sociality and individuality could be made, as Liederbach (2012: 126) notes, it is not exactly clear what it would necessarily mean to negate the totality of *ningen*.

Unfortunately, Watsuji never quite clears up this ambiguity. That is, he never goes into detail on how this negation could be understood within the context of human existence and practice. Although Watsuji is stressing the temporal and spatial nature of being human, in the *Ethics*, we are unable to gain an understanding of areas of conflict and social strife at the level of the ontic, the level of the everyday. One may be intellectually generous and argue that the key to understanding emptiness and the double negation is to point to quotes such as, "Neither the one nor the other has 'precedence.'" Therefore, it is irrelevant to state whether individuality or totality comes first. However, such a reading of emptiness' operation within society would not be compatible with other ways that Watsuji himself discusses dialectics.

According to interpretations of Watsuji's work that stress the "return to totality" of the individual, on the level of everyday existence, rather than theoretical claim, the individual has to submit itself to society because it is ontologically permanently oriented toward *aidagara*. This ontological anchoring of the individual to *aidagara* has two aspects and is the cause of much confusion and criticism of Watsuji's work. However, for the moment, the notion of the individual is grasped only in its negative relationship with a totality and provides little understanding of how, under such ontologically conditions, new *aidagara* may be created: social reform for instance. Therefore, it may be reasonable to claim, following Sakai, that the individual is a nonentity within the movement of dual negation. However, while Watsuji does give seemingly ambiguous accounts, therefore, is there a way to break this deadlock? Liederbach (2012) in an ambitious endeavor of cross-cultural engagement argues that an explication of Watsuji's understanding of *fūdo* provides the key to overcome the deadlock: that Watsuji, in the *Ethics*, fails to account for the ontic and ontological distinction.

UNRAVELING THE ONTIC FROM THE ONTOLOGICAL

Liederbach initiates the unraveling the problem by turning to Watsuji's investigation of spatiality. He makes the argument that the movement involved in the double negation hints at the problem of spatiality as the negation of the individual and its return to totality must, for Watsuji, be understood, as

---

[14] Of course, the reader will see the influence of Watsuji's reading of Confucius thought here.

"movement of disruption and then of unification" (WTZ 10: 27; Watsuji 1996: 24; Liederbach 2012: 127). As this is a negation of multiple individuals, then it is necessary for Watsuji to give a phenomenological description.

Methodically, Watsuji's investigation starts from the spatial factuality of everyday life through which to then unravel its ontological structure. In doing so, Watsuji follows Heidegger's insight when he argues that *ningen* is not oriented toward abstract points in an objective space, but toward a space of a symbolic life-world, or, as he puts it, a space that is structured by "*expressions.*" These are the correlates of *ningen's* "practical understanding." Watsuji writes:

> [T]he spatiality of human being is known to everybody in an ontic way. People use transportation facilities and behave in a spatial fashion for the benefit of their ordinary lives. It is doubtful whether this facticity is grasped theoretically. (WTZ 10: 163; Watsuji 1996: 156)

It is this inquiry into the structure of spatiality that serves the purpose of disclosing "the practical interconnectedness of acts . . . in its concrete structure" (WTZ 10: 28; Watsuji 1996: 24), and "give expression to a wide variety of relations between human beings" (WTZ 10: 169; Watsuji 1996: 161). In applying the movement of double negation to the problem of spatiality transforms it into that of "division/disruption and connection," which is to point to the fact that societies are made up many individuals with diverse perspectives and experiences, but which, through the imaginary, connect with each other to form totalities. However, as Liederbach notes (2012: 129), in transferring the double negation to the problem of spatiality merely replicates the issue of the subsuming of the individual by the totality. Equally, in respect of temporality:

> [J]ust as the movement of negation was, in its extreme, the self activity of absolute negativity, so temporality is precisely the manner in which absolute negativity exhibits itself. That is to say, an established betweenness is, in its extreme, the absolute wholeness that consists of the nonduality of the self and the other [. . .] At the same time, possible betweenness is absolute wholeness, which also consists of the nonduality of self and other. By bringing to realization the nondual relationship between self and other, we return to our authentic home ground. This ultimate ground out of which we come is the ultimate *terminus ad quem* to which we return. (WTZ 10: 195; Watsuji 1996: 187; Liederbach 2012: 130)

Regrettably, once again, we see that in respect of temporality *ningen* cannot help but return to totality as it is ontologically determined and lacks the potential to transcend *aidagara*. This is due, contends Liederbach (2012: 130), to Watsuji's accounts of spatiality and temporality lacking a sufficient appreciation of the "notion of existence at the cost of facticity." This also has implications for Watsuji's understanding of agency. Watsuji writes:

> [A]n act is not something constructed out of various activities of the individual consciousness but the movement itself in which subject, although splitting into self and other, combines in a nonduality of self and other to form a betweenness. (WTZ 10: 36; Watsuji 1996: 34)

If we restrict ourselves to Liederbach's analysis on the ontological structure of spatiality and temporality, in a strict sense for Watsuji, individual agency does not exist. Rather, for Watsuji, agency is permanently anchored within the structure of betweenness. As Liederbach states, "agency [for Watsuji] is characterized by the movement from an established betweenness towards a possible one, whose movement is possible only because *ningen* is characterized by extendedness and is always oriented towards betweenness" (Liederbach 2012: 130. My parenthesis). That is, all the possibilities available to the individual for transcendence are predetermined by *aidagara*. In terms of the aim of this chapter in providing an epistemic basis for critical cosmopolitanism such a predetermination of agency would fail to allow for a critique of ideology and would be fatal for this project.

In the introduction, I argued that it was possible to provide a synthesis of Delanty and Mignolo that held out the possibility of providing the basis for a critical cosmopolitan account of social theory capable of overcoming the book's critique of cosmopolitanism. However, it was stressed at the time that this remained at the level of abstraction and that a grounded account of socio-epistemology was needed to fully address the criticisms of the project of cosmopolitanism. We have also discussed that rather than being opposed to "modernity" that the Kyoto School in general and Watsuji in particular, had engaged in a critique of modernity through the perspective of East-Asian thought as well as Western methodologies. Here it was claimed that Watsuji, in basing his socio-epistemology on Confucius and Buddhist thought, provided an opportunity to alter the lens and the imagination of social theory through which to engage in a critique of our received notions of terms such as the individual, democracy, globalization, and capitalism. However, in identifying Watsuji's vacillation between different forms of social ontology, has raised the concern that Watsuji's work, while providing a means of analysis beyond individualistic or holistic societal analysis, would nevertheless fail to accommodate a critique of existing ideologies (existing *aidagara*). Therefore, the questions to be addressed are what is the cause of Watsuji's apparent vacillation between a creative sense of *aidagara* and are there resources in Watsuji's account of socio-epistemology capable of providing a means of critique?

Following Liederbach's argument, it is possible to distinguish two meanings of *aidagara* that Watsuji presents in his analysis. First, following Watsuji's application of his *Confucius* thought, it is concrete relationships such as the family, children, and community that structure social relationships. Second, there is the use of the term to designate the ontological structure of human existence. Liederbach is right to object that the problem arises in Watsuji presentation in that he makes no effort to distinguish both meanings. This is because his articulation of *ningen sonzai* can only be understood primarily in the context of ethical concreteness (Liederbach 2012: 132). Therefore, despite Watsuji's criticism of Heidegger's supposed neglect of the factuality of life, this conceptual deficiency does not provide an account of authenticity for the everyday as it never gains concreteness. How did this arise in Watsuji's work?

In identifying the lack of distinction between the ontic and the ontological, Liederbach points the way to Watsuji's interchangeably use of emptiness and nothingness. As Cestari notes, nothingness is Buddhist insofar as it is engaged in self-negation, and it is not Buddhist insofar as it is conceived realistically as a negative universal that lies at the immediate foundation of the world. Buddhist emptiness does not have to do only with awakening to the transiency of things and the self but also with the emptiness of dualistic thinking itself. Vacillating between ontology (nothingness) and nonfoundationalism (emptiness), Watsuji shows his clearest affinity to Buddhism in his notion of self-negation, which lies closer to the core of his idea of absolute nothingness than its metaphysical overtones.

The lack of distinction between the two concepts leads Watsuji to propose finite totalities such as culture, family, nation, or the state as ontological categories that are neither Buddhist nor a correct interpretation of emptiness. In fact, the two concepts are incompatible in respect of social analysis. Nothingness derives from Sino-Japanese history as well as through the influence of Hegelianism on Japanese philosophy and is prescriptive, while emptiness is descriptive. For the project of forming a conceptually post-western account of critical cosmopolitan social theory that the term is best understood as a heuristic device used to describe the interdependence of subject and object, and that if we misunderstand this then the cure is worse than the disease (Loy 2002: 84). A cure that ends in the creation of diametric dualities of totalities.

Furthermore, the concepts from Buddhist or Confucius thought that he drew from do not rely on an understanding of societal dynamics as static. They are open to the potential of critique as we transcend a present *aidagara* to the creation of new areas of *aidagara*. Briefly, rather than offer an understanding of proprietary rituals as being static and conformist through drawing on these intellectual traditions had provided Watsuji with a critical and reflexive source. However, although Watsuji developed a critical engagement with the world through a dialectic of enlightenment and ontic location, his inability to distinguish between the ontic and ontology meant that he was unable to provide an account capable of the critique of ideology.

And yet, there are instances of Watsuji tending toward societal models capable of subsuming the individual into a totality, there are equally clear indications that he did not support such an account. For instance, when he writes that in terms of the "division/disruption and connection" of *aidagara* he is clearly stressing the importance of individual and social creativity:

> The first point to be argued is that of the double structure of a human being itself . . . An individual who does not imply the meaning of negation, that is, an essentially self-sufficient individual, *is nothing but an imaginative construction.* On the other hand, the totality of *ningen* comes to be established as the negation of individuality. A totality that does not include the individual negatively is also *nothing but a product of the imagination.* These two negations constitute the dual character of a human being. And what is more, they constitute a single movement. On the very ground that it is the negation of totality, the individual is, fundamentally speaking, none other than that totality. If this is true, then this negation is also the self-awareness of that totality. Hence, when an individual realizes herself through negation, *a door is opened to the realization of totality* through the negation of the individual. (Watsuji 1996 [1937, 1942, 1949]: 22. Emphasis added)

Here five claims can be made concerning the effort to find "openings" for creativity out of the functioning of emptiness through *aidagara* which has a direct bearing on the present project. For Watsuji, the ontic and the ontological are intertwined. In supporting "this negation is also the self- awareness of that totality," allows for *ningen*, through standing out into *aidagara*, in the ontological sense, to realize the structure of its own existence (Liederbach 2012). It is only in this account of Watsujian transcendence within the continual model of negation[15] that can provide the potential for societal change and individual transformation. We have here the individual as a generative agent, a theory proposing actor, enunciating from the inbetweenness of the cavernous ravine of the imaginary of *becoming* and what she experiences as reality. It is an account capable of accommodating our heuristic devices of diametric and concentric dualities. In realizing the structure of its own existence and in recognizing both the limitations of its own existence and that of the totality as a nondualistic movement, allows one to gain an awareness

---

[15] The reader will recall this quotation from his work:We cannot first presuppose individuals, and then explain the establishment of social relationships among them. Nor can we presuppose society and from there explain the occurrence of individuals. Neither the one nor the other has "precedence" (Watsuji T,1996 [1938]: 102).

of both. This is in direct contradiction to Sakai's argument. For Watsuji, if anyone thinks that individuality or totality is the whole story, then they are talking about a figment of the imagination. It is the double movement of individuality and totality, without privilege, that is the underlying premise of being human. Any distortion of either as privileged is an illusion but social change out of the incessant spatial tension between the totality and individuality. Watsuji is making the claim that every society produces a public universe of meaning for itself, which is not determined by necessity—history is characteristically the existence of a multiplicity of such worlds. This is in the sense that it is embodied in the whole of social life, in social practices and institutions, determining personal identities as well as the collective-social reality. However, it is not entirely contingent either since it must consider the existent. In turn, this means that we move from necessity to contingency and contains the possibility of societal transformation. In stressing the realization of "herself," Watsuji is arguing that it is in self-realization, without grounds, that totalities, communities, develop. It is through one's own rejection, one's own engagement with the rationality of the norms of a society through which "I" provide models for change.

THE EMPTINESS OF CRITICAL COSMOPOLITANISM

Cosmopolitanism is a spatial critique of the axiomatic claims of the temporal. The issues facing the critical cosmopolitan imagination are predicated on its temporal understanding of the social. Here, rather than providing a spatial critique of the temporal process of globalization and how it is effecting space, or providing a spatial critique of the convention of self as an economic unit of analysis, existing social spaces are reduced to the narrative to the dominant discourse of the everyday. This emphasizes a vertical understanding of tradition. Delanty maintains verticality through pursuing the agenda of human rights and democracy, tradition. Doing so is to ignore the spaces within the space of globalization. Delanty is surely correct to place emphasis on, in a negative sense, *freedom from* structures or conditions which may be constraints on the *self-realization* of an agent. For example, the global extension of human rights. However, by relying on a modernist account of time, he does not provide an account that extends beyond the assumptions of the reification of everyday language games. Nor does he provide for the possibility of self-realization, to question the production of truths through which to reconfigure knowledge. This positive sense is really a *freedom to*. Certain capacities must be generated by the agent, if that agent wishes to be free, and these capacities depend in part on external conditions which must include the spaces within space.

Equally, Mignolo maintains the enunciation of the vertical through his emphasis on the ideal of a totalized community. Mirroring Delanty and the Eurocentrism that he denounces through the adoption of the mirror image of a totalizing otherness, Mignolo does not accommodate the insight that there are spaces within space in which the marginalized, my other's other, resides. Though he is right to call for the means to articulate the *self-realization* of a people, in a positive sense a freedom *to be*, in a negative sense in rejecting the account of the everyday this is only partial. This is due to his failure to recognize that if an agent wishes to be free, for self-realization, such a capacity depends in part on external conditions which cannot be reduced to a totality. For example, for an agent to move away from perceptual and conceptual reification, they must gain autonomy *from* certain endogenous as well as exogenous limitations of the conceptual conventions of the everyday. These reifications of language are not only global; they are local too. Though it may be reasonable to argue that the "worldview" of neoliberalism oppresses me and restricts my self-realization, on the scale of the everyday it may also be my neighbour.

These considerations lead to the assertion that a critical account of cosmopolitanism must be epistemically predicated on a principle which is necessarily capable of both a negative *and* a positive form. Negative in the sense that some structures or conditions might be pernicious constraints which agents must gain *freedom from*, for example, ordinary assumptions and discourses about reality which give a reified conception of reality. Positive in the sense that some structures or conditions might be necessary conditions *for* the possibility of self-realization. Their function within the conceptual persona that will be developed in the chapter on *aidagara* is not necessarily the guarantee of rights but to provide a point of critique from outside the dominant modes of social, economic, and political conventions.

Therefore, to predicate the enunciation of the cosmopolitan imagination on a temporal account of locale, universalism, or being, individual or social, reduces it to reification. The acclaimed notion of the transcendent imagination of modernity is confined within its own view and fails to acknowledge the legacy of colonialism for the subjectivity of both colonized peoples and colonizing peoples. Though the effects of colonialism, slavery, and more recently, the exportation of neoliberalism to the south are evident in the fact of "southern" theory or decolonial theory, the effects of colonialism on the sociopsychological of "Western" communities, are pernicious, We encounter these socio-psycho-historical tropes in the symbols and materiality of conquest and colonialism in our meeting places, our legislators, our language, our knowledge, our universities and their curriculum, in our "common-sense," and in the history of our jurisprudence and theories of the political. Race, colour, sexuality, gender, and disability, should be understood as implied rather than as a foregrounding signifier for identity. To foreground such signifiers only essentializes and extinguishes differences and the creativity made possible when differences encounter each other. However, the complete lack of acknowledgment or exploration of race and identity-attributions of colour by critical theory means that it is caught within a universalism of its own mind.

In the context of critical theory as a cosmopolitan endeavour, such a universalism, whether veiled as immanent transcendence or the cosmopolitan imagination can only lead to assimilation of the other. Cosmopolitanism can only be authentic if it (a) accepts the notion of incompleteness in respect of its own social structures, that the relations within social space are less concrete, and that the production of knowledge is based on cooperation and critique, rather than certainties that set up diametric dualities, that is: cosmopolitan versus noncosmopolitan; (b) in recognizing that incompleteness allows for a mechanism of epistemic change that in itself leads to ontic transformation-changes in the production of knowledge, which will lead to changes in social arrangements. However, such an account will need to reintroduce the human being, as an embodied and located being into the imagination of critical thought. The process of critique and cooperation that we are undertaking in this book reaches out from the confines of the European theoretic horizons to engage the universal imagination, in its partialities, to then return back to be a resource for such a being.

What emptiness provides cosmopolitanism is a means to take the conventional to be only that, conventional within the fluidity of intra- and intercultural exchange, and to maintain a "bite in reality" (immanent transcendence/border-thinking). The standpoint of emptiness is not at odds with the conventional standpoint, only with any claim to closure. It recognizes the enunciation of injustices in the face of claims of ideals and objectivity. The account of emptiness presented here does not require the critical theorist to "transcend" her own milieu in the name of some abstraction such as reason or humanity or even God? Rather, it is in the overcoming of the conventional knowledge of social reality. Emptiness, as a form of reflexive negation, provides a means to acknowledge epistemic location though reject closure—it is the acknowledgment of incompleteness beyond sematic elegance, and is the basis for critical cosmopolitanism.

The account of emptiness developed in this chapter, as Tillemans (2016: 9) suggests, is a form of pragmatism: what we do as societies and individuals is adopt or choose certain objects that are "convenient fictions." Socially, this represents the possibility of the reimagining of truths through the exposure of social conventions to emptiness as a heuristic tool that destabilizes conventional knowledge. What does that mean for the dialectic between the critical theories of Delanty and Mignolo? A postfoundationalist, or positionless account, immanent transcendence or border-thinking must be characterized in such a way that proposes an ecology of knowledges and intercultural translation as an alternative to a general theory that cannot grasp the infinite diversity of the world. To imagine other than thought, our own thought, needs a neutral "place," an unbiased universal medium in which various cultures can meet, converse, and consider our interdependence and the effects on our own sense of reality. It also assumes that different experiences of reality, even incommensurable experiences, are available to experience and learn from.

In predicating the cosmopolitan imagination on units of analysis, the individual and social, and universalisms, that recognize their codependent arising nature, their emptiness, allows thought to reflect upon itself critically. This does not mean that the concept is an empty signifier, or that it lacks any creative potential. On the contrary, as we shall see, such an account of cosmopolitanism becomes a site of contestation, globally and locally. However, if cosmopolitanism is aligned to decontextualized normative claims, such as human rights, democracy, or decolonialism, then its critical function is lost. Instead, it becomes a means of assimilation, a consensus. This is not to suggest that these things are not important or pernicious, but only to state that in tying cosmopolitanism to such concept's shreds cosmopolitanism of its critical function. This leaves the authentic philosophical and social questions left continuously open though without being incapable of being addressed due to a paralysis of the fear of uncertainty.

In *Ethics III* Watsuji demonstrated his commitment to the cosmopolitan project through the application of emptiness to the international realm. The epistemic principle of emptiness applied by Watsuji to the international realm moves away from the imposition of parochial abstract accounts to the human condition, time, and social space. Here, anticipating Eisenstadt's account of Multiple Modernities (2003) by some sixty years, Watsuji's account, in analytically emphasizing the nonduality of self and other and an understanding of global history as a nonteleological or nonhierarchical order, provides an account of decolonial critical cosmopolitanism which accepts existing, multiple imagined and lived ideas of progress, or "modernities," and their underside. As a precursor to decolonial theory, this analysis is designed to show that morality is ontically and epistemically specific, and that the imposition of "outside" ethical systems amounts to violence. However, his study is also designed to show that various global ethical systems are grounded in and expressive of universal morality. Like history, nations only realize their climatic character in contrast to other nations. This represents the description of "self-realization of identity through difference," nondialectical heterogeneity, or concentric duality, wherein the self-awareness of finite totality is only possible through the realization of what one doesn't share with those outside of one's own totality. Reason, in this conception, cuts through the dualism of bounded and detached conceptions of reason and reasoning and aims to intertwine the local and the universal. The goal of universal reason to seek unity, which is the cosmopolitan idea of humanity, supervenes on the negotiation of difference through adjustments: cosmopolitanism changes as it travels which must be attuned to the local.

It is important to note that this is not at the level of abstraction but of experiential accounts; rather, it is dependent upon reason's articulation of the universal through an engagement with the local. In other words, reason can make it possible for one tradition to converse with another; it is possible to widen one's own tradition by importing elements into it from another. However, this view of humanity and reason also works within and across cultures. Otherness, in this view, is not a fixed universal artifact open to the gaze of abstract reason but within the space of cultural flows, when not taken as either/or, there is every reason to expect that my tradition can develop to include features from other traditions. Importantly, the introduction of emptiness as a reflexive negation provides a basis to overcome societal limitations, diametric dualities, that maintains closure, through understanding the encounter between self, other and the world through the space of concentric dualities: critical cosmopolitanism.

Chapter 5

Cosmopolitan Transmodernity

Reimagining the Loci of Enunciation

INTRODUCTION

In *Post-Western Account of Critical Cosmopolitan Social Theory*, we are concerned with providing a means to draw from global resources to find new questions to address the issues that we all face now, but also as a resource for future generations. In this chapter, we will be setting out how that space can be provided with context for being and acting in a more democratic way. Put bluntly, the argument that will be developed in this chapter is that interculturally and intraculturally we share consciousness. That is, rather than understanding human agency as being mediated within a neutral space, the recognition of our shared consciousness with a commitment to the positive articulation of injustices allows the rethinking of the loci of enunciation to strengthen democratic ways of being in the world.

To move away from abstract or essentializing notions of human space in this chapter, the methodology of critique and cooperation is applied to the decolonial project of Walter Mignolo and the Buddhist/Confucius inspired social theory of Watsuji Tetsurō. Mignolo introduces the concepts of trans-modernity and relative universalism to provide a means of enunciation and connection between societies around the world that had been affected by slavery, colonialism, and empire. His argument is that these communities experienced this epistemic and ontic violence in diverse ways, but recogniz-ing the diverse condition of this trauma provides the cosmopolitan connectors between these different communities. Transmodernity, a function of relative universalism, offers the promise of different forms of social and political consciousness coming together to bring about newness and a more humane and compassionate form of societal thinking. The hope is to bring into being novel ways of political and social experimentation. It is a noble endeavor that aims to bring light from the wound of the past and is centered on the production, consumption, and exchange of knowledge.

However, in reducing this encounter to the sociohistorically, traumatized experience of colonialism moves transmodernity toward a new totality and relative universalism to a new absolute universalism. The problems that we are faced with is that in the need to provide an epistemic difference between the colonizer and colonized peoples, the decolonial project followed Levinas in establishing an account of absolute otherness. This was a concrete totalizing account that separated the colonizer and colonized. The problem with this, of course, is that in the effort to illuminate the exceptionalism of the trauma of colonialism it refuses to recognize internal difference. Mignolo's account of relative universalism cannot provide the means of authentically fulfilling the potential of critical cosmopolitanism as he remains within the realm of the "other." This has the tendency to reduce difference to an abstraction and subsume internal heterogeneity. As will be apparent, this abstractness fails to accommodate the role of the body, of how it is used by itself and by others. Furthermore, in transmodernity and relative universalism, Mignolo represents an example of our heuristic device of diametric duality as it positions the present conditions of colonized peoples in comparison with the west as relative, but which assumes separation. Though transmodernity and relative universalism do offer the potential to rethink global and local political and social structures, in the context of theory as a cosmopolitan endeavour, such a universalism, whether veiled as immanent transcendence, the cosmopolitan imagination, or border thinking, fails to provide a means of cross-cultural exchange based on humility. Yet, decolonialism makes the claim that transmodernity offers the potential to overcome the limitations of the underside of modernity. Therefore, it is necessary for it to engage with the subjectivity of the "west." Not the west of ideals, but a west of pluralistic community formation and agency.

Watsuji, too, was interested in the loci of enunciation and a concern with the imposition of "West" cultural and intellectual forms as universal. Through a two-stage account of socioepistemology, *fūdo* and *aidagara*, Watsuji sought to recover the focus on embodied, practical relationships that are situated in concrete society. This places emphasis on our enactment with self, other, and the world as spatial. Through this process, Watsuji wished to take our descent into hermeneutical understanding, through which we uncover the particularity of our own being but to then reconstruct, even further into the expressions of the everyday. For Watsuji, the hermeneutic method, in recognizing that it cannot remove us from our climatic and historical "burden" must somehow destroy this "burden." In doing so, he admits that what is likely to be discovered is the particularity of one's own. However, he argues, that through the process of communication and exchange with other cultures, we can "come[s] to grips with their respective particularity," and thereby collectively recon-struct the fundamental nature of being a human being as relational (Watsuji 1996 [1937, 1942, 1949]: 45). This has the potential, through critique and cooperation, to address one's own and one's society's limitations.

In his work, *Fūdo* (1988 [1935]), Watsuji claims that he was inspired to write due to Heidegger's failure in *Sein und Zeit* to fully develop the theme of existential spatiality. His theory of *fūdo* is a deceptively simple though an admittedly unusual one to the "Western" understanding of reality. While *fūdo* means "wind and earth . . . the natural environment of a given land" (Watsuji [1935] 1961: 1), it also includes the social environment of school, family, society, customs, and localized practices. In this view, *fūdo* is a theory of practices of the relational space in which life unfolds and forms realities. In terms of social analysis, the imposition of social norms of one *fūdo* to another *fūdo* distorts the meaning and context of a practice or text. For Watsuji, Heidegger had placed too much emphasis on time and the individual and too little on space and the social aspects of being human. For him, spatiality and temporality are in "mutual relation" (Watsuji [1937] 1996: 223) with each other. This means that they are balancing concepts for grasping ontologically the structure of existence (sonzai) and necessary for authentic social analysis.

Watsuji's understanding of *fūdo* certainly foreshadows Mignolo's account of the loci of enunciation. It is reasonable to suggest that Watsuji would agree with Mignolo's argument for the development of a decolonial epis-temic critique as one that rejected the epistemic and ontic violence imposed through colonialism. And again, the criticism of cultural totalities levelled against Mignolo has been equally applied to Watsuji. However, through introducing Watsuji's *fūdo* to Mignolo's loci of enunciation, the potential creativity of human space moves away from an emphasis on comparative ideological, sociological, or philosophical analysis, at the level of ideals, to a level of analysis at the meeting point of the ideals of a society and the prac-tices of everyday life. However, because Watsuji's work lacks the potential for critique or an account of power through introducing Mignolo's account of relative universalism and loci of enunciation, with its emphasis on the articulation of injustices to Watsuji's *fūdo* allows us to overcome this limita-tion. This encounter, in the spirit of critique and cooperation, points toward, first, an account of the relationship between different *fūdo* below the level of the state and toward a more localized loci of enunciation. This indicates a reorientation of the relationship between the state, the local, and the interna-tional in political terms. Second, it sets out a restructuring of the relationship between self, society, and state, and between being a citizen and being a member of humanity. Bring the emancipatory ethic of Mignolo together with the grounded account of human existence of Watsuji allows us to develop an account of human space which aims to find more democratic ways of acting and living in the world through critique and cooperation.

Emptiness, our form of reflexive negation, was introduced to provide a conceptual means to critically navigate social space. I will argue that when this reading of emptiness is introduced to Watsuji's account of *fūdo* that the conventional view of circumscribed and distinct communities, the totalities of encounters found in Mignolo's account of loci enunciation, is transformed to one predicated on change and creativity. That is, they lack inherent essence and are themselves open to heuristic deconstruction. This is not to deny identity, only to suggest that this should not be the foreground of analysis but should instead be implied. Doing so would allow for the loci of enunciation to provide an authentic ground which recognizes internal heterogeneity. Significantly, the incorporating reflexive negation into the cosmopolitan project as an epistemic principle overcomes the problem of over-positioning and lacks any claim to a teleology. Following our adoption of the decolonial rejection of absolute universalism allows us to posit the dynamics of nullification by jury to provide a localized and grounded locus of enunciation capable to resetting the one-directionality of power between ruled and rulers.

MIGNOLO, TRANSMODERNITY, AND THE LOCI OF ENUNCIATION

The merit of Mignolo's (2005) conception of modernity/coloniality as a horizon of comprehension is that it manages to capture the darker side of modernity. As a project of emancipation, it endeavors to move beyond the confines of critical theory's 'event horizon' through the incorporation of the negative legacies of modernity. Coloniality is, it is argued, "alive in books, in the criteria for academic performance, in cultural patterns, in common sense, in the self-image of peoples, in aspirations of self, and so many other aspects of our modern experience" (Maldonado-Torres 2007: 243). The violence and repression that was and is instrumental in the victory of modernity, yet which is hidden in the rhetorical power of ideas such as "progress," "civilization," "justice," and latterly "development." In claiming that knowledge production is situated, or context-bound, the decolonial approach makes its central concern the ways in which differences are formed and sustained through references to cultural identities.

For Mignolo "if knowledge is an instrument of imperial colonization, one of the urgent tasks ahead is the decolonization of knowledge" (Mignolo 2010). What becomes clear here is not just the intimate bond between modernity and coloniality but also the ways in which the universal can be read as rooted in a particular history, loaded with multiple layers of cultural assumptions, ideological choices, and philosophical and religious persuasions that all connect back to Europe. Therefore, decolonial readings take as their point of departure the belief that intersubjective inequalities are shaped and sustained by the colonization of knowledge that has turned a regional locus of enunciation into a universal one. What decolonial theorist's argue is that universality is premised on the assertion of radical difference amid sections of humanity in which one part of humanity is sacrificed to assert the universality of the "West's" notions of progress and modernity (Aman 2014). From this perspective, Europe not only affirms itself as the center of space and the site from which newness emerges but also has the epistemic privilege of being the center of enunciation (Mignolo 2002a).

Therefore, while Delanty sees modernity as signaling the translation of all cultures, by contrast the decolonial movement sees this as a mode of absolute universalism, expecting everyone to become intercultural in a prescribed way. To overcome this, what is needed is, "a kind of thinking that moves along the diversity of historical processes" (Mignolo 2001: 9). If modernity is linked to Eurocentrism, then the notion of "transmodernity" is proposed as a way out of the impasses of postliberalism and postmodernity. Dussel's, and Mignolo's use of the term "transmodernity," can be interpreted as both a call for moving beyond modernity and its effects but, most importantly, as critically engaging and supporting non-Western knowledges. As Aman argues, the goal of the "other paradigm" is the overcoming of the categories associated with modernity, the state, race, class, and gender, to reimagine new forms of social organization within contemporary debates (Aman 2014: 48).[1] What Mignolo and the decolonial movement are arguing for is a situated epistemology through which to base critical cosmopolitanism. This, as a form of "barbaric epistemology," sets out an intercultural position not tied to modernity but as *interculturalidad*. Beginning with a nonexcluding sense of rationality and reason, such a perspective stresses the historical and sociopolitical conditions of the *inter* (Lenkersdorf 1996). Such a reconstructive project means giving voice to those perspectives on the world that have been silenced and excluded (Mignolo 2000b: 722; Suárez-Krabbe 2009: 2). Based on histories that do not necessarily begin in the Enlightenment, it is formulated to acknowledge that language and knowledges are not only tangled up with each other, but that they are *interdependent with territory*. Through shifting the *geography of reason* interculturalidad points toward other assemblages of meaning, understanding, and transformation. But how is this possible?

Such a reconstructive project comes about through Mignolo's adoption of Gloria Anzaldúa's (1999), concept of border thinking. Defined by epistemic

---

[1] See also Ruggie (1993, 2000), who identifies the spatial-social and political-effects of epistemological claims.

difference and geographical distance, it provides the opportunity for societal transformation at the epistemic and ontic border between the marginalized and modernity. In drawing on the aspects of life understood through aesthesis and transmodernity, it expresses a pragmatic nondualistic heterogeneity, in that it recognizes that people "living" at the "border" already "live" the theories that have the capacity to overcome the oppression of the colonial matrix of power. Therefore, "border thinking is the epistemology of the exteriority; that is, of the outside created from the inside" (Mignolo and Tlostanova 2006: 206).

"Border thinking" stems from the "subaltern perspective" and arises at the intersection of local histories enacting global designs and local histories dealing with them. For Mignolo, this concept of the border is meant to signify that the locality of subaltern knowing, far from simply being "the other side" of "Western" knowing, has a border-like quality. Though this may be reminiscent of some of postcolonial theory's concern with hybridity, mestizaje, and creolization (Venn 2006: 18–19; Bhabha 1994; Anzaldúa 1999), here Mignolo denotes a more radical stance toward transcending the celebration of postcolonial liminal, hybrid, and ambiguous consciousness mediated through modernity. Through resituating Anzaldúa's image of the border into the field of coloniality, Mignolo posits the opportunity of "thinking otherwise," from the interior exteriority of the border. It also asserts that simultaneously spaces for alternative thinking emerge from the places where indigenous and Eurocentric paradigms meet to create a consciousness stemming from the relative exteriority of the world system.

FŪDO: SHARING CONSCIOUSNESS

Watsuji's account of *fūdo* provides a much deeper and systematic account, within a localized though expansive context, both natural and artificial, of our means of engagement with the world. Watsuji rejects cultural isolation, by placing humanity, nations, state, cultures, within the universalism of infinite humanity; there is no end to development.[2] He precedes Mignolo's loci of enunciation, its relationship to modernity and intercultural exchange, and the possibilities of imagining "other than." However, though he provides the "deep structure" of a shared consciousness that we experience spatially,

---

[2] It is important to clear at this point as an element of misunderstanding could arise. Following the discussion on emptiness in the earlier chapter, this is not to claim that borders do not exist. Clearly, borders do function as a result of structural, historical, and agential reasoning. However, what it is to claim is that they do not have ontological priority as they are dependently coarising political reality. Their existence is dependent on other causal factors. Therefore, they are open to heuristic deconstruction to solve complex problems in a way that does not reify them.

his work is explicitly unable to provide a critical perspective on social real-ity. And yet, Mignolo and Watsuji share affinity in drawing on the local resources as a cosmopolitan endeavour allows us, through the process of critique and cooperation, to move beyond their respective limitations while respecting their contributions. That is, this process of mutual interaction is beneficial in exploiting the positive contributions of both thinkers. For the decolonialist, it provides a theoretical horizon through which it can enrich itself of internal heterogeneity through the contribution of the *fūdo's* epis-temic principle of emptiness (reflective negation). In exploiting a reading of Watsuji's account of emptiness as a reflexive negation operating within *fūdo* together with Mignolo's rejection of ideals, to instead focus on the articula-tion of injustices, provides criticality for *fūdo*. This spatial critique, observed at the meeting place of the ideals of a society and practices of everyday life, undermines the modernity's solution to the contradictions between unity and diversity, between the inside and the outside, and between space and time. Intraculturally this provides a space from which 'I' can enunciate between the famished ravine of the imaginary of *becoming* and what I experience as reality.[3] From such a space is formed a critique of the normativity of tempo-rality through which to develop new localized forms and new temporalities of social and political experimentation. This shifts the analytical and conver-sational perspective in intercultural terms to the relationship of intercultural interlocutors from the vertical relationship of an authorities of tradition to a horizontal relationship between interlocutors. The theoretical ambition of such an encounter would not be the prolongation of one's own ideals but of becoming by revealing the shadows within one's own thought.

Drawing on the Sino-Japanese linguistic tradition, *fūdo* literally means wind and earth.[4] However, as stated in the introduction, Watsuji's treatment of *fūdo* goes beyond an understanding of the role of the natural environment in terms of the development of societies purely in respect of physical and geographical features, but to also elucidate its effect on societal customs, practices, and consciousness. Through *fūdo*, he endeavoured to overcome the duality between subject and object and argues that the proposition that "man" and nature are treated as two separate entities misses the more fundamental bond between "'man" and climatic phenomena. While *fūdo* does indicate

---

[3] We will be returning to the topic of enactive personhood in the next chapter. Our concern in this chapter is to provide a space for such an account of agency.

[4] While climate means the pattern of weather, in its extended meaning, climate means the character of the landscape, the soil, the flora, and fauna of a given land, and the qualities of local natural elements such as light, wind, and rainwater. Augustin Berque (2004), translating fūdo as "milieu," argues that this does not represent a determinist account of culture, but rather about the *essential consideration* of humanity's immediate relationship with our environment, both natural and artifi-cial. As stated earlier, the book has used the original term "fūdo" to offer the opportunity for the expansion of the sociological vocabulary, and therefore, its imagination.

concrete phenomena, "as a mountain blast or the cold, dry wind that sweeps through Tokyo at the end of the winter" (Watsuji 1961: 5), it is never apprehended as a scientific fact. *Fūdo* is, "the agent by which human life is objectified, and it is here that man comprehends himself; there is self-discovery" in it (1961: 14). It is this subjectivity that interests Watsuji: "the climatic character is the character of subjective human existence" (1961: 16). Warmth is not only a corporeal quality of a body of air with a certain degree of temperature, it is also a quality that characterizes the connection between "man" and "man." Here we are understood not as passive beings within the vortex of a chaotic "outside." Rather, biologically and socially, given the multitude of separate ways of being in the world and their interdependence and interconnectedness with the world, human beings form a part of an unfolding experiment in which they can transform their environment.

More curiously, he argued that climatic phenomenon is pervasive. Reaching across to Heidegger, Watsuji's idea of "ex-sistere" is like Heidegger's. "'Ex-sistere' is the fundamental principle of the structure of ourselves, and it is on this principle that intentionality depends" (Watsuji 1961: 4). Of course, this is related to the second stage of Watsuji's account of socioepistemology. As the reader will recall from the introduction to Watsuji, one of his primary intellectual concerns was the rise of "individualism." However, he was also greatly concerned that "Western" theoretical developments and societal "progress" had discarded the relationship between humanity and nature, as well as between individuals. Though Watsuji does expand on Heidegger's notion of ex-sistere which he argued was temporally and historically bounded, the crucial point is that his spatial perspective does not offer a totalizing account of the relationship between self, other, and the world. In fact, his is a quite radical contribution in that he is saying that we share consciousness, and we share in fūdo and aidagara (See Krueger 2020: 11–12). This by necessity is localized and embodied. He writes:

> The problem of climate affords a pointer for any attempt to analyse the structure of human existence. The ontological comprehension of human existence is not to be attained by a mere transcendence which regards the structure as one of temporality, for this has to be transcendence in the sense of, first and above all, the discovery of the self in the other and the subsequent return to absolute negativity in the union of self and other. Therefore, the "betweenness" of man and man has to be the *locus* for transcendence. That is to say, the betweenness as the basis for discovering the self and other must be originally the place that "stands out." (*ex-sistere*) (WTZ 8: 18; Watsuji 1961: 12)

While the relationship between oneself and coldness is that of intentionality, the relationship between different "I"s in the coldness is that of mutuality.

The "I" that is here and the "I" that is in the middle of coldness, fashion the formula of reflection in which one sees one's own self. Expressed differently, the realization of "I" is only possible based on "I" being unexpectedly outside the "I" of a restricted sense of self as "being only in my head." It formulates a context in which different individuals are located. He provides a second example of this shared consciousness in the act of staring at a wall (Watsuji 1996: 73). As Watsuji tells us:

> The consciousness we possess in our daily lives is never a collection of sensations. Even when we remain in our study alone, we are still conscious of a wall as a wall, of a desk as a desk, and of a book as a book . . . from the beginning we must concern ourselves with tools and assume there is no more primitive consciousness than this concern.

However, Watsuji is not rejecting this "common-sense" description of this action. Rather, he is pointing to the fact that "social consciousness has already intervened" when you see a wall as a wall (Watsuji 1996: 73). Of course, in one sense, this experience of seeing a wall can only be described as an individual experience. It is distinctly yours. This distinct act of seeing a wall includes not only your act of conscious perception but also sociocultural forms—meanings. That is, rather than understand the act of perceiving the desk as being an act which is unmediated prior to interpretation and the assigning of meaning, that the desk is saturated in meaning prior to perception. This is preconscious and gains immediate awareness within the consciousness of self through the material and symbolic forms of society. In bridging the gap between individual and the self, Watsuji's account of *fūdo* offers an account of space in which we are inter/intracorporeally immersed, interconnected, and in which cognitive production is distributed within the dynamics of the human and natural worlds. Such cognitive cooperation radicalizes notions of co-cognitivity as, "language-mediated cooperative thinking" (Heal 2013: 339), to propose that an individual's self-discovery is not self-sufficient or self-focused but becomes part of "we." It is through "we" that we discover ourselves and not merely as fragmented individuals. What we begin to get a sense of is the individual's struggle with individuality, drawing further into her own being, through which to contribute to the development of society. However, rather than providing a communitarian deterministic account that fails to provide an account of "free-will,", Watsuji is pointing toward a moment of transformation as "in this self-apprehension we are directed to our free creation" (Watsuji 1961: 6). Furthermore, it is through a "hermeneutic destruction" of the *practices* of a society that we reveal its limitations.

NATIONAL EXISTENCE

The self's immersion in a wider geocultural environment establishes a platform for a cultural ethos represented by the practices of life. Watsuji seeks to
situate human existence in time. He describes the basic structure of temporality as follows:

> *Ningen sonzai* [human existence] is subjectively extended. On the other hand,
> as a subjective connection, this extendedness must possess a structure that,
> although shouldering the established betweenness, aims at achieving a possible
> betweenness in and through its present activities. That is to say, subjective
> extendedness is temporal in structure. (WZT10, 196 (186); Cited Sevilla 2015:
> 181–182)

The concept of interest here is "Established betweenness." What Watsuji is
referring to is history and its relationship to territory. The past, seen through
Watsuji's relational ontology is the concrete past, but which, in the context
of each nation, is a relational past. The past shapes the present in the context
of the practices of life and is unique to a particular territory. Should we be
cautious about retreating to the past of a particular territory?

Cornelius Castoriadis also expressed that the universal is accessible only
through the particular. He wrote:

> It is because we are attached to a given view, categorical structure, and project
> that we are able to say something meaningful about the past. It is only when the
> present is intensely present that it makes us see in the past something more than
> the past saw in itself. (Castoriadis 1987: 34)

This follows Watsuji as he also argued that such knowledge allows us to
appreciate that there is no "truth specific" to each society. For Castoriadis,
what

> can be termed the truth of each society is its truth in history, for itself but
> also for all the others, for the paradox of history consists in the fact that every
> civilization and every epoch, because it is particular and dominated by its own
> obsessions, manages to evoke and to unveil new meanings in the societies that
> preceded or surround it. (Castoriadis 1987: 34–35)

This paradox of historical knowledge, as discussed by Watsuji, is not only
necessary but also productive in how we as communities go about addressing our own limitations. The chapter will now turn to Watsuji's discussion in
Ethics III of history and begin to integrate the book's reading of emptiness.

Despite what may appear as a hermetically sealed cultural entity, that ties history to territory, it can only be viewed in relation to its other.

FŪDO AND WORLD HISTORY

Watsuji writes:

> History is revealed in the trans-state stage. The state's self- consciousness is mediated by other states. Thus, the self-consciousness of history occurs when the people that composes this state comes into contact with other peoples and experiences various forms of excitement and peril. (*WTZ11*: 34: Cited Sevilla 2015: 206–207)

As Sevilla notes, finite totalities, states, within an infinite totality by necessity place individual national histories in relation to each other. Pursuing his mediated relational logic within a concentric duality of global space, the "privacy" of the finite state, though essential, cannot form an identity without the mediation of other historical finite agents (Sevilla 2015: 204). Such incompleteness derives from the very fact that there is a plurality of cultures (Santos 2002: 46–47). What Santos is signaling here is that no culture, social gathering, or individual is individuated, distinct, or hermetically sealed. Cosmopolitanism merely reflects this observation; if we are complete, individuated, autonomous, or distinct, how could we learn? Like Sousa Santos, Watsuji is arguing that no culture is hermetically sealed. For Watsuji such an account, based in the historical and particular is rooted in a universal history that can never rest completed. Rather, culture and values all need to be constantly renewed.

What would this require?

> Thinking of it in this way, the realization of moral difference in each nation is indispensable for the fulfillment of the universal socio-ethical path. It saves each nation from conceit and spurs them to work to overcome their individual limitations. (WTZ11, 348[, quoted in Sevilla 2015: 215)

Therefore, it is in appreciating one's culture, its limits, and discovering innovative approaches to overcome these that one requires an intercultural relationship with other nations. For not only is it in meeting other nations that a nation becomes self-aware, but it is also in seeing how things might have gone otherwise that we see limitations in our own social structures and find inspiration to do things otherwise. However, while learning from other countries is crucial, Watsuji, again foreshadowing Castoriadis, stresses the need to respect the national morality of other nations as being their own means to recognize universal values:

> The true unity of humankind ought to be a unity wherein the included nations and states would no longer *desire liberation*, that is, each nation and state's *individuality is sufficiently respected*, and without oppressing such, completely fulfills the proper mission of each. . . . The ideal of the unity of humankind would definitely break through an *abstract unity*, a *homogenous* unity where individuality is discarded. (WTZ11: 72. Cited Sevilla 2015: 211. Emphasis in original)

The model that Watsuji develops is cosmopolitan in the sense of self-awareness of history.

> The *ideal* finally arose in history that we should form humankind into *one community* with no divisions of nation or state, and in so doing realize the law of *ningen sonzai* at the level of humankind. This is the *ideal of the unity of humankind*. In this ideal, humankind can be said to have become *self-conscious* of its essence, that is, that the same law of *ningen sonzai* makes humankind into what it is. (*WTZ11*, 68: Cited Sevilla 2015: 209)

However, rather than ideals of humanity, reason, god, for Watsuji humankind is hardly a unity:

> When *ningen* began its historic self-realization, *the unity of humankind* did *not exist*, and all there was conflict and war. After that, humankind's history was still a history of conflict and war. Humankind attaining one *socioethical unity*, in other words, humankind forming a *living totality* has never occurred. Therefore, humankind is, factually speaking, none other than *the space for conflict and war* between all states and all nations. (WTZ11: 68. Cited Sevilla 2015: 210. Emphasis in the original)

It was within the sphere of warfare, through economic, epistemic, and military expansion that the cosmopolitan imagination was kindled (Mignolo 2000a, 2000b). However, for Watsuji, such imperialism, "oppresses the *characteristic individuality* of each nation and state, making it submit to an external power. Consequently, as the destruction of freedom, it can even be said to be a step backward" (WTZ11: 71. Cited in Sevilla 2015: 211. Emphasis in original). "If this is coerced using military force, the nation thus coerced will probably become *without personality* and *spineless*" (WTZ11: 197. Cited Sevilla 2015: 209. Emphasis in the original). Therefore, changes to a culture must be spontaneous and internal, rather than imposed. Given what appears as a homogenizing account of mutuality such an account does not acknowledge somatic difference and how this is experienced as *practices* within a society. Wasn't this Sakai's argument? To put this in a basic form, what Watsuji, like Mignolo, does not articulate is that there are spaces within space, and that these are experienced differently. But just because Watsuji did not articulate the presence of such spaces within space, does not mean that they are not there to be found.

ENUNCIATING THE IMAGINATION

Can Watsuji's concept of *fūdo*, when interpreted through the book's reading of emptiness, help to overcome the difficulties identified in Mignolo's concept of loci of enunciation? *Fūdo* represents a proto-decolonial account of relative universalism, the attempt to move beyond the absolute universalism of modernity. To argue, as Mignolo does, for the construction of cultural space as a locus of enunciation misses the point that loci of enunciation are continuous movements internally which also develop through their relationships to other cultural spaces. This conception of cultural transfer is in direct contrast to "thick" concepts of culture maintained by Mignolo, which assign specific cultural traits and habits to communities. Equally, though Watsuji would side with Mignolo's proposition of developing a "post" universalistic account of modernity, and if we concede that the structure that he puts forward of *fūdo* is capable of intercultural fluidity and learning, there still remains a concern of totality. While Watsuji's account of the phenomenology of the social imaginary has merit in linking inner consciousness with the co-cognitive creativity of societal practices, does such a theoretical proposition leave it open to distortion in the real world?

However, Watsuji does go much further than the decolonialist in two respects. First, he and his entire project were predicated on the belief that we as individuals and as societies develop through our interaction with the other: self is in other, other is in self. That is, that the encounter between self and other is a reciprocal process of self and societal transformation. Here, while linking the interaction of cultures "outside" with developments "inside" cultures, he points toward a way beyond the captivity of the decolonial imagination to engage in intercultural communication below the level of the state. Second, he provides in greater detail the dynamics of location through which to resist absolute accounts of cosmopolitan universalism. However, this was not a claim to exceptionalism but a move away from hubris.

We can develop this further by arguing that with the introduction of reflexive concepts such as the state can be, ultimately, said to lack inherent existence. This is not to argue that the state does not exist, only, ultimately, to argue that its existence is dependent on other causal factors. This provides for the imposition of structural blockages to individual self-realization and societal openness. These support the dominant modes of social, economic, and political conventions and which govern the enunciation of reasoning and rationality within a society. The notion of the state is a recent invention that captures a deep historical, theological, and philosophical teleology of human progress. The term the "state" signifies an abstract political community which structures the relationship between itself, as an example of universal reason and legitimacy, and individual agency. That is, we are immersed in the symbolic and material structure of the state. Through this symbolic and material structure, it provides the basis for rationality between the state and the individual as citizen and mediates the relationship between itself and other states. In addition, it mediates your agency through the dichotomy of the individual as citizen and humanity. This highlights that our consciousness in the world, a world that structures our bodies, our minds, our emotions, is structured by the hegemonic forces of the state which are corralled through institutional linkages. The implication is that although such demarcations may be justified and pragmatically very useful, because they are merely conventional (in this case, merely in the linguistic sense), there may be good reasons to consider them lacking independent existence but are dependent on other causal factors. Put less abstractly, "I" is in a large measure defined through its relationship with an abstract entity which is itself dependent on a diverse range of vested interests with their own agendas. And these are states that ordain the rationality of modernity though which can exist alongside war, discrimination, inequality, political violence, and poverty.

Though Watsuji relied on Hegelian structures, such as the state, emptiness as an example of reflexive negation provides a means to re-inscribe into contemporary debates categories of thought, social organizations, and economic conceptions that have been silenced by the progressive discourse of modernity. The application of the heuristics devices of concentric and diametric dualities onto the account of social space provided through relative universalism and fūdo allows for identification of structural and internal blockages and to provide structural options to enhance self and societal well-being that nurture openness and assumed interconnection. It does so by not just to challenging the diametric dualities of modernity that maintain reifications and separations, but to also offer a means for new affirmations of social and political conditions to arise from silence. The concepts of the loci of enunciation and *fūdo* are an attempt to move away from absolute notions of universalism and to set out a paradigm of account of relative immanent universalism for cross-cultural transformation and communication. The application of the heuristics devices of concentric and diametric dualities onto the account of social space provided through relative universalism and fūdo allows for identification of structural and internal blockages and to provide structural options to enhance self and societal well-being that nurture openness and assumed interconnection. This will require the development of an innovative range of analytical categories, conceptual devices, and sensitizing metaphors to enable us to envision the unfamiliar and relatively uncharted dimensions of social space. However, though the challenges that global populations face are interconnected, these can only be addressed, initially at the level of the personal and local.

To advance the argument for the first stage of an intercultural imagination, the chapter needs to introduce the vertical and horizontal axes of a society. Much in line with Watsuji's argument that to understand a community and the ideas that motivate it would necessitate understanding practices, and the ways in which social practices are influenced by ideas, methodologically Jenco (2007) moves this further. She suggests that the social consciousness needs to be understood in its own terms. This, following Watsuji and Mignolo, implies that in terms of the recognition of difference, the use in social theory of exogenously determined categories to structure analysis erases the ontological dimension of the practices of the cultures to which they are applied. Echoing Watsuji, she argues that social and political thought is not always articulated through text, and so forth, but can be communicated through rituals, memorials, churches, temples, song, poetry, and so forth. The secondary methods that she identifies of political articulation are logicoepistemological spaces/practices. They are affective and somatic in that they are produced and act to produce the "slide" from "I" to "We," (Parsons 1977; Lefebvre 1991 [1974]).

Watsuji's socioepistemological account would support this logic of practice that presupposes a cultural and social habitus and which becomes internalized in the form of behavioral dispositions to think, to reason, to perceive, and even to feel in a certain way (Bourdieu 1998; see also Elias 1939 [1978]).⁵ Equally, Mignolo would identify with such an approach concerning the internalization by the colonized subject of symbols of social practice. However, in recognizing the effects of colonialism on the colonized as well as the colonizer this would also allow a reciprocity of intercultural conversation. Therefore, the methodological approach put forward here is designed to take advantage of the systematic relationship between the vertical and horizontal

---

⁵ An examination of emotions though important—say in the anger generated by colonialism, sexism, or racism—would take the thesis too far from its remit. However, emotions do play a significant role in politics and society in general, yet they have so far received surprisingly little attention in the field of political theory (Bleiker and Hutchinson 2007; but note Durkheim 1893 [1997]). Part of this neglect has to do with a "tradition" that misconceived the "nature" of emotions as follows: (1) irrational and disruptive; (2) are things that merely happen to people rather than that people do voluntarily; and that (3) the impact of emotions on action is at best indirect and insignificant (Zhu and Thagard 2002).

axes of a society with its underside: inter- and intraculturally. Vertical, in the context of a philosophical system within a continuing tradition, and horizontally in the context of life practices, practices that are not always self-consciously articulated. An analysis that isolates either part distorts both the intentional effect of the practices or scholarship as well as the epistemic and ontic structure into which it is located.

This is because there may be a tendency to include only elite articulations of the political and social. As Simpson notes (2014), in the construction of intellectual edifices, whether it is the abstraction of life as distinct and autonomous or bridled with an inheritance of ethnicity, the theorist runs the risk, in respect of intercultural communication, of relying on the authority of text or an amorphous notion of "we" rather than representing a loci enunciation centered on the concerns that matter to people. The decolonial insight minds us at the level of the general analysis of life-worlds to entwine the ontological claims of a community, the political, with the ontic facts. Here the framework challenges discourse through its use of Mignolo, to instead focus on "injustice" rather than idealized norms of Law or Justice. The adoption of the decolonial perspective has drawn out the importance of finding a means of politically articulating social and political injustices that are hidden from discourse through the application of the self-satisfying and self-rewarding arrogance of unaccountable power.

Following Simpson (2014), in effect this rotates the analytical, and conversational perspective in intercultural terms, to the relationship of intercultural interlocutors from the vertical relationship of an authorities of tradition to a horizontal relationship between interlocutors. Though remaining sensitive to the asymmetries between dominating and dominated languages and practices, interculturally and intraculturally, this would not take for granted notions of shared traditions. Rather, it would seek an expressive, embodied lexicon through which to locate the reciprocal recognition of interlocutors to open up the possibility of other ways of thinking that produces a form of interculturality with the aim of undercutting the normativity of modernity (Simpson 2014). This draws in and integrates the manifold loci of enunciation, including the body, social practices, time, and physical space, beyond singularities such as the individual, democracy, globalization, or the social. Such a space is ontologically prior to the reason, the discourse, of a culture and its institutions, and makes communicative exchange conceivable and fecund. This maintains that the perspective of the other of my Other may also be enunciated. Here there are spaces within space, with the focus of analytical and normative attention being at the intersection of ideals and the practices of life.

This enables us to overcome the difficulties in Leigh Jenco's account of social analysis (2007). Though Jenco recognizes that to understand a community and the ideas that motivate it necessitates understanding practices, and the ways in which social practices are influenced by ideas, adopting such a methodology could lead to the book replicating models of critical cosmopolitanism that it has found problematic. Intraculturally, reflexive negation asks us not to look for absolute universal space of cultures, nations, states, peoples, but to look to the "spaces within spaces." In this sense, consciousness if understood temporally relates to social reality by limiting possibilities. That is defining sole legitimators of rationality creates diametric dualities internally and externally. While Ricoeur, Habermas, and Gadamer look to the European experience through which to critique the affirmations of our time, of an immanent critique, this cannot be provided by endogenous means alone, as the endogenous and the exogenous are interconnected. Rather, the cosmopolitan imagination proposed in this book suggests that cosmopolitan social theory must be capable of intertwining endogenous and exogenous sociohistorical experiences. Any descent into societal hermeneutics needs to incorporate the relationships within these "other" spaces that provide blockages to self-realization, us and them, old and young, black and white, men and women, rich and poor, human and nonhuman (including the environment) if it is to maintain an expansive imagination critique. I stress, this is not to suggest the adoption of another totalizing view of the world, the eradication of difference. Rather it is only to point out that "we" share in the consciousness that structures the space we exist in and how this effect is mutual.

Fūdo aims to show us that we share consciousness. It is in "sharing" consciousness that we are inter/intracorporeally immersed and interconnected, and through which "we" as "I" discover ourselves. Introducing the criticality of Mignolo to Watsuji makes us cognizant how this "withness" has the potential to be controlled by vested interests. Introducing criticality to Watsuji's concepts of *fūdo* has two key goals. Taken together, this enables us to distinguish the underlying characteristics of sociocultural blockage in systems that hinder heuristic inclusivity (diametric dualities) and to provide pluralistic conceptions of agentic immediacy that allows the enunciation of those aspects of material or bodily reality that are not knowable or understandable in rational terms. This should not be understood as a rejection of intellectual criticality. Quite the contrary, in recognizing the limitations of social reality is to provide further critical resources to enunciate injustices.

Therefore, rather than rely on the reification of cultural or political life as an enunciation of intracultural analysis for intercultural exchange, drawing on our epistemic premise of incompleteness looks to the meeting place of ideals of a community and existing social practices. It does so in the belief that such an undertaking will allow for the articulation of novel forms of evidence gathering, empirical design, and to allow for the emergence of new spaces of innovative individual, societal, and intercommunal reflexive engagement. At the level of intercultural exchange, the methodological approach to critical cosmopolitan social theory proposed here, of critique and cooperation, is premised on our use of reflexive negation. This has the potential to rejuvenate world philosophies through an engagement of mutual humility. The parochialism of claims to a philosophy, a philosophy of the west, the east, the north, or the south, is enriched through the recognition that the many different paths that civilizations have ventured down have brought about different conceptions of being human. Though acknowledging the strength of the ties between place and space to beliefs, the process of critique and cooperation does not understand the encounter with the other as the meeting of incommensurable theoretic-ontic understandings of reality, but as partial accounts which have developed, within the context of a global history, as a mutual phase of development. As such, the power of cosmopolitanism does not come from confining thought to the illusionary grandeur of a specific time and place which is then projected out on to the world. Instead, we have suggested that cosmopolitanism occurs and provides an internal critical perspective, where relational sociologies can pursue the practical activity of critique and cooperate.

A SPACE FOR BEING AND ACTING
MORE DEMOCRATICALLY

If, for the reform of the space of democracy, we can longer look to our immanent ideals or essentialize our identity, where are we to look? Where are we to look for inspiration to change the way we do the political? What is needed is a practical capacity within the matrix of institutions capable of offering the enunciation of injustice to allow human well-being to flourish. If our aim is the revitalization of democracy, then we need to find a way of reconnecting the individual with politics. As will apparent, the proposal that follows for understanding the spatial dynamics of democratic life is not one predicated on the distinct and autonomous individual or of a "people." Rather, we must begin in the observation of human creativity through our enactive engagement with the world. In bridging the gap between the individual and society and in sharing consciousness allow for the reconsideration of the space of democracy. Not based on axiomatic claims, such an imaginative perspective understands totalities, such as nations, groups, identities, and processes, globalization, as real though imaginary. Instead, it focuses analytical attention on the co-cognitive interconnections that give rise to their formation and how over-positioning takes places within them. This is theoretically enabled through the shifting of to the crossing of the axes of ideals and the practices of life. However, it is not entirely contingent either since it must consider the existent. Rather, the *political* cannot consist in a vision for the future, institutions, or simply social practices as necessary but must necessarily intertwine the ontological vision and ontic reality as a never ceasing practical activity. To do otherwise is the surrender of political will by the individual and of society to the *political*.

Of course, the democratization of the state that took place during the nineteenth and twentieth centuries was not accompanied by a parallel democratization of the public sphere. Writers from Durkheim, Marx, and Habermas were highly skeptical about the state's willingness to realize social freedom as enabling political opinion-formation. However, recent events within Western democracies have led to a revisiting of the question of democracy and its relationship to social freedom. Two prominent examples for the reform of representative democracy within the EU region have recently come from Richard Bellamy and Thomas Piketty. Bellamy (2019), argues that the challenges facing democracy within national and European contexts can be addressed not by strengthening the European Parliament, but by "reconnecting" the EU through empowering national parliaments of the member states in the formulation of EU policy-making. Such a "reconnection" would allow a relinking between the different demoi of the European Union.

In a somewhat more "radical" approach, Piketty et al. (Piketty 2018), in a manifesto for the democratization of Europe, calls for the creation of a new European assembly. Such an assembly would have the ability to implement taxes and to affect the democratic, fiscal, and social compacts of states and the European Union. For Piketty, partially mirroring Bellamy, national and European parliamentarians must be central to the new assembly. Here, in an innovative move, to maintain the legitimacy of the new assembly, it would need to be populated by members of both national and the existing European parliaments. This would provide, they claim, in bringing together national and European parliamentarians in a single assembly, a habitus,[6] of co-governance, and therefore connecting legislator with the administrated, a role that presently only exists between heads of state and ministers of finance.

While admittedly from important sources, given the recorded concerns in respect of trust, fairness, and the truth values of representative democracy set out above, it appears difficult to imagine how such proposals would address such grievances. All that these proposals appear to offer is more of what the populations of democratic society are clearly objecting to. Rather than Piketty et al.'s and Bellamy's proposals offering a means to address the concerns of the citizen, to connect citizen with the representative political will-formation, they would only further avoid or delay resolving the tensions between the citizenry and mainstream political institutions and parties.

---

[6] The authors use the English word "habits," however, I feel Bourdieu's notion of habitus better conveys what they are meaning to create in such a co-cognitive policy forming environment.

The decolonial insight minds us at the level of the general analysis of the democratic life-world to entwine the ontological claims of a community, the *political*, with the ontic facts. Here the framework challenges discourse through its use of Mignolo, to instead focus on "injustice" rather than idealized norms of Law or Justice. Here the emphasis is on the co-cognitive creativity of knowledge that is mindful to the abuses of economic, social, and political over-positioning. The primary concern of citizens within democratic nations is the creation within the practical act-connections of democratic life of an increased distance between themselves and centers of power and the one-directionality of power.[7] A better-informed citizenry, locally and globally, has given rise to the articulation of observable inequality and the decline in trust of social and political institutions and actors as mainstream parties have struggled to find policy-solutions to endemic social and political questions. However, though this may be indicative of a "crisis of trust" in public services, institutions, and the people who run them, as the Jones' inquiry on the Hillsborough disaster set out (Jones 2017), it is far from clear whether trust can be restored by making people and institutions more accountable, or whether it is the systems in which these institutions operate as a "patronising disposition of unaccountable power" that itself damages trust (O'Neill 2002). Such political paralysis has been accompanied by the growing appeal for citizens of populist parties. The act of participation in the life of the polity is a crucial aspect of part of a "Good Life" for the citizen (Sen 1999: 10; see also Bellamy 2008). In enriching their lives through democratic participation allows for the expression of social claims that lead to political change, but it also provides a forum for the citizen's education. Indeed, as Hermans notes, (Hermans 2018: 353), "a well functioning society needs well-functioning selves, and, in reverse, the self needs a society that creates not only constraints on it development but also, foremost, opportunities." However, if the act of participation is temporal, that is in the forms of periodicity and finality, is it impotent and open to manipulation. Instead, our emphasis is on our creative enactment with the world, to begin to provide a means of transforming the present in a way that undercuts the dominant mood of existence. Being human is creativity. Not beginning in the temporal, *to be*, in the transitivity of the cultural, social, political, and economic world, identified through

---

[7] We see the implications of these developments in the evidence that electoral participation has declined in recent years (Oser and Hooghe 2018; Dassonneville and Hooghe 2018), that trust in national parliaments dropped from 38 percent in 2004 to 28 percent in 2016, being accompanied with a decline in trust of national governments from 34 percent to 27 percent (European Commission, Spring 2016; July 2016), and political parties were ranking as the most distrusted institution in Western Democracies (Mungiu-Pippidi et al. 2015). Additionally, the 2017 Pew Global Attitudes Survey revealed a large gap in satisfaction with democracy between those Europeans who think the economy is doing well and those who do not (Wike et al. October 2017; See also, Brechenmacher 2018).

constituted power. Rather, understanding agency as a constant enactment of creativity we have argued, that it is in the meeting of the transitivity *to be*, the temporal, with the intransitivity of our spatial experience, *fūdo/aidagara*, provides the energy for the creativity of *constitute power*.

What is required is the extension of people's potential to address one's own and one's society's limitations within their workplaces, communities, and public services. The account of intracultural analysis put forward here is designed to take advantage of the systematic relationship between the vertical and horizontal axis of a society with its underside: inter- and intraculturally. Vertical, in the context of a philosophical system within a continuing tradition, and horizontally in the context of life practices, practices that are not always self-consciously articulated. Bringing the critical edge of decolonial thought with *fūdo* provides the opportunity to incorporate both singularity, relationality and difference as a phenomenological analysis and the articulation of injustices beyond modernity, rationality, and totality. This destabilizes the state as the sole legitimate arbiter of rationality and indicates the localization of democracy, spatially, at every level of human development from the constituting space of reality. This is made possible through the spatial evacuation of temporal claims of necessity and objectivity to develop new forms, new temporalities, of social and political experimentation. Temporal prerogatives are always accompanied with claims of necessity, objectivity or with the caveat of "that is the way things are." Recalling Dussel's and Mignolo's argument for the concept of transmodernity such an opening, a negation of the ideals of its time, allows for the affirmation of new ways of living and acting within a vibrant democratic community.

Rather than political and social creativity beginning in the temporal, to be, creativity is the outcome of the collision between the transitivity of the cultural, social, political, and economic world, *constituted power*, with our intransitivity, our multitudinous and interconnected ways of being in the world. This represents the *constitute power* of creativity. Immanent transcendence/border thinking springs from the individual through their engagement and exchange with the liminality and potentially dangerous space between what is and what is imagined. This allows us/we to dismantle our self-conceptions as often as it allows to reach some understanding of our circumstances. Rather than being, we have proposed that it is *becoming* within the an open community, through the constant negation of transitivity and intransitivity, between objectivity and subjectivity, which allows us to provide a third space through which to initiate personal, social, and political change. Drawing on the decolonial notion of relative universalism and Watsuji's epistemology, this book's support of pluralistic and open community identity and agency carries with it an obligation to reject boundaries between diverse political identities.

In stressing a move away from an overly concrete and diametric dualistic understanding of space and the public, it would have to focus on an inter-dependent and co-cognitivist form of communication as the space of demo-cratic politics. This would allow for the identification of appropriate societal mechanism to carry such principles. Therefore, what epistemic mechanism for democracy would be available from the spatial account of cosmopolitan-ism set out above?

In the face of sustained attempts to impose diametric dualities on human cultures, we continue to stake a claim to creative co-cognitive individuality. We find one such claim in English common law: the principle of nullification by jury. Many will be not be common with this, so it may be worth providing a brief sketch. The original cases of nullification by jury represent positive acts by a jury to return legislation to the public arena for continued discus-sion. One of the most prominent early cases are the cases of Sir Nicholas Throckmorton, who had openly participated in Wyatt's Rebellion (1544), and the Bushell Case which arose from the arrest and prosecution of Quaker leader William Penn and his associate William Mead (1670). In both cases, the jury reached a verdict of not guilty of the stated charge, despite the weight of evidence against the defendants being overwhelming. However, it is the Bushell case that is intriguing for this chapter as it defined the independence of the jury from state inference. What jury nullification is about is particular-ized justice; it is about citizen's oversight of prosecutorial discretion; and it is about limiting the power and intrusiveness of the legislature and of the criminal sanction (Clayton 1999). Of course, its application within the cre-ation of epistemic value would represent the use of the principle in a new context. However, as presently understood, nullification by jury serves the purpose of addressing immoral or social inequality as "most instances of jury nullification are in response to what the members of the jury perceive as unlawful government behaviour, unjust laws, or the inequitable application of the law" (McKnight 2013: 1104). The example of nullification by jury gives us a concrete representation of the expression of our heuristic devices of diametric and concentric dualities. In identifying structural blockages to well-being, diametric dualities, the jury provides a forum in which the question is returned to the public arena for further discussion, concentric dualities. This does not act as a mere arena for deliberation. Rather, acting as independent and local sources of legitimate rationality, the practical act of the jury, acts an incessant and permanent spatial bridging of the gap between the individual and society to provide an affirmation of will through the articulation of injus-tice. Here we see an offer of Watsujian transcendence in a spatial continual model of negation, to provide the potential for societal change and individual transformation.

Acting as an informed forum alongside existing representative bodies, following the established rules of jury participation, and with oversight, advocacy, and evidence de jure powers, such a body, at the local, national, and international level, could provide an effective counterweight to statist, political parties, and corporate over-positioning and for the instigation of democratic innovation. Such a communicative space, at the meeting place of ideals and practices, contains the possibility of societal transformation. Its application within the creation of epistemic value would represent the use of the principle in a new context extended to the political, social, and economic spheres. As a spatial institutional observation of the political, the practical act of politics of the jury could provide a significant means of realizing, uncovering, and preserving the practical act-connections of democratic life.

Chapter 6

Aidagara and the Imagination of Being and Acting in the World

INTRODUCTION

Cosmopolitanism does not begin in the word, a discipline, or doctrine, but begins in our enactive and generative engagement with the world. The objective of this chapter is to fulfil the promise of providing a decolonized and phenomenological account of the agent as being and acting in a democratic world. Here, a decolonized agent is not reliant on the individual as the ultimate unit of analysis but also moves beyond notions of an essentialized sociohistorical informed identities. This is gained through synthesizing the relational sociology of Delanty, the Mignolo's concept of aesthesis, which is captured within Watsuji's socio-epistemology concept, *aidagara*.

The last chapter brought together the relative universalism of the decolonial theorist with Watsuji's socio-epistemology concept of fūdo. What emerged through that encounter is that in "sharing" consciousness we are inter/intra-corporeally immersed and interconnected. Cognitive production, subjectivity, intersubjectivity, and objectivity are distributed and mediated within the dynamics of the material, symbolic signs, and natural worlds, through which "we" as "I" discover ourselves. In exploiting a reading of Watsuji's account of emptiness as a form of reflexive negation operating within *fūdo* together with Mignolo's rejection of ideals, shifts normative and analytical attention from ideals to instead focus on the articulation of injustices. Such an account of the human condition allows us to propose an account of the ultimate unit of analysis for a critical cosmopolitan social theory as intersubjective and inter/intracorporeal. Here agency is exercised as exchanges distributed phenomenon within the dynamics of the reification of material, earthly, and social worlds, *fūdo*. This also provides criticality for *fūdo* through understanding social space through the heuristic devices diametric and concentric dualities. However, such an account cannot take us further down the road of providing an authentic account of cosmopolitanism as what is still required is an understanding of how one, the self, engages with the world and how we can bring change into being. It is this task for cosmopolitanism, the ultimate unit of analysis, to which this chapter now turns.

In this chapter, I am concerned with developing a means to explore social practices and to provide a means of articulating the limitations of a society. Watsuji's concepts of *fūdo* and *aidagara* are the interconnected parts of his account of socioepistemology. Through the concept of *aidagara*, Watsuji wished to take our descent into hermeneutically understanding into the expressions of the everyday. For Watsuji, the hermeneutic method, in recognizing that it cannot remove us from our climatic and historical "burden" must be somehow destroy it to address each society's limitations (Watsuji 1996 [1937, 1942, 1949]: 45). As he argues, "...hermeneutic destruction reveals traditions, comes to grips with their respective particularity, and thereby gains the clarity to reconstruct the fundamental of a human being's Sonzai"[1] (Watsuji 1996 [1937, 1942, 1949]: 45). But, it is only in the encounter with the other in a genuine dialogue are we able to uncover our own limitations and to provide new ways of being human.

Cosmopolitanism maintains its critical edge when it is in genuine and revealing conversation with the other. It is only through the process of critique and cooperation, that one's own limitations can be revealed and new affirmations proposed. This chapter brings together the ultimate units of analysis of Delanty and Mignolo. What Delanty seeks to find are sources of dialogue for the cultivation of critical thought. In stressing a relational account of social ontology, mediated through an account of culture that stresses the cognitive over the symbolic, it aims to go beyond the simple excavation of cultures to find globally shared values or occurrences of exchange and multiplicity. As an account of "cognitive universalistic principles" and "moments of openness," though not stated in such terms, the implication is the development of a global account of *negative liberty*.

In setting out a sociohistorical informed unit of analysis, Mignolo's focus is the development of an account capable of bridging the gap between theory and practice to provide loci of enunciation for claims of injustice. Within such a framework, like the case of the emperor's new clothes, the grand claims of the universalizing impartiality of modernity are shown to be merely an eloquent secularized mysticism. This obscures the profound dehumanizing

---

[1] Existence.

effects of sociogenic norms on the interpenetrative "practical-act connections" of self-other-world.

Of course, these can only ever provide partial accounts of societal dynamics. However, though partial, they do capture important aspects of the human condition and the process of theoretical development. I have suggested that cosmopolitanism can only be possible as a theoretical endeavour when the cosmopolitan imagination, when focussed on matters of common concern, reaches out to its negation. Through understanding the encounter between Mignolo's decolonial project and Delanty's critical cosmopolitanism as an originary though nonbinary phases of social development allows us to begin a moment of cosmopolitan creativity. In what follows, the encounter of Delanty with decolonial theory shatters critical theory's commitment to an inherently Eurocentric idea of historical progress, of the competences of modernity, to stress the effects of social power and nonrationality. In the contrary movement, of introducing Delanty to Mignolo, equally shatters the totalities of decolonial theory through which the decolonial theorist represents the world, to reveal a principle autonomy enhanced through the multiplicity provided through relative universalism.

Though this may be a development, we are still left with the feeling of abstraction as this nascent "conceptual persona" would still carry with it fragments of the totalizing social ontologies in which they were created. For instance, though this movement would shatter and disrupt, the certainty of the decolonial movement, it would still leave it within its own bounds of intelligibility. What we need is an account of social ontology that can capture and respond to the tensions of individuality and the overcoming of social injustices to reveal the underside of ideals within and beyond its horizons of intelligibility. We find such an account in Watsuji's concept of *aidagara*. However, though it maintains the tension between individuality and sociality, here, applying emptiness as an epistemic principle allows us to premise negative and positive liberties not as universal rights, but as points of critique.

This chapter will develop as follows: The first sections will set out the relational social of Delanty and Mignolo's account of aesthesis. Mignolo's account of aesthesis is a stimulating account as it apparently offers the opportunity to move beyond monadic accounts of the individual to incorporate the human, social, material, and natural worlds into our analysis of the human condition. The next section of the chapter brings these accounts together within the social ontology of *aidagara*. Predicating on the reflexive negation of emptiness, *aidagara*, allows to draw out the critical potential of the conceptual persona of Delanty and Mignolo's account. The final section sets out an account of a democratic decolonial being and acting in the world.

DELANTY'S RELATIONAL ONTOLOGY

For the cosmopolitan theorist, the imagination provides the basis through which "...human agency can radically transform the present in the image of an imagined future" (Delanty 2006: 38). It can provide a "site of resistance and alterity,"[2] which can interrupt and transform normative orders and ideologies that are oppressive. It provides the opportunity to find "fissures" within stabilized texts and meanings of how things should be in order to create "...the possibilities for imagining differently, for a radical politics from 'elsewhere'" (Latimer and Skeggs 2011: 404). As an account of the possibilities of the cosmopolitan imagination for social analysis, "[T]he notion of Critical cosmopolitanism sees the category of the world in terms of openness rather than in terms of a universal system. It is this that defines the cosmopolitan imagination" (Delanty 2006: 38). The primary ontological focus of cosmopolitan analysis, for Delanty, is the relationality between self, other, and the world. It is the interplay through this encounter, set against the context of an increasingly globalized and reflective world, which initiates a cosmopolitan moment of self and societal transformation (Delanty 2006: 41). And it is through the extension of Cornelius Castoriadis' universal project of autonomy that provides the imaginative resources from which to draw on to effect social change within the context of globalization.

While previous accounts of the imaginary had highlighted its societal aspects, it was not until the work of Castoriadis that we find an emphasis on the inherent creative and radical nature of the imagination. Delanty draws on Castoriadis' notion of the imaginary as the way in which societies symbolically constitute themselves to define the cosmopolitan imagination not in universal terms but in terms of openness (Delanty 2006: 38). Castoriadis does not conceive of the imagination as a merely individual faculty. Imaginaries give meaning to symbols, goods, institutions, and are "not so far removed from what Hegel called 'the spirit of a people'" (Castoriadis 1987 [1975]: 128). He argues that we are immersed in the social imaginary, all societies possess an imaginary dimension, since they must answer certain symbolic questions as to their basic identity, their goals, and limits. Every society, collectively, institutes itself by creating its own laws, rules, values, and shared meaning. It does so by changing its "instituted social imaginary," namely the "existing" truths which it embraces and subscribes to what is sensible, true or false, fair or unfair and of course, what is meaningful and what is meaningless. Put otherwise, the definition of the "real" is the result of a dialectical movement between the instituted and the instituting side of the social

---

[2] My emphasis.

imaginary. The imaginary in this sense is not in contrast to reality, since it itself is something real. In reemphasizing the importance of social context in shaping the free imagination of individuals through a process of socialization by the imaginary significations of society, Castoriadis claims to have overcome the problems of the philosophy of the individual. He also emphasized the need to rethink the concept of the imagination to answer the question of what its potential use in terms of what is are social and political projects. His work represents a transitional moment from a theory of imagination, as an individual faculty, to one of the imaginaries, which emphasizes the social context of the radicality of the imagination.

For Delanty, cosmopolitanism can be one such imaginary constituent of society. It appears more like a concept for representing a process of interaction which is based on the principle of openness and which leads toward the formation of a global public sphere. However, in a world of growing interconnections, this is not an abstract ideal at the interface of the local and global, the social and individual, of materiality and imagination (Meskimmon 2011: 6–7). It is these interconnections that offer the opportunity to explore new ways of living. However, he is aware of the social, economic, and political instability that has been brought about through increased globalization. Therefore, Delanty's focus is on the use of the cosmopolitan imagination as a continuing process of other and self-transformation, "...which can be realized only by taking the cosmopolitan perspective of the Other as well as global principles of justice" (Delanty 2009: 3). This signifies an account that enables the transformation of everyday consciousness and identities. But how is this to be achieved?

He begins the development of this argument through an account of a relational social ontology. Culture, like cosmopolitanism, is both discursive and an arena of claim-making which entails the imagination, and which raises the possibility of critique of the status quo (Delanty 2011: 641). Where traditional accounts of culture have stressed closure or symbolic order Delanty draws on research that emphasizes the open-ended nature of culture, and which critically emphasizes cultures cognitive and narrative aspects (Eder 2009; Somers 1994, 1995; Delanty 2011: 638). Here we understand the social as referring less to an unambiguous characterization of "society" as a national society or as a geographical location or cultural bounded entity but as a field of social relations and interconnectedness. Culture and social structures, like cosmopolitanism itself,[3] are sites of dialectical tension in which conflicting orientations are played out. It is situated in the present in relation to the past and future, and through which new solutions to societal problems are

---

[3] Recalling the link between "world disclosure" and immanent transcendence.

formulated (Delanty 2012: 341, 350). On this basis, then, cultural phenomena can be theorized as more than simply differentiated but as fluid, fragmented, contested, diverse, and open to new forms of sense-making and narrative construction. This should not be understood as denying the importance of social actors and the need to identify the carriers of cultural values, beliefs, and so forth, but rather as an endeavour that seeks to explain the mechanisms and processes by which such cultural phenomena are generated and have impacts on the shaping of political community.

Through separating the normative, symbolic, and cognitive dimensions of culture and in emphasizing the latter (Delanty 2011: 640), allows Delanty to posit a cognitive universalism with the potential to overcome not only objections of Eurocentrism but also all ethnocentric methods (Delanty 2014: 10). It follows from this account that what are taken as European values are not specific to Europe but only represent historical "germs" that were simply developed there first. Following Habermas, but more pertinently for the book drawing on the project of autonomy of Castoriadis (1987), he argues that we can make certain assumptions about the nature of the individual and of political community while leaving open the specific solutions in a way that recognizes the specific context of the community (Delanty 2014: 4).

MIGNOLO, THE OTHER AND THE SPACE IN-BETWEEN

To speak of an "other" critical thought, for the decolonial thinker, is to give credence to ongoing struggles that are epistemic as well as political in character through which to confront postcoloniality. This marks a radical form of critical thought that is distinct from that which locates critical theory simply *within* the interior of modernity. Here the decolonial project develops a de-colonized "other" through which to infuse liberation philosophy with Levinassian depth (Dussel 1973: 161). Dussel writes, "[T]he real overcoming of the [ontological and dialectical] tradition . . . is found in the philosophy of Levinas. Our overcoming will consist in re-thinking the discourse from Latin America." (Enrique Dussel 1973). This critical perspective was always present within modernity and points toward a way of formulating a political program based on the experiences and aspirations of the peoples displaying such consciousness. Therefore, in contrast to Delanty's development of *connectors*, Mignolo's project of decolonial cosmopolitanism aims to offer *connectors* on grounds that maintain the ontic and epistemic location of the subject. One possible outcome of this process is an understanding of the social sciences and of social and political thought that develops from this, that is, relational: different perspectives on the experience of being human. This call hopes to escape the Habermasian consensus, in which the symbolic and material signifiers of society are intertwined with a society's cultural, social, economic, and political institutional, to instead move toward an equal horizontal relationship among citizens as humanity and between cultures.

There is an aspect of Mignolo's work that we haven't covered yet, but which offers a stimulating view on the human condition, a view that links with Watsuji. This is Mignolo application of the notion of aesthesis. If "Modernity" was imagined in the house of epistemology (Mignolo 2006: 93), this has also included the distinguishing and defining of reason from the aesthetic. If "...decolonial corpo-politics of knowledge, perception, and being" (Tlostanova 2017: 38), stresses the exploration of the aesthesis of society, such a "corpo-politics of knowledge" emphasizes that global localities are not only a "...geohistorical location of the knowing subject, but also an epistemological correlation with the sensing body, perceiving the world from a particular locale and specific local history" (Tlostanova 2017: 38). At its most fundamental, such an account of aesthesis is about heightened alertness to the world as experienced through space and time combined; it involves "perception" beyond mere "recognition" or representation.

Aesthesis literally refers to our ability to perceive through the senses and the process of sensual perception itself. Mario Perniolo, describing Hans Robert Jauss's principle of aesthesis (1921–1997) understands it as providing:

> ...the access to a perception of the world different from the utilitarian and instrumental one. It is an intuitive knowledge that deconceptualizes the world and allows access to a cosmological vision capable of establishing connections between its different manifestations. (Perniola 2013: 79)

In the concept of aesthesis, Mignolo and others capture something fundamental about the human experience; how the self, as body and mind, relate and connect to the external world beyond the cognitive, but which saturates it with expressive meaning. At its most fundamental, aesthesis is about heightened alertness to the world as experienced through space and time combined; it involves "perception" beyond mere "recognition" or representation. In stating such a multidimensional account of the access to knowledge as ontology draws our attention to the "perceptual abstraction" or "semblance" whereby through symbolic forms the human actor partakes—physically or imaginatively—in an experience where he or she "does not remain a cold spectator" (Dewey 1958: 5), but through which the vital dynamics of a life are captured. Within the sociohistorical context of colonialism, an account of aesthesis merges that transforms the "the goals of art, its ontological, ethical, existential, and political status." To create art becomes an act of dissidence, a compassionate perception of other lives or as an act of healing and reopening the old colonial wounds (Saadawi 1998 [1983]: 157–175; Lugones 2003;

Anzaldúa 1999). As an embodied form, aesthesis springs from the function of human creativity, our enacting and generative interaction with the world. Such a multidimensional account of the access to knowledge draws our attention to the "perceptual abstraction" or "semblance" whereby we coordinate our inner life with an outer world through symbolic forms. This recognizes the immanence of the everyday. However, aesthesis draws out from the realm of temporality's perceptual and conceptual reification the real, to enunciate what has been silent and confined within limitations of one's societies ideals. Aesthesis is the outcome of the collision between the transitivity of the cultural, social, political, and economic world, *constituted power*, with our intransitivity, our multitudinous, and interconnected ways of being in the world. This provides for the infinity of otherness and simultaneously recognizes the infinity of self within a necessarily contingent, hetero-plural account of space. In setting out a spatial account of the self is not to reject the idea of the individual only to enrich it. This is not a fragmentary self of postmodernity, but an epistemic perspective that places the individual within the prevailing social conditions of the time but allows them to question their normativity. It is a conscious and self-reflective critical movement for the development of practices of subversion and emancipation of experience, corporality, and its ontological, ethical, existential, and political status. As Tlostanova (2017) argues, though recalling Delanty's claim for the possibilities for resistance at the site of the cosmopolitan imagination, the creativity of such a transmodern sensibility becomes a method of liberating knowledge through subversion. It is to undercut reality through the enunciation of a sensuous account of agency. Through reaching out, from within a world of relative universalism, provides the opportunity for redefining self-other-world, and the institutions that frame our imagination(s).

WATSUJI ON RELATIONAL EXISTENCE AND EMBODIED INTERSUBJECTIVITY

For Watsuji, it is an understanding of these interconnections, the space or place in which people are located, and in which the various crossroads of relational interconnection as practices, that are prior to the moment of art and philosophy. It is through *aidagara* that Watsuji wishes to take our descent into hermeneutical understanding even further through " understanding of the expressions of life" (Watsuji 1996 [1937, 1942, 1949]: 42). Therefore, the task of "hermeneutics [is] to elucidate the possibility of knowledge about living connections in the historical world" for its destruction and reconstruction (Watsuji 1996 [1937, 1942, 1949]: 42). It is only by conducting such a task, argues Watsuji, that will enable a culture to identify and to then overcome its historical and climatic conditions and limitations. This will not be merely a cognitive account but presents a socio-aesthesis of being that involves the body, the feelings, the will, and the consciousness, and how these are mediated through concrete things that are necessarily both spatial and temporal.

The embedded and embodied principle of aesthesis contained within *aidagara*, conceptually highlights how we coordinate our inner experience with outer reality through the "nervous system of society." However, one must not understand this as simply the created, the diametric duality of social existence, because for Watsuji *aidagara* is both objective and subjective. It is objective in that it must be mediated by actual things—trade relations, education, shared emotions, a shared environment, and so forth. But, as subjective, these media are not given. Rather, they are subject to dynamic reinterpretation and renegotiation—just as cultural products are constantly produced and reproduced. Thus, objective subjectivity illuminates the concealed spaces of life's act-connections (See Shields notes 2011: Watsuji 1996 [1937, 1942, 1949]: 160).

RELATIONAL EXISTENCE

The aim of Watsuji's project was to move away from an "individualist" view of ethical life and toward a "relational" view of being human. However, anyone who claims that social reality rested on solely individual or communal foundations were, for Watsuji, speaking merely in terms of figments of the imagination. Emptiness, acting as a means of illuminating the barriers to human well-being allows us to provide a means of overcoming these barriers, allows us to overcome the totalizing effects of hard ontological accounts and the dichotomies that such approaches bring into being: the world of us and them. Rather, this is a world in which "I" am part of "we." This provides a space "within *aidagara*" through which the individual and society could view its limitations.

However, in proposing such a relational system, Watsuji sees the paradox of individuality and totality:

> What I have described as a human being's existence as betweenness is that which renders individuals and societies capable of occurring in their reciprocal negations. Therefore, for human beings, we cannot first presuppose individuals, and then explain the establishment of social relationships among them. Nor can we presuppose society and from there explain the occurrence of individuals. Neither the one nor the other has "precedence." (Watsuji 1996 [1937, 1942, 1949]: 102)

To explore this paradox, Watsuji examines the act of writing. In Western thought, the conceit continues of the certain existence of the ego, even to the point of lapsing into solipsism.[4] However, Watsuji shows that rather that than sinking into the solipsistic trap of the solitary author in a room, that the very method of ethics, as the act of ethical inquiry, is relational. In doing so, through his exploration of ethical questions, Watsuji is arguing that something very special is taking place. He states:

> For writing is an expression of words, and words are what have come to shape themselves in anticipation of partners who live and talk together. Even though words are written in a foreign language and perhaps with the intention of allowing no one else to read them, this does not mean that these words have come into being without there being partners to talk with, but only that the author is without partners with whom to talk. (WTZ10, 52 (50))

This needs an understanding of the relationship between the individual and society as a co-creative demand as participants within a shared and intersubjective horizon of knowledge that is ontic and epistemic. To do so also assumes that the participants have achieved social integration that must contend with the tasks of interpreting their relations to one another. This also needs a framing narrative about personal and collective identification and the justification of the demotic, of everyday speech, its signifiers and signification. Given this, Watsuji concludes:

> No matter how much we concern ourselves with the consciousness of I, this concern itself implies our going beyond the consciousness of I and being connected with others" WTZ10, 52 (50). And: [T]his relationship is constructed, through and through in the betweenness between an author and his readers. Neither can exist prior to and independent of the other. They exist only by depending on one another. WTZ10 55 (52)

---

[4] There continues a story, inevitably linked to progress and modernity, of the "invention" of the ego, most notably in Descartes' cogito. This goes largely unchallenged. However, Day (2007) points to examples of "subjectivity" with clear sexual, political religious characteristics and which carry what we, as moderns, would understand as emotional interiors, although from "premodern" societies. A relevant example is the poem entitled "*On being a concubine*" through which the eighteenth-century Vietnamese poet Ho Xuan Huong examined her own sexuality and laid claim to both a private subjectivity and an independent, public self. "One wife gets quilts, the other wife must freeze. To share a husband—damn it, what a fate! I'd settle for just ten, nay, just five times. But fancy, it's not even twice a month! I take it all for rice: some musty rice. I labor as a maid: a wageless maid. Had I but known I should end up like this, I would have sooner stayed the way I was." (Day 2007: 25). See also (Houng 1996: 214).

Our everyday experience is not from the point of view of a reader-less author nor an author-less reader, but between the author and the reader. He then defines relationality as follows:

> We take our departure not from the intentional consciousness of "I" but from "betweenness." The essential feature of betweenness lies in this, that the intentionality of the I is from the outset prescribed by its counterpart, which is also conversely prescribed by the former. (WTZ10, 53-54 (51))

While on the one hand, Watsuji is pointing to the clear fact that when an individual utters a word, or sets down a sentence, the act cannot be construed through a Charybdisian or Scyllaian configuration of bounded identities of the self or the social. As Sevilla points out (2015: 76), Watsuji is claiming that when we make ethical enquires this means that "I" as an individual is asking ethical questions. However, we can only make such an enquiry within the context of a collective space. While "I" may make the enquiry within the privacy of "my" own mind, "my" enquires can only be raised within the context of language which carries our relationality. If we accept that all communities have entered such discourses about the nature of being human leads Sevilla to conclude that:

> while the question is undoubtedly raised by the individual, the question is, in a sense, also asked by humankind by communities, by relationships. Ningen is asking about ningen—and in ethics, ningen in a sense comes home to itself. And we seek ourselves in our shared expressions—words, literature, paintings, religious practices, political life, and so on. With these, Watsuji paints a thoroughly relational picture of human life and its ethical quest. (2015: 76)

And in pointing to our fundamental relationality vis-à-vis our roles Watsuji notes:

> We can now confirm an obvious everyday fact, that we always act with a certain capacity and that this capacity is prescribed by something whole, further that this whole is the relationship we construct by means of possessing a certain capacity. Simply speaking, we exist in our daily life in the being in betweenness. (WTZ10, 61 (57)

The idea of "capacity" has a key function in Watsuji's argument.[5] For Watsuji, a capacity/role is the meeting point between the individuals and the

---

[5] Once again, we see an example of Watsuji drawing on his commitment to the relational ontology provided through Confucius thought.

totality-not in the individual being but in *aidagara*. What this suggests is that life is informed by praxis and thought and is constructed and experienced through the body, emotions, memory, cultural knowledge, by what is, to use a metaphor, "the smoke of culture." Relational being means being constantly situated in these capacities, as both a singular member, and as a part of the whole, in one's "plural" existence simultaneously. In his insistence on the importance of human spatial relations in terms of social analysis, what he is concerned with "...are not objective relations that established through subjective unity, as is the case with spatial relations between subject and object. Rather, they are act-connections between person and person like communication or association" (Watsuji 1996 [1937, 1942, 1949]: 10).

What we begin to see is a sign of a relational ontology, a breaking-down of inside-outside of my head distinction. Though maintaining the protection of the individual, this has the potential to release the creativity of internal heterogeneity through a move away from essentialist notions of concepts of the individual, cultural, and society. However, what is perhaps the most philosophically stimulating aspect of Watsuji's account is his insistence that the body is simultaneously an object as well as an experiential dimension, a bodily subjectivity.

EMBODIED INTERSUBJECTIVITY

Much of Watsuji's thinking turns on a phenomenological analysis of the body that inhabits and negotiates social space. In his work, *The Body* (1987: 47), Yuasa Yasuo, writes that

> Watsuji's concept of betweenness, the subjective interconnection of meanings, must be grasped as a *carnal* interconnection. Moreover, this interconnection must not be thought of as either a psychological or physical relatedness, nor even their conjunction. Moreover, this interconnection must not be thought of as either a psychological or physical relatedness, nor even their conjunction.

As such, the physical body is our point of contact with the world.[6] It is what allows us to interact causally with the world, to act but at the same to be acted upon. However, signalling a point explored at length by phenomenological

---

[6] We shall be returning to this point in the next chapter. However, to pre-empt that discussion Yuasa connects Watsuji's theory of fūdo to his theory of the body where the person, understood as ningen, embodies its entire spatial locus of the social interconnections and nature. For Watsuji the body, is not a physical object situated in the world alongside other physical objects, "an organism of the sort that physiology expounds" (Watsuji 1996 [1937, 1942, 1949]: 59).

thinkers such as Husserl, Sartre, Merleau-Ponty, and Levinas, the body is furthermore, and correspondingly, a subjective body: a lived, first-person perspective on the world. As Joel Krueger notes, what this translates into phenomenologically is that the lived body is not just a container of consciousness such as perception or memory (2013: 129). Rather, the lived body is much more than this; it is hybrid with an irreducibly "dual structure" (Watsuji 1996 [1937, 1942, 1949]: 19).

It is in the "activity" of the subject, and its relationship to *aidagara*, to which Watsuji wants to draw our attention. While for Watsuji "[W]hether considered theoretically or practically, a human body is subjective through and through, so long as it is an element in the activity of a subject" (Watsuji 1996 [1937, 1942, 1949]: 65). To further develop his book on the phenomenological aspects of social space, Watsuji appeals to interpersonal interactions and gives several phenomenological descriptions. Watsuji brings our individual to life within the tensions and strains between our individuality and the totality of the world. Watsuji argues that this immediate connection with another is possible because the physical body is an expressive vehicle that externalizes, via "practical act-connections," aspects of another's subjectivity in such a way that I have immediate perceptual and emotional access to them.[7] We can get a sense of this when he writes about the parents' grief on hearing of the death of their child:

> The interpenetration of the consciousness of self and other is conspicuously recognizable in emotion . . . We share the same emotions as others in situations in which the relationship between oneself and the other is quite intimate and in which a sense of community is to a considerable extent realized. For parents who have lost a child, concern for their child is shared by both. In such cases the independence of the consciousness of the ego is almost completely lost sight of. (Watsuji 1996 [1937, 1942, 1949]: 70)

What we can note here is a description of the direct perception view of social cognition, the basis of interpersonal understanding consists of empathic perception: an immediate and direct perceptual grasp of another person's feelings and intentions (Kruger 2014). Though aspects of their subjectivity stay transcendent, it is the case that the body, as a communicative modality, makes manifest other aspects of subjectivity within the *aidagara* of social interaction: we are sharing consciousness (Krueger 2014: 57). This provides "...the material scaffolding both structuring the lived space of betweenness (i.e., by making aspects of one's 'inner' subjectivity available for direct perception),

---

[7] See accounts of "direct perception" in Gallagher (2005, 2008).

as well as motivating the back-and-forth dialectic" (2014: 62–63). It is the carnally based, practical, everyday action-connections gestures and vocal and bodily expressions, that indicates for Watsuji the "subjective extendedness" of the social self.

Rather than being a content-holder for consciousness, consciousness as only being in the head, Watsuji's phenomenological account offers the body as our anchored first perspective on the world. This grounds our egocentric frame of spatial orientation through which we are also revealed to ourselves as somatic subjects situated in the world. It is through these *practical interconnections* of acts, of a *habitus*, that we acquire roles or capacities, neither as abstract theoretical beings nor as automatons. Rather, these interconnections function in shaping our thinking and feeling as embodied subjects within emotional systems. Furthermore, it is only through the participation in these practical interconnections that the subject internalizes their community and reproduces it. In sharing consciousness, we play out our roles *between* the self and society. To argue otherwise is simply to argue from the point of view of the imagination (Watsuji 1996 [1937, 1942, 1949]: 22). However, being in *aidagara*, and following on from the discussion of *fūdo* the community has no *essence* but exists only in the ongoing process of interaction and creativity. This suggests that although the body is affected through material, social, and philosophical relations, it also is a site of enactive experimentation with the capacity for cultural, social, and philosophical creativity. It is in this gap, *aidagara*, that we find a shared ground with the other, in which we also have the potential to see not only the other's infinite depth but also infinity within ourselves. And this, has important implications for critical cosmopolitanism.

A CRITIQUE OF COSMOPOLITAN CREATIVITY

Delanty's account of a cosmopolitanism imagination, and the relational sociology through, rests largely on the work of Castoriadis. Of course, the merit of Castoriadis' concept of radical social imaginary is to point out that the instituting social imaginary is always at the same time instituted. No society could ever exist if the individuals created by the society itself had not created it. Society can exist concretely only through the fragmentary and complementary incarnation and incorporation of its institution and its imaginary significations in the living, talking, and acting individuals of that society. However, as Bottici (2011, 2014) has highlighted, all that was achieved was to shift the difficulties raised from a subject-situated problematic ontology of the subject and the associated unsolvable problem of the reality of imagination, onto the similarly challenging ontology context-oriented concept of the imaginary. Behind this total rupture of self and society lies the tension between an "individual imagination" and the "social imaginary"' from which Castoriadis's account was meant to philosophically free us.

Besides this broad point, there are two specific limitations to Castoriadis' work that I want to focus on at present as they important for the development of the rest of this chapter. First, it would appear to be a remarkable suggestion from Castoriadis that if the "monadic" self with the radical possibilities of creativity is a universal of humanity, that it was only the ancient Greeks and modern Europeans that have took advantage of such a notion (Gaonkar 2002: 9). More importantly, Whitehead notes that Castoriadis creates an untenable metaphysical opposition in placing a gap between the self and society; a problem that his project was meant to address and overcome. Once we find ourselves within the monadic isolation of the unconscious, it becomes difficult to explain how communication is possible in the first place (Whitebook 1989). Such a proposition, of the monadic nature of the self, repeats the conceptual problems raised in chapter 2 in respect of Delanty's inclusion of the individual in his theoretical model. Such a conceptual device can be understood as a "blob" of data hanging freely in space. Its means of communication, not information, with other "blobs" seems to not only be problematic but also abstract in the extreme. If social contexts are assumed to be neutral, that is issues of power, language domination, and so forth, are excluded from any social analysis this raises the specter of assimilation of the less powerful by the strong. Therefore, any form of communication would only be on the terms that are valued the dominant party.

Second, Castoriadis' characterization of the body does not acknowledge the deep way in which it is functionally interwoven into biological, cultural, and historical contexts via how it is represented, imagined, does to itself or has done to it (See Kopf 2001: and Krueger 2008). Though Castoriadis argues that people can exist only within and through society, he maintains that there are aspects in the individual human being which are "not social" (Castoriadis 2010: 45). Here rather than putting forward an emancipatory account that separates the "biological substratum, the animal being," that is our somatic needs, he elevates the "mind" as it is "which is infinitely more important" than the biological substratum (Castoriadis 2007: 184). This implies that the body and any radical critique of the body's role in society or how bodies are used, would lack the force of reason. Rather, than the lived body being our anchored first-person perspective on the world, it is reduced to a mere assemblage of biological parts that have useful capacities.

While Delanty's relational social ontology does try to move away from abstraction through maintaining an account of absolute universalism he fails to appreciate the interdependency (though expressed as plural spatial and temporal modalities) of being human. Delanty's individual inhabits a one-dimensional and homogenous social space and of temporality through which Western social theory has developed its questions and solutions (Domingues 1995: 236). Such an account of space cannot account for the multiple interconnections locally or globally as it sets in place a totalizing set of assumptions of the human condition. These function as barriers between individuals and global cultures. Such assumptions have restricted the scope of investigation into alternative accounts of sovereignty, identity, agency, and the nature of the state and inter-state relationships. Therefore, rather than offering alternatives to the logic of the singular perspective, of either/or logic, such an account supports the diametric duality between self, other, and the world, which cosmopolitanism is meant to overcome. This is something he did not intend.

Mignolo does appreciate how space has been affected by temporal claims to universalism. From such a perspective, it resists the ethical universalism of Eurocentrism. However, though derived from the acknowledgment of the co-cognitivity of space and for the articulation of injustices through the medium of transmodernity, it fails to provide a site of enunciation in terms of the face-to-face encounter. Focusing further, it fails in two respects, to provide a conceptual space to release the creative societal forces that it itself brings to the fore. First, it still maintains a diametric duality of space and time through relying on a systemic account that builds on totalities in absolute terms. It misses the relationships "in and between." A result of this totalizing of space and time is to produce a reductivist method which excludes the internal heterogeneity that his very method is claiming to represent (Mignolo 2000: 103; see also Alcoff 2007: 99). Though the resources for such analysis are present within the decolonial project, aesthesis, and transmodernity, it fails to follow through on the potential of its own fundamental proposition for the creation of new and inclusive forms of social and political experimentation. Once again, social theory fails as it has no resources through which to identify the infinity within self, internal heterogeneity, as well as the infinity of the other, beyond the rejection of the other: the West. Second, as the potential of the globally enhanced imagination of the critical theorist is frustrated, the potential for transmodernity to offer transcendence is restricted by its insistence of a diametric duality of the world—the West and the rest. In doing so, in proclaiming with righteous anger, "I have been wronged and I will now find my own way in this world, alone," it sets itself apart from humanity. Not a humanity of reason that it has rightly cursed, but the humanity of the tapestry of the human condition that decolonialism, by its very existence, proclaims into existence. Though it recognizes how the outside effects the inside, to justify its righteous anger it creates an account of space that builds on totalities in absolute terms. Yes, the signification of ethnic identity is important, but not as a foreground, as to do so extinguishes individual rebellion that adds further colour and scent to the world. This is not to say the race, for example, is not important, only to suggest that you are more than one signifier.

A DECOLONIAL PHENOMENOLOGY
OF EXISTENCE: PART TWO

Being human is creativity. The account of loci of enunciation sees us embedded within the norms, values, and standards of objectivity of our societies. Exploring the intersection of ideals and the practices of life and appreciating the encounter with self, other, and the world as less distinct and concrete but relational, entangled, and conditional, allows us to step outside the temporal-modalities of time to rethink who we are. Here, noting our heuristic spatial devices of concentric and diametric dualities, we are concerned with existing social practices with our body being our interdependent contact with the world. This is opposed to an understanding of the human condition as being one in which we are autonomous and distinct individual centers of rationality or as an essentialized identity. If we appreciate agency through our notion of reflexive negation, then the tension between individuality and totality allows us to understand agency as being constantly enactive between self, other, and the world to provide the energy for the creativity of *constitute power*. Cultural reproduction and production are brought about *between* the self and its poly-modal interaction with totality. This recognizes the immanence of the everyday but draws the real from out of the realm of temporality's perceptual and conceptual reification to enunciate what has been silent and confined within the objectivity of the limitations of one's societies ideals. The moment of change is elicited with the silent suggestion, the silent thought as negation, that is already present in the affirmation, and which emerges in the individual through their engagement with the greater whole. This allows us to recognize not only the infinity with other but also the infinite within ourselves. The point here to stress that though the self is centered, it is at the same time part of an enactive interaction with other and the world through which new ways of being and acting in the world come to light. However, unlike the notion of a rationality of self or social identity, identities that have no real power for change, the recognition of the pluralistic nature of agency provides the mechanism the localization of democracy, spatially, at every level of human development.

Mignolo's focus on ethnicity appears to present a considerable limitation in respect of reimaging the state, society, gender, and other accoutrements of modernity. Yet, as remarked above, and in spite himself, though he is correct to put forward the voice of those marginalized outside the "West," when his thought is brought into contact with that of the critical theorist, he de-stabilizes the subjectivity of the "West" too. In drawing our attention to the creative possibilities found at the intersection where antagonistic forms of consciousness collide, Mignolo does appear to open a promising theoretical mechanism through which to enunciate new forms of social and political practices. However, by adopting an account of the singularity of ethnic identity it cannot provide, beyond abstraction, a basis for social analysis that would move beyond textuality and move into the heterogeneity of existing social systems. These are always at some distance from textual accounts of an imaginary ideal. In his focus on an ethnic, he strips the situated individual of individuality. This provides no mechanism through which "ethnic" communities may address internal social pathologies. While an account of double critique may be called into action here, if this is based on an equally abstract account it seems difficult to understand how "I" may critique my own community. What we gain is a "gap" between "I" and society.

What is required to overcome the limitations of decolonial thought is to engage in a theoretical *en passant* move: of passing the decolonial imagination through that of critical theory's but to move beyond both accounts. This theoretical movement is made possible through our development of Watsuji's notion of *aidagara*, predicated on our account of reflexive negation. This brings the social dynamics of the decolonial unit of analysis, the sociohistorically, informed identity of the colonized, together with the exclusive abstraction of the individual. The tension between these two aspects of life, individuality and our social being, is "docked" within the account of socio-epistemology of Watsuji. Though maintaining the positive protection of the individual, this shatters the ideal of subjectivity of critical theory to overcome the imposition of an account of the decontextualized individual as an ultimate unit of concern. At the same moment, the introduction of the imagination of critical theorist to that of decolonial theorists provides a space for the protection of the individual. This allows for social power to be articulated against though not at the expense of individuality as it de-essentializes identity to nurture of internal heterogeneity. The normative commitment of such a model is the articulation of injustice.

Given the concern raised about the totalizing account of Watsuji's work, can such a theoretical move provide a means of representing the tension between individuality and sociality, while protecting positive and negative rights? In an example that expresses the need for social change, or the addressing of social ills, Watsuji writes:

> When an individual resolutely rebels against something that up to that point had held currency, and through strife and sacrifice finally *manages to change the consciousness of totality, [it can be said that in this case,] that individual had become clearly conscious of something that had already been vaguely felt in collective consciousness* (zentai ishiki), and ahead of the masses had tried

to form things toward how they ought to be, thus leading collective consciousness to self-awareness. (WTZ11: 648; Sevilla 2015: 11. Sevilla's emphasis and
added parenthesis)

What Watsuji is putting forward here is the idea of the individual returning
to the absolute to lead social change. It is important to note that this functions
as a process of individualization. What we get is a sense of the individual's
struggle with individuality, drawing further into her own being, through
which to contribute to the development of society. Furthermore, despite
Watsuji's views on language, he sees it as something that is also dynamically
created:

In expressing this mutual intelligibility, [and] while bearing the pre-existing
linkages between subjects, linguistic activity constantly creates the linkages
between subjects anew. If one pays attention to this working, one can say that
linguistic activity is the working that creates relationality (aidagara) . . . [It is] a
double creative activity that, in making language as a meaningful form, creates
relationality [as well]. (WTZ10, 531; Cited Sevilla: 140. Sevilla's parenthesis)

Language can be a means of control and of power, but it can also be a
means of resistance. The language of the everyday, limits consciousness
and shapes social reality. In pointing to such a process, Farah Godrej shows
how the language of the public sphere, say racist, effects the consciousness
of the individual (Godrej 2011). However, language, and its reclamation as
Godrej demonstrates, can be an expression of dissensus: social reality can
be altered through the altering language or the inclusion of new theoretical
understanding. To be clear, Watsuji is arguing that freedom comes through
the conscious engagement with the space of our lives and that through such
efforts, we recognize our own and our society's its limitations. This is not
necessarily at the level of political or social institutional activity, but through
the self's enactment with society through which change occurs. Now this is
deeply abstract. But if we look at the life of one of the most important writers
in the English language, we get a glimpse of this movement between self and
society that Watsuji was thinking about.

Mary Ann Evans, George Eliot, was born into a comfortable English
middle-class family in 1819. Her early life and education were dominated by
the traditional Christian teachings of the day. She had an especially strong
relationship with her father, but this would be damaged as she developed
her intellectual interests. Before Eliot was a novelist and poet, she was
involved with the positivist movement of Auguste Comte, and was a transla-
tor of David Strauss's *Life of Jesus* in 1846, Ludwig Feuerbach's *Essence
of Christianity* in 1854, and Spinoza's *Ethics* in 1856. Her love-life was

disreputable for the time as she lived and had a lasting relationship with a man who was separated from his wife. Eliot's novels rejoice in her views of cultural, social, and political reform and emancipation. Largely based in rural settings, Eliot's novels drew on her own life experiences, and carry with them the message that if you want to be free, rather than rely solely on structural reform, look toward internal liberation from staid ways of understanding yourself and your world. Recognize that, she is saying, and one moves toward emancipation and social reform.

When we view Watsuji's account of reflexive negation, emptiness, through the life of Eliot, we get the sense that being free is not something to which we gain immediate access. Our means of understanding of self, other, and the world has been mediated through a singular, one-dimensional account of being-in-the-world. This conception moderates the inside and outside of the nation, subjective, intersubjective, and objective reason, and distances "I" as a citizen from "I" as a member of humanity. This is a conception of the world that is historically and temporally bound. The world occurs to the agent of Delanty and Mignolo, but in the proposed unit of analysis, the agent enacts with the world for change. The proposed ultimate unit of analysis, a post-individual combines, the individual, though as individuality, of critical theory and the sociohistorical identity of decolonial thought. But if the singular per-spective, the one-dimensional "man" of the present has shaped our view of self, other, and the world, the discussion of this chapter has tried to reimagine the life of an enactive agent. The decolonial experience has provided us with an imaginative perspective on the paucity of ideal-seeking societies. The *en passant* move of the ethnic-historical-social identity of the decolonial self with critical theory's abstract individual shows us that rather than the histori-cal concept of the individual providing protection against the wants of vested interests, that the individual is, in fact, left defenseless without the ability to provide a counterweight to the problem of over-positioning. In demonstrating the spatial dimensions of diametric duality in the acquisition and maintenance of power, the decolonial project provides a key through which *reality springs forward*. It is a key that has significance not only for those that live through the application of colonialism but also for many of the existential issues of the day.

We have conceptualized this critique of cosmopolitanism the heuristic device of diametric dualistic space. Such space has the characteristics of though the symmetry as a mirror image and of a relative closure. We see examples of diametric dualistic representations of reality in the dichotomies of modernity versus nonmodernity, a West and the rest, of self and other. Such an epistemic stance maintains closure and therefore supports notions of completeness. From such a position, the imaginative potential of cosmopoli-tanism can never be realized. To realize the critical and heuristic potential of cosmopolitanism, we have applied to these supposed dichotomies the heuristic device of concentric duality. As discussed, this account of space stresses the assumed connection as a symmetry of unity, understands the interaction of self and other, or the encounter with a culture alien to one's own as a process of reciprocal self or societal development. In emphasizing openness, this maintains the ethos of incompleteness.

Incompleteness alerts to the dangers of understanding the human condition as merely *to be* or of essentializing our being through our multitudinous, relational, and interconnected ways of being in the world. This would have to acknowledge one's consciousness' is not fixed within an unchanging perceptual world accompanied by a stable conceptual system, but still capable of being grounded. As a heuristic project cosmopolitanism is concerned with the opportunity for self-realization provided in the encounter with other and the world. But cosmopolitanism is not merely the recognition of our incompleteness; that things could have been otherwise. Incompleteness indicates to us that, like the unceasing creativity of being human, cosmopolitanism as an ethico-political agenda of unceasing activity. Its constructive criticality begins with a human being's constant enactive with the social forms of their time that either provide blockages for human realiaztion or a means of mutual self-development. Cultural reproduction is sustained but new cultural forms are brought into being through the poly-modal interaction *between* the self and totality. Beginning in the deconstruction of temporal claims of objectivity, the movement of cosmopolitanism then proceeds to find new affirmations of the human journey unceasingly. Transformation occurs through this space.

There is no sovereign self. Through the application of emptiness as our principle of reflexive negation, the proposed ultimate unit of analysis, combines the individual of critical theory and the sociohistorical identity of decolonial thought within the concentric duality of Watsuji's account of socioepistemology. To overcome the abstraction of both thinker's social ontologies, incapable of self-reflexivity, Watsuji's account of *aidagara* positions subjectivity as post-individual. In drawing on our notion of *aidagara*, that carries with it the criticality of Mignolo and Delanty, allow us to maintain a commitment to contestation, contingency, and interconnectedness. In contrast to positioning the relationship of self, other, and world within a space of diametric duality, the application of a concentric understanding of space reveals a social landscape that characterizes the dynamic of change as connection, a symmetry of unity, the co-cognitivity of knowledge, and relative openness. But this enaction can also lead to significant social, cultural, and political change, as evidenced through the life of Eliot. This negation of temporal affirmations, the ideals of the time, emerges in the individual through their engagement with the greater whole. Cultural reproduction and production are brought about *between* the self and its poly-modal interaction with totality.

The synthesis of Delanty's relational social ontology with the notion of aesthesis must be accompanied by the imperative of rights as a right of enunciation. Can the reading of emptiness as a logic of reflexive negation offer a means of *freedom from* and *freedom to* be, that cannot be guaranteed through Watsuji?[8] His understanding of being human emphasizes our relational essence. This stresses that apparent contradictions may be at best penultimate statements and that more profound insights may be found when we position these contradictions within an underlying system. What is added is the idea that all individual entities are unique and separated and yet are mutually constrained and interdependent, and that the two concepts, positive and negative liberties, are needed to give a fuller account of experiential public space. Here our heuristic devices of diametric and concentric dualities offer us a means of bridging the gap between the self and society for the enunciation of silenced claims of injustice. The immediate spatial dynamics provided through the process of nullification by jury offers us a means for the articulation of dissent that was beyond the dominant social, political, cultural, and economic conventions. However, this would not necessarily the guarantee of rights, as they developed alongside modernities temporal-spatial understanding of political and social space. Based locally, and within the dynamics of diametric and concentric dualities, the identification of injustices and their creative solution, provided by the reciprocity of power between the ruled and rulers through nullification by jury, makes available alternative decision-making procedures, means of reasoning, forms of knowing and knowledge.

"Unity" lies in the fact that we are all connected because of our relational insertion into hierarchies of domination and subordination, hierarchies that we also can resist and transform. It is toward such transformations that this book is geared. Drawing on the decolonial notion of relative universalism and Watsuji's notions of *aidagara* this book's rejection of closure around objective, subjective, and intersubjective identities and political and social commitments, which carries with it an obligation to empower political and social creativity, implies a concomitant obligation to reject closure of boundaries between diverse political communities. As we have noted in the introduction, temporal claims are always accompanied with claims of necessity,

---

[8] A conventional picture is often painted of Berlin prioritising negative liberty over positive liberty. However, Berlin always took care to explain that negative and positive liberty "overlap" (2002 [1957]: 169) or "cannot be kept wholly distinct" (2002 [1969]: 36), and he was clear that his two concepts of liberty have to coexist and cannot be substituted for each other: "I am not offering a blank endorsement of the 'negative' concept as opposed to its 'positive' twin brother, since this would itself constitute precisely the kind of intolerant monism against which the entire argument is directed" (2002 [1969]: 50, n. 1).

objectivity, or with the caveat of "that is the way things are." However, these claims have been used to justify what are perceived as grave social, political, and economic injustices. If incompleteness breaks the tension between an abstract "I" and an abstract "state," with the state being the arbiter of rationality, then the spatial injunction looks to localized democracy as independent sources of rational legitimacy. The account of the societal imagination developed through this chapter breaks down the barrier between in-here and out-there and recognizes the role of capacities that are governed through conventions. Rather than respond to the singular perspective, that encases self within the rationality of society, our discussion has aimed to provide an account which recognizes individual plurality. Instead of relying on instrumental or utilitarian accounts of reason, such an account of social knowledge, through the enunciation of heterogenous sensibility, is based on an analytic of practices. Here the body is not merely a contingent aspect of selfhood but is integral to identity which cannot be thought of as separate from mind; the body is thus an ethical and epistemological site.

In recognizing that we live out our lives in the creativity of *aidagara*, allows us to recognize the structure, mechanisms, and effects of society on our own existence. Proceeding in this dialogic way, self and other provide a means of moving beyond the scripts of our lives. Transformation, a radical cosmopolitan imagination occurs through such an account of the space "in between" when focused on matters of common concern. For sure, on the everyday level of existence, these may be small interventions. The point to stress here is that though the self is centered, it is at the same time part of a poly-modal interaction with other and the world. We recognize ourselves through our enaction with the other; this, if we step outside of 'I' to discover 'self', provides an opportunity for change. We develop as individuals and communities when we come face-to-face with the effects of ourselves on the other. This is not a self or other of an autonomous and distinct identity, but a self and other of blood and feelings. Change comes about through understanding agency as the individual emerging through the constant enactive creation between self, other, and the world. This reaches inside of self and requires it to contribute to the greater whole. Rather than the closure of the affirmation, a way of life, life continues, but the epistemic principle at work, emptiness, implies that when focused on matters of common concern this creativity is supported through structural reform based on reciprocity. Such structural reform must bridge the gap between an abstract 'I' and an abstract state. This would bring to life new thoughts through which lives can re-appropriate life. This overcomes the present restrictions of the cosmopolitan imagination through expanding agency by safeguarding the infinity of otherness and simultaneously requiring the opening of infinity within self within a necessarily contingent, non-rational and hetero-plural account of space.

Glossary of Important Terms

Aidagara: *Aidagara* is a Japanese term which is used commonly to describe the social relationship between two people. However, Watsuji's use of the term is intended to provide a way beyond the antinomy between methodological individualism and communitarian accounts of social dynamics. In methodological individualism, the individual is assumed to be autonomous and distinct. In contrast, aidagara assumes that the boundary between individuals includes their social relations. For example, the interaction between male or female individuals is not simply understood as the interaction between two autonomous units of analysis, holders of individual rights. Rather, when viewed through the analytical lens of aidagara, would consider aspects of social, economic, political, and cultural capital when concerning this interaction. This shift from an idealized bearer of rights to a focus on the articulation of points of critique is considered in this book. It is important to note that in Japan, the notion of aidagara is not considered a result of their intentional acts as it is considered to be created by a power beyond human control. This is reflected in the lack of critical perspective in Watsuji's work. My introduction of Mignolo to aidagara provides such critical perspective.

Cosmopolitan social theory: The aim of cosmopolitan social theory is to understand social transformation by discovering the new and emerging social and personal identities that come about through increased global interconnection.

Enactive: In the approach presented here, understanding human agency as enactive looks at the circular relationship between our bodies, how we feel, how we act, our sensorimotor activity, and cultural and environmental influences.

Epistemic: Epistemic is related to the act of knowledge or knowing in the everyday. Miranda Fricker provides a useful way of understanding how epistemic knowledge, in particular epistemic injustices, is presented in this book (2007). She identifies two distinctive kinds of epistemic injustices: testimonial injustice and hermeneutical injustice. Testimonial injustice occurs when someone is disregarded or disbelieved because of their identity. Hermeneutical injustice is injustice associated with how an individual interpret their own lives and when their experiences, racist, sexism, agism are not accommodated in current concepts.

Epistemology: Epistemology is concerned with the techniques, legitimacy, and scope of a theory of knowledge and its difference between justified belief and opinion.

Fūdo: Fūdo, from the Sino-Japanese linguistic tradition, is presented by Watsuji to comprehend the interpersonal merging of different individuals within a given geographical/climatic area. Importantly, fūdo provides a metaphor for the subjectivity but not in the context of individual self-actualization but as a part of a collective (see also aidagara).

Generative: This understands the individual as a theory-forming agent. That is, a generative agent is one who through their engagement with everyday reality forms theories about the world.

Ningen sonzai: Ningen sonzai provides the twofold structure and refers to human nature as individual yet social, private as well as public, with our coming together in relationships occurring in the aidagara between us through the unceasing negation of self and society.

Ningen: Ningen refers to both individual human beings, and in the realm of ningen, we are both individual and social. Ningen refers not only to the individuality of being human but also to society. Watsuji was concerned with overcoming a view of being human that focused solely on temporality to instead look at the temporal and spatial aspects of individual/social life. As such, when viewed spatially, as in existing social relations and their effect on the individual, it appears difficult to maintain a view of being human reduced to an autonomous and distinct self.

Ontic: In terms of philosophical ontology, see below, ontic refers to the physical, real, or factual existence.

Ontological: Ontology relates to being, to what is, to what exists, to the constituent units of reality; political ontology, by extension, relates to political being, to what units that comprise political reality. Liberal theorists such as John Rawls have argued that given the enduring and unavoidable disagreements concerning ontological claims the political theory needs to avoid making such claims about the constitution of political units of analysis. Of course, this requires the substantiation of the "neutral" nature of the social and political world, however, theorist such as Oliver Marchart (2007) that this claim of a neutrality of the social and political world itself requires an ontological claim which must be critically investigated. The purpose of such investigations is to develop alternative political ontologies capable of providing novel and creative languages for contemporary societies. An example of this approach would be this book introduction of Watsuji's account of socio-epistemology.

Overpositioning: Overpositioning occurs when a person, an institution, an organisation, has adominant position without a sufficient counter-weight through which to provide an adequate response.

Reflexive negation: A logic of reflexive negation is an epistemic approach to social analysis that suggests that the negation of a social ideal or practice possesses a reflexive structure that can provide new affirmations of social praxis. Beginning with the incompleteness principle inherent in cosmopolitanism as an example of reflexive negation, we have used the concept in this book through drawing on the social/political implications for social theory from the concept of emptiness. In the discussion of the spatiality of aidagara, emptiness points to understanding the relationship between self and other as a constant process of self-reflexivity that has no grounds other than itself, from which a unique critical perspective can be gained.

Social epistemology: Social epistemology understands human knowledge as a collective achievement. Specifically, social epistemologies are concerned with the evaluation of the social dimensions of knowledge production and reproduction.

Sonzai: With sonzai, Watsuji is attempting to go beyond the ontic description of the fact of a self in relation, as in two distinct units encountering each and to radically reconsider existence (sonzai) spatiotemporal existence that is fundamentally relational.

Bibliography

Adam, B. (1994). *Time and Social Theory*. Cambridge: Polity Press.

Adorno, T. W. (1977). The actuality of philosophy. *Telos*, 1977(31), 120–133.

Agger, B. (1998). *Critical Social Theories: An Introduction*. Boulder: Westview Press.

Allen, A. (2016). *The End of Progress: Decolonizing the Normative Foundations of Critical Theory*. New York: Columbia University Press.

Allen, Amy. (2017). Critical theory in postcolonial times. In Cristina Lafont & Penelope Deutscher (Eds.), *Critical Theory in Critical Times* (pp. 183–207). New York: Columbia University Press.

Allen, Amy, & Mendieta, Eduardo. (2018). *From Alienation to Forms of Life: The Critical Theory of Rahel Jaeggi*. State College: Penn State Press.

Almond, G., & Verba, S. (1963). *The Civic Culture: Political Attitudes in Five Nations*. Princeton, NJ: Princeton University Press.

Aman, R. (2014). *Impossible Interculturality? Education and the Colonial Difference in a Multicultural World*. LiU-tryck: Linköping.

Ames, R. T. (1994). Introduction to part one. In R. T. Ames, W. Dissanayake, & T. P. Kasulis (Eds.), *Self as Person in Asian Theory and Practice*. New York: State University of New York Press.

Anderson, B. (1983 [2006]). *Imagined Communities*. London: Verso.

Anzaldúa, G. (1999). *Borderlands/La Frontera: The New Mestiza*. San Francisco: Aunt Lutte Books.

Apffel-Marglin, F., & Marglin, S. A. (1996). *Decolonizing Knowledge: From Development to Dialogue*. Oxford: Clarendon Press.

Appadurai, A. (1996). *Modernity at Large*. Minneapolis: University of Minnesota Press.

Araújo, Marta, & Maeso, Silvia R. (2015). *Eurocentrism, Racism and Knowledge: Debates on History and Power in Europe and the Americas*. Basingstoke: Palgrave Macmillan.

Archibugi, D., Held, D., & Köhler, M. (Eds.). (1998). *Re-Imagining Political Community: Studies in Cosmopolitan Democracy.* Stanford, CA: Stanford University Press.

Arisaka, Yoko. (1993). *Haiku, Nishida, and Heidegger: Toward a New Metaphysics of Experience* (1993 manuscript).

Arisaka, Yoko. (1997). Beyond "east and west": Nishida's universalism and postcolonial critique. *The Review of Politics,* 59(3), 541–560. Reprinted in Fred Dallmayr (Ed.). (1999). *Border Crossings: Toward a Comparative Political Theory* (pp. 236–252). Lanham: Lexington Books.

Arnason, J. P. (2003). *Civilizations in Dispute: Historical Questions and Theoretical Traditions.* Leiden: Brill.

Arnold, D. A. (2005). *Buddhists, Brahmins, and Belief: Epistemology in South Asian Philosophy of Religion.* New York: Columbia University Press.

Arrowsmith, R. R. (2011). *Modernism and the Museum.* Oxford: University of Oxford.

Asch, S. (1952). *Social Psychology.* Englewood Cliffs, NJ: Prentice-Hall.

Ascione, Gennaro. (2016). *Science and the Decolonization of Social Theory: Unthinking Modernity.* London: Palgrave.

Atkinson, A. B. (2018). *Inequality: What Can Be Done?* Cambridge, MA: Harvard University Press.

Baek, J. (2011). Re-conceptualizing critical subjectivity and identity in critical regionalism: Phenomenological inputs. *Architectural Research,* 13(2), 23–30.

Baldwin, R. (2016). *The Great Convergence: Information Technology and the New Globalization.* Cambridge, MA: Bleknap Press of Harvard University Press. .

Balestra, Carlotta, & Tonkin, Richard. (2018). *Inequalities in Household Wealth Across OECD Countries: Evidence from the OECD Wealth Distribution Database.* OECD Statistics Working Papers 2018/01, OECD Publishing.

Barad, K. (2007). *Meeting the Universe Halfway: Quantum Physics and the Entanglement of Matter and Meaning.* Durham, London: Duke University Press.

Barber, B. (1996). Constitutional faith. In J. Cohen (Ed.), *For Love of Country?* (pp. 30–37). Boston: Beacon Press.

Barber, M. D. (1998). *Ethical Hermeneutics: Rationalism in Enrique Dussel's Philosophy of Liberation.* New York: Fordham University Press.

Bardhan, N., & Sobré-Denton, M. (2015). Interculturality, cosmopolitanism, and the role of the imagination: A perspective for communicating as global citizens. In M. Rozbicki (Ed.), *Perspectives on Interculturality: The Construction of Meaning in Relationships of Difference* (pp. 131–160). London: Palgrave.

Barnett, C. (2017). *The Priority of Injustice: Locating Democracy in Critical Theory.* Athens: The University of Georgia Press.

Bauman, Z. (2003, February). Utopia with no topos. *History of the Human Sciences,* 16(1), 11–25.

Beck, U. (2006). *The Cosmopolitan Vision.* Cambridge: Polity Press.

Beck, U., Giddens, A., & Lash, S. (1994). *Reflexive Modernization: Politics, Tradition and Aesthetics in the Modern Social Order.* Cambridge: Polity Press.

Becker, A. L. (1982). Beyond translation: Esthetics and language description. In Heidi Byrnes (Ed.), *Georgetown University Round Table on Languages and Linguistics* (pp. 124–138). Washington, DC: Georgetown University Press.

Bellah, R. (1964). Japan's cultural identity: Some reflections on the work of Watsuji Tetsurō. *The Journal of Asian Studies*, 24(4), 573–594.

Bellamy, R. (2008). Evaluating union citizenship: Belonging, rights and participation within the EU. *Citizenship Studies*, 12, 597–611.

Bellamy, R. (2019). *A Republican Europe of States: Cosmopolitanism, Intergovernmentalism and Democracy in the EU*. Cambridge: Cambridge University Press.

Benhabib, S. (1992). *Situating Self; Gender, Community and Postmoderism in Contemporary Ethics*. Cambridge: Polity Press.

Benhabib, S., Butler, J., Cornell, D., & Fraser, N. (1995). *Feminist Contentions: A Philosophical Exchange*. London: Routledge.

Berlin, I. (2002 [1958]). Two concepts of liberty. In *Four Essays on Liberty* (pp. 166–217). Oxford: Oxford University Press.

Bernard, Manin. (1997). *The Principles of Representative Government*. Cambridge: Cambridge University Press.

Bernasconi, Robert. (1997). Philosophy's paradoxical parochialism: The reinvention of philosophy as Greek. In Keith Ansell-Pearson, Benita Parry, & Judith Squires (Eds.), *Cultural Readings of Imperialism: Edward Said and the Gravity of History* (pp. 212–226). London: Lawrence and Wishart.

Bernier, B. (2006). National communion: Watsuji Tetsurô's conception of ethics, power, and the Japanese Imperial State. *Philosophy East & West*, 56(1), 84–105.

Berque, A. (2004). Offspring of Watsuji's theory of milieu (Fûdo). *Geojournal*, 60, 389–396.

Berque, A. (2013). *Thinking Through Landscape* (A.-M. Feenberg-Dibon, Trans.). London: Routledge.

Best, S., & Kellner, D. (1991). *Postmodern Theory: Critical Interrogations*. New York: Guilford.

Bhabha, H. K. (1994). *The Location of Culture*. London: Routledge.

Bhambra, G. K. (2009). Postcolonial Europe or understanding Europe in times of the postcolonial. In C. Rumford (Ed.), *The Sage Handbook of European Studies* (pp. 69–85). London: SAGE.

Bhambra, G. K. (2016). Whither Europe? Postcolonial versus neocolonial cosmopolitanism. *Interventions: International Journal of Postcolonial Studies*, 18(2), 187–202. doi: 10.1080/1369801X.2015.1106964.

Bhambra, G. K. (2017). The current crisis of Europe: Refugees, colonialism, and the limits of cosmopolitanism. *European Law Journal*, 23, 395–405. doi: 10.1111/eulj.12234.

Bird-Pollan, S. (2015). *Hegel, Freud and Fanon: The Dialectic of Emancipation*. London: Rowman &Littlefield International.

Bleiker, Roland, & Hutchinson, Emma. (2007). *Understanding Emotions in World Politics: Reflections on 168*.

Bohman, J. (2004). Toward a critical theory of globalization: Democratic practice and multiperspectival inquiry. *Concepts and Transformation*, 9(2), 121–146.

Bok, S. (1996). From part to whole. In J. Cohen (Ed.), *For Love of Country: Debating the Limits of Patriotism: Martha Nussbaum with Respondents* (pp. 38–44). Boston: Beacon.

Bose, S. (2006). *A Hundred Horizons: The Indian Ocean in the Age of Global Empire*. Cambridge, MA: Harvard University Press.

Bosworth, A. (2014). A comparison of dual and non-dual logic in a dialectical method of analyzing towards transcending intractable and polarized political conflicts. *Global Journal of Human-Social Science*, 14(2), 42–49.

Bottici, C. (2014). *Imaginal Politics: Images Beyond Imagination and the Imaginary (New Directions in Critical Theory)*. New York, Chichester, West Sussex: Columbia University Press.

Bourdieu, P. (1977). *The Outline of a Theory of Practice* (R. Nice, Trans.). Cambridge: Cambridge University Press.

Braidotti, R., Bhavnani, K. K., Holm, P., & Ping-chen, H. (2013). The humanities and changing global environments. In *UNESCO, World Social Science Report 2013 Changing Global Environments: Changing Global Environments* (pp. 506–508). Paris: UNESCO Publishing.

Braidotti, Rosi, Blaagaard, Bolette, & Hanafin, Patrick. (2013). *After Cosmopolitanism: A Glasshouse Book*. Abingdon: Routledge.

Brechenmacher, S. (2018). Comparing Democratic Distress in the United States and Europe. Carnegie Endowment for International Peace. Retrieved May 12, 2018, from https://carnegieendowment.org/2018/06/21/comparing-democratic-distress -in-united-states-and- europe-pub-76646.

Breckman, Warren. (2013). *Adventures of the Symbolic: Post-Marxism and Radical Democracy*. Foreword by Dick Howard (Columbia Studies in Political Thought/ Political History). New York: Columbia University Press.

Brivio, C. (2009). *The Human Being: When Philosophy Meets History: Miki Kiyoshi, Watsuji Tetsurô and Their Quest for a New Ningen*. Netherlands: Wöhrmann Print Service.

Brooks, T. (2004). A defence of jury nullification. *Res Publica*, 10, 401–423. doi: 10.1007/s11158-004- 2329-3.

Brooks, T. (2013). Philosophy unbound. *Metaphilosophy*, 44, 254–266. doi: 10.1111/ meta.12027.

Browitt, J. (2004). (Un)common ground? A comparative genealogy of British and Latin American cultural studies. In S. King & J. Browitt (Eds.), *The Space of Culture: Critical Readings in Hispanic Studies* (pp. 54–80). Newark: University of Delaware Press. Retrieved July 12, 2015, from http://www.class.uh.edu/mcl/fa culty/zimmerman/lacasa/Estudios%20Culturales%20Articles/Jeff%20Browitt.pdf.

Brown, G. W. (2009). *Grounding Cosmopolitanism: From Kant to the Idea of a Cosmopolitan Constitution*. Edinburgh: Edinburgh University Press.

Burton, David. (1999). *Emptiness Appraised: A Critical Study of Nagarjuna's Philosophy*. London: Curzon.

Butler, Judith. (1990). *Gender Trouble*. London: Routledge.

Cain, B., Dalton, R., & Scarrow, S. (2003). *Democracy Transformed? Expanding Political Opportunities in Advanced Industrial Democracies*. Oxford: Oxford University Press.

Calhoun, C. (2003a). The class consciousness of frequent travelers: Towards a critique of actually existing cosmopolitanism. In D. Archibugi (Ed.), *Debating Cosmopolitics* (pp. 86–116). London: Verso.

Calhoun, C. (2003b). 'Belonging' in the cosmopolitan imaginary. *Ethnicities*, 3(4), 531–553.

Canclini, N. G. (2014 [1999]). *Imagined Globalization* (G. Yúdice, Trans.). Durham, London: Duke University Press.

Caney, Simon. (1992). Liberalism and communitarianism: A misconceived debate. *Political Studies*, 40, 273–289.

Caney, Simon. (2005). *Justice Beyond Borders: A Global Political Theory.* Oxford: Oxford University Press.

Caraus, T., & Lazea, D. (Eds.). (2015). *Cosmopolitanism Without Foundations?* Bucharest: Zeta Books.

Carter, A. (2001). *The Political Theory of Global Citizenship.* London and New York: Routledge.

Caruth, Cathy. (2015 [1996]). *Unclaimed Experience: Trauma, Narrative, and History.* Baltimore: John Hopkins University Press.

Castells, Manuel. (2000). The contours of the network society. *Foresight*, 2(2), 151–157. doi: 10.1108/14636680010802591.

Castoriadis, C. (1987 [1975]). *The Imaginary Institution of Society* (K. Blamey, Trans.). Cambridge, MA: MIT Press.

Cazdyn, E. (2015). Enlightenment, revolution, cure: The problem of praxis and the radical nothingness of the future. In *Nothing: Three Inquiries in Buddhism* (pp. 105–184). Chicago and London: University of Chicago Press.

Césaire, Aimé, & Robin, D. G. Kelley. (2000). *Discourse on Colonialism.* New York: Monthly Review Press.

Cestari, M. (2010). Between emptiness and absolute nothingness: Reflections on negation in Nishida and Buddhism (J. W. Raud, Ed.) Frontiers of Japanese Philosophy. *Classical Japanese Philosophy*, 7, 320–346.

Chakrabarty, D. (2000). *Provincializing Europe: Postcolonial Thought and Historical Difference.* Princeton: Princeton University Press.

Chanady, Amaryll. (1995). The territorialization of the imaginary in Latin America: Self-affirmation and resistance to metropolitan paradigms. In Lois Parkinson Zamora & Wendy B. Faris (Eds.), *Magical Realism: Theory, History, Community* (pp. 125–144). Durham and London: Duke University Press.

Chandler, D. C. (2013). Contemporary critiques of human rights. In M. Goodhart (Ed.), *Human Rights: Politics and Practice* (pp. 107–122). Oxford: Oxford University Press.

Cheah, P. (2006). Cosmopolitanism. *Theory, Culture & Society*, 23(2–3), 486–496.

Clammer, John. (1999). Transcending modernity? Individualism, ethics and Japanese discourses of difference in the post-war world. *Thesis Eleven*, 57(1), 65–80.

Clammer, John. (2018). Nature, culture and the debate with modernity: Critical social theory in Japan. In A. K. Giri (Ed.), *Social Theory and Asian Dialogues*. Singapore: Palgrave Macmillan.

Clifford, J. (1998). Mixed feelings. In P. C. Robbins (Ed.), *Cosmopolitics: Thinking and Feeling Beyond* (pp. 362–370). Minnesota: University of Minnesota Press.

Cohn, B. S. (1996). The command of language and the language of command. In *Colonialism and Its Forms of Knowledge: The British in 170.*

Comte, Auguste, & Andreski, Stanislav. (2015). The Essential Comte: Selected from Cours de philosophie Positive by Auguste Comte: First Published in Paris 1830–42. Retrieved from http://public.ebookcentral.proquest.com/choice/publicfu llrecord.aspx?p=1770581.

Conrad, Clay. (1999). *Jury Nullification: The Evolution of a Doctrine.* Durham, NC: Carolina Academic Press.

Corrias, L. (2017). The empty place of European power: Contested democracy and the technocratic threat. *European Law Journal,* 23, 482–494.

Cox, R. (1986). Social forces, states and world orders: Beyond international relations theory. In R. Keohane (Ed.), *Neorealism and Its Critics* (pp. 204–254). New York: Columbia University Press.

Crosby, Kevin. (2012). Bushell's case and the Juror's soul. *Journal of Legal History,* 33(3), 251–252.

Curato, Nicole, Dryzek, John S., Ercan, Selen A., Hendriks, Carolyn M., & Niemeyer, Simon. (2017). Twelve key findings in deliberative democracy research. *Dædalus: The Journal of the American Academy of Arts & Sciences,* 146(3), 28–38.

Dahl, Robert. (1998). *Democracy and Its Critics.* New Haven, CT: Yale University Press.

Dale, P. (1995). *The Myth of Japanese Uniqueness.* London: Routledge.

Dallmayr, F. (2006). Encounters between European and Asian social theory. In G. Delanty (Ed.), *Handbook of Contemporary European Social Theory* (pp. 372–380). Abingdon, Oxon: Routledge.

Dassonneville, R., & Hooghe, M. (2018). Indifference and alienation: Diverging dimensions of electoral dealignment in Europe. *Acta Politica,* 53(1), 1–23.

Davidson, M. (2015). Compassion and the death penalty. *Journal of Theoretical & Philosophical Criminology,* 7(2), 1–20.

Davis, B. W. (2014). Conversing in emptiness: Rethinking cross-cultural dialogue with the Kyoto School. *Royal Institute of Philosophy Supplement,* 74, 171–194.

Daye, D. (1975). Major schools of the Mahāyāna: Mādhyamika. In C. S. Prebish (Ed.), *Buddhism: A Modern Perspective* (pp. 76–96). Pennsylvania: The Penn State University Press.

Delanty, G. (2000). *Citizenship in a Global Age: Society, Culture, Politics.* Buckingham: Open University Press.

Delanty, G. (2006a). Introduction: Social theory in Europe today. In G. Delanty (Ed.), *Handbook of Contemporary European Social Theory* (pp. xvi–xxv). Abingdon, Oxon: Routledge.

Delanty, G. (2006b). The cosmopolitan imagination: Critical cosmopolitanism and social theory. *British Journal of Sociology,* 57(1), 25–47.

Delanty, G. (2009a). *The Cosmopolitan Imagination: The Renewal of Critical Social Theory.* Cambridge: Cambridge University Press.

Delanty, G. (2009b). The foundations of social theory. In B. S. Turner (Ed.), *The New Blackwell Companion to Social Theory* (pp. 19–37). Oxford: Blackwell Publishing Ltd.

Delanty, G. (2012). The idea of critical cosmopolitanism. In G. Delanty (Ed.), *Routledge Handbook of Cosmopolitanism Studies* (pp. 38–49). Abingdon, Oxon: Routledge.

Delanty, G. (2014). Not all is lost in translation: World varieties of cosmopolitanism. *Cultural Sociology*, 8(4), 374–391.

Delanty, G., & Mota, A. (2017). Governing the anthropocene: Agency, governance, knowledge. *European Journal of Social Theory*, 20(1), 9–38. doi: 10.1177/1368431016668535.

Delanty, G., & Turner, S. P. (Eds.). (2011). *Routledge International Handbook of Contemporary Social and Political Theory*. Abingdon, Oxon: Routledge.

Deleuze, G., & Guattari, F. (1983). *Anti-Oedipus: Capitalism and Schizophrenia* (R. Hurley, S. Mark, & H. R. Lane, Trans.). Minneapolis: University of Minnesota Press.

Deleuze, G., & Guattari, F. (2003 [1994]). *What Is Philosophy?* (H. Tomlinson & G. Burchell, Trans.). London: Verso.

Dessaix, R. (1996). *Night Letters*. Sydney: Macmillan.

Dewey, J. (1958). *Experience and Nature*. New York: Dover Publications.

Dhanda, A., & Parashar, A. (2009). Introduction: Decolonisation of knowledge: Whose responsibility? In A. Dhanda & A. Parashar (Eds.), *Decolonisation of Legal Knowledge* (pp. xi–xxxv). London: Routledge.

Dharwadker, V. (2001). *Cosmopolitanism in Its Time and Place*, p. 171.

Dietrich, E., & Fields, C. (2015). Science generates limit paradoxes. *Axiomathes*, 25(4), 409–432.

Dilthey, Wilhelm. (1985 [1887]). *Wilhelm Dilthey Selected Works, Volume V* (Rudolf A. Makkreel & Frithjof Rodi, Eds.). Princeton, NJ: Princeton University Press.

Dilworth, D. (1974). Watsuji Tetsurō (1889–1960): Cultural phenomenologist and ethician. *Philosophy East and West*, 24(1), 3–22.

DiMaggio, Paul. (1997). Culture and cognition. *Annual Review of Sociology*, 23, 263–287.

Diversi, M., & Moreira, C. (2009). *Betweener Talk: Decolonizing Knowledge Production, Pedagogy, and Praxis*. Walnut Creek, CA: Left Coast Press, Inc.

Domingues, J. (1995). Sociological theory and the space-time dimension of social theory. *Time & Society*, 4(2), 233–250.

Douzinas, C. (2007). *Human Rights and Empire: The Political Philosophy of Cosmopolitanism*. Abingdon: Routledge Cavendish.

Downes, P. (2012). *The Primordial Dance: Diametric and Concentric Spaces in the Unconscious World*. Oxford/Bern: Peter Lang.

Drabinski, J. (2011). *Levinas and the Postcolonial: Race, Nation, Other*. Edinburgh: Edinburgh University Press.

Dryzek, J. S., Bächtiger, A., Chambers, S., Cohen, J., Druckman, J. N., Felicetti, A., Fishkin, J. S., Farrell, D. M., Fung, A., Gutmann, A., Landemore, H., Mansbridge, J., Marien, S., Neblo, M., Niemeyer, S., Setälä, M., Slothuus, R., Suiter, J., Thompson, D., & Warren, M. E. (2019). The crisis of democracy and the science of deliberation. *Science*, 363, 1144–1146. doi: 10.1126/scienceaaw2694.

Dumont, Louis. (1970a). The individual as an impediment to sociological comparison and Indian history. In *Religion, Politics and History in India: Collected Papers in Indian Sociology*. The Hague: Mouton.

Dumont, Louis. (1970b). *Homo Hierarchicus: The Caste System and Its Implications*. Chicago: University of Chicago Press.

Durkheim, E. (1897 [1997]). *Suicide: A Study in Sociology*. New York: Free Press.

Dussel, E. (1985 [1980]). *Philosophy of Liberation* (A. Martinez & C. Morkovsky, Trans.). New York: Orbis Books.

Dussel, E. (1993). Eurocentrism and modernity (introduction to the Frankfurt lectures). *Boundary 2: The Postmodernism Debate in Latin America*, 20(3), 67–76.

Dussel, E. (1999). "Sensibility" and "otherness" in Emmanuel Lévinas. *Philosophy Today*, 126, 1. Retrieved March 14, 2014, from http://biblioteca.clacso.edu.ar/ar/libros/dussel/artics/sensi.pdf.

Dussel, E. (2002). World-system and 'trans' modernity. *Nepantla: Views from South*, 2(3), 221–245.

Dussel, E. D., & Barber, M. D. (1995). *The Invention of the Americas: Eclipse of "the Other" and the Myth of Modernity*. New York: Continuum.

Eco, U. (1999). *Serendipities: Language and Lunacy*. London: Orion Books.

Eder, K. (2009). A theory of collective identity making sense of the debate on a 'European identity.' *European Journal of Social Theory*, 12(4), 427–447. doi: 10.1177/1368431009345050.

Eisenstadt, S. (1986). *The Origins and Diversity of the Axial Civilisations*. New York: Suny Press.

Eisenstadt, S. (2003). *Comparative Civilisations and Multiple Modernities, Vols. 1 and 2*. Leiden: Brill.

Elias, N. (1978 [1939]). *The Civilizing Process*. Oxford: Blackwell.

Elias, N. (1992 [1987]). *Time: An Essay*. Oxford: Blackwell.

Eno, R. (2015, Version 2.21). The Analects of Confucius an Online Teaching Translation. Retrieved March 5, 2018, from http://www.indiana.edu/~p374/Analects_of_Confucius_(Eno-2015).pdf.

Epstein, J. (2006). *Generative Social Science: Studies in Agent-Based Computational Modeling*. Princeton, Oxford: Princeton University Press. doi: 10.2307/j.ctt7rxj1.

Escobar, A. (2004). The Latin American modernity/coloniality research program: Worlds and knowledges otherwise. *Cuadernos del Cedla*, 16, 31–67.

Escobar, Arturo. (2007). Worlds and knowledges otherwise. *Cultural Studies*, 21(2–3), 179–210. doi: 10.1080/09502380601162506.

European Commission, Standard Eurobarometer 85, Spring 2016, published July 2016, European Commission, Directorate-General for Communication. Retrieved from https://ec.europa.eu/commfrontoffice/publicopinion/index.cfm/ResultDoc/download/DocumentKy/75902.

Fanon, F. (2008 [1952]). *Black Skin, White Masks* (R. Philcox, Trans.). New York: Grove Press.

Feenberg, Andrew. (1995). The problem of modernity in the philosophy of Nishida. In J. Heisig & J. Maraldo (Eds.), *Rude Awakenings: Zen, the Kyoto School and the Question of Nationalism, University of Hawaii* (pp. 151–173).

Fine, R. (2006). Cosmopolitanism: A social science research agenda. In G. Delanty (Ed.), *Handbook of Contemporary European Social Theory* (pp. 242–256). Abingdon: Routledge.

Fine, R., & Cohen, R. (2002). Four cosmopolitan moments. In S. A. Vertovec (Ed.), *Conceiving Cosmopolitanism: Theory, Context, and Practice* (pp. 137–164). Oxford: Oxford University Press.

Fishkin, J. S. (2011). *When the People Speak: Deliberative Democracy and Public Consultation*. Oxford: Oxford University Press.

Fitz, Hope K. (2011). A comparison of confucius' notion of Jen/Ren as inner-humanity and human-heartedness with Gandhi's view of ahimsa as compassion. *Dialogue and Universalism*, 2(1).

Flax, J. (1990). *Thinking Fragments: Psychoanalysis, Feminism, and Postmodernism in the Contemporary West*. Berkeley, CA: University of California Press.

Flikschuh, Katrin, & Ypi, Lea (Eds.). (2014). *Kant and Colonialism: Historical and Critical Perspectives*. Oxford: Oxford University Press.

Flores, M. J. (2010). *Cosmopolitan Liberalism: Expanding the Boundaries of the Individual*. New York: Palgrave Macmillan.

Foa, R. S., Klassen, A., Slade, M., Rand, A., & Williams, R. (2020). *The Global Satisfaction with Democracy Report 2020*. Cambridge, United Kingdom: Centre for the Future of Democracy.

Foster, C., & Frieden, J. (2017). Crisis of trust: Socio-economic determinants of European's confidence in government. *European Union Politics*, 18(4), 511–535. doi: 10.1177/1465116517723499.

Foucault, M. (2011). *The Courage of the Truth Lectures at the Collège de France*. New York: Palgrave Macmillan.

Fox, N. (2013). Creativity, anti-humanism and the 'new sociology of art'. *Journal of Sociology*, 1–15. doi: 10.1177/1440783313498947.

Fox, N. (2017, May 29). A Sociology of Creativity: The Deleuzian Canvas. Retrieved from https://humuscreativity.files.wordpress.com/2015/09/a-sociology-of-creativity-v2.pdf.

Fraser, N. (1989). *Unruly Practices: Power, Discourse, and Gender in Contemporary Social Theory*. Minneapolis: University of Minnesota Press.

Fricker, Miranda. (2007). *Epistemic Injustice: Power and the Ethics of Knowing*. Oxford: Oxford University Press.

Fuente, Eduardo de la. (2013). Why aesthetic patterns matter: Art and a "qualitative" social theory. *Journal for the Theory of Social Behaviour*, 44(2), 168–185.

Fukuyama, Francis. (1995). *Trust: The Social Virtues and the Creation of Prosperity*. New York: Free Press.

Galison, P. (1997). *Image and Logic: A Material Culture of Microphysics*. Chicago: Chicago University Press.

Gallagher, S. (2005). *How the Body Shapes the Mind*. Oxford: Oxford University Press.

Gallagher, S. (2008). Direct perception in the intersubjective context. *Consciousness and Cognition*, 17(2), 535–543.

Gallie, W. B. (1955–56). Essentially contested concepts. *Proceedings of the Aristotelian Society*, 56, 173.

Gaonkar, D. P. (2002). Toward new imaginaries: An introduction. *Public Culture*, 14, 1–19.

Garfield, J. (1995). *The Fundamental Wisdom of the Middle Way. Translation and Commentary of Nāgārjuna's Mūlamadhyamakakārikā*. Oxford: Oxford University Press.

Garfield, J. (2005). *Empty Words: Buddhist Philosophy and Cross-Cultural Interpretation*. Oxford: University of Oxford Press.

Gastil, John, & Wright, Erik Olin. (2019). *Legislature by Lot: Transformative Designs for Deliberative*. London, New York: Verso Books.

Geleta, E. B. (2014). The politics of identity and methodology in African development ethnography. *Qualitative Research*, 14(1), 131–146.

Giddens, Anthony. (1979). *Central Problems in Social Theory: Action, Structure and Contradiction in Social Analysis*. London: Macmillan.

Giddens, Anthony. (1984). *The Constitution of Society: Outline of the Theory of Structuration*. Cambridge: Polity Press.

Gilbert, J. (2006). Cultural imperialism revisited: Counselling and globalisation. *International Journal of Critical Psychology, Special Issue: Critical Psychology in Africa*, 17, 10–28.

Gilroy, P. (2005). A new cosmopolitanism. *Interventions: International Journal of Postcolonial Studies*, 7(3), 287–292.

Gloria, Anzaldúa. (1987). *Borderlands/La Frontera: The New Mestiza*. San Francisco: Aunt Lute.

Godrej, F. (2011a). *Cosmopolitan Political Thought: Method, Practice, Discipline*. Oxford: Oxford University Press.

Godrej, F. (2011b). Spaces for counter-narratives: The phenomenology of reclamation. *Frontiers: A Journal of Women Studies*, 32(3), 111–133.

Gopal, Priyamvada. (2019). *Insurgent Empire: Anticolonial Resistance and British Dissent*. London: Verso Books.

Gordon, L. R. (2010). Fanon on decolonizing knowledge. In E. A. Hoppe & T. Nicholls (Eds.), *Fanon and the Decolonization of Philosophy* (pp. 3–18). Lanham, MD: Lexington Books.

Grosz, E. (1994). *Volatile Bodies*. Bloomington: Indiana University Press.

Gutmann, Amy, & Thompson, Dennis. (2002). *Why Deliberative Democracy?* Princeton, NJ: Princeton University Press.

Habermas, J. (1996). *Between Facts and Norms: Contributions to a Discourse Theory of Law and Democracy* (W. Rehg, Trans.). Cambridge: Polity Press.

Habermas, J. (2001). *Postnational Constellation: Political Essays*. Cambridge: Polity.

Hall, D. L., & Ames, R. T. (1987). *Thinking Through Confucius*. Albany: State University of New York Press.

Hall, D. L., & Ames, R. T. (1998). *Thinking from the Han: Self, Truth, and Transcendence in Chinese and Western Culture*. Albany: State University of New York Press. Hall, S. (1992). Race, culture and communications: Looking backward and forward at cultural studies. *Rethinking Marxism*, 5, 10–18.

Hannerz, U. (1996). *Transnational Connections: Culture, People, Places*. London: Routledge.

Hansen, C. (1989). Language in the heart-mind. In R. E. Allison (Ed.), *Understanding the Chinese Mind: The Philosophical Roots* (pp. 75–124). Hong Kong: Oxford University Press.

Hardt, M., & Negri, A. (2001). *Empire*. Cambridge MA and London: Harvard University.

Harootunian, H. D. (2000). *Overcome by Modernity: History, Culture and Community in Interwar Japan*. Princeton: Princeton University Press.

Hattam, R. (2004). *Awakening-Struggle: Towards Buddhist Critical Social Theory*. Flaxton: PostPressed.

Hay, C. (2007). *Why We Hate Politics*. Cambridge, UK: Polity.

Hayward, M. J. (2014). *Contesting Buddhist Narratives: Democratisation, Nationalism, and Communal Violence in Myanmar* (D. Ernest & M. Mietsner, Eds.). Honolulu: East West Center.

Heater, D. (1990). *Citizenship: The Civic Ideal in World History, Politics and Education*. London and New York: Longman.

Hegel, G. (1976). *Phenomenology of Spirit* (A. Millar, Trans.). Oxford: Oxford University Press.

Heidegger, M. (1973 [1962]). *Being and Time* (J. Macquarrie & E. Robinson, Trans.). Oxford: Basil Blackwell.

Held, D. (1996). *Models of Democracy* (2nd ed.). Cambridge: Polity Press.

Held, D. (2002). Law of states, law of peoples. *Legal Theory*, 8(2), 1–44.

Held, D. (2010). *Cosmopolitanism: Ideals, Realities and Deficits*. Cambridge: Polity Press.

Held, David. (1995). *Democracy and the Global Order: From the Modern State to Cosmopolitan Governance*. Cambridge: Polity Press.

Hermans, H. J. (2018). *Society in the Self: A Theory of Identity in Democracy*. Oxford: Oxford University Press.

Hobson, John. (2004). *The Eastern Origins of Western Civilization*. Cambridge: Cambridge University Press.

Holton, R. J. (2009). *Cosmopolitanism: New Thinking and New Directions*. Hampshire: Palgrave Macmillan.

Honneth, A. (2000). The possibility of a disclosing critique of society: The dialectic of enlightenment in light of current debates in social criticism. *Constellations*, 7, 116–127.

Honneth. Axel. (2003). The point of recognition: A rejoinder to the rejoinder (Joel Golb, et al., Trans.). In Nancy Fraser & Axel Honneth (Eds.), *Redistribution of Recognition? A Political-Philosophical Exchange*. London: Verso.

Hooghe, M., & Kern, A. (2017). The tipping point between stability and decline: Trends in voter turnout, 1950–1980–2012. *European Political Science*, 535–552.

Hoppe, E. A., & Nicholls, T. (2010). *Fanon and the Decolonization of Philosophy*. Lanham, MD: Lexington Books.

Horkheimer, M. (1972). *Critical Theory: Selected Essays*. New York: Seabury Press.

Horkheimer, M. (1982). *Critical Theory*. New York: Seabury Press.

Huntington, C. (1989). *The Emptiness of Emptiness: A Study of Early Indian Mādhyamika*. Honolulu: University of Hawaii Press.

Huntington, Samuel P. (1993). The clash of civilizations? *Foreign Affairs*, 72(3), 22–49. Retrieved JSTOR: May 26, 2020, from www.jstor.org/stable/20045621.

Hutchings, K. (2004). World politics and the question of progress. In: *Redescriptions: Yearbook of Political Thought and Conceptual History* (pp. 211–234). SoPhi.

Inglis, D. (2014). Cosmopolitanism's sociology and sociology's cosmopolitanism: Retelling the history of cosmopolitan theory from Stoicism to Durkheim and beyond. *Distinktion: Scandinavian Journal of Social Theory*, 15(1), 69–87.

Irigaray, Luce. (1999 [2002]). *Between East and West: From Singularity to Community*. New York: Columbia University Press.

Irvine, A. B. (2011). An ontological critique of the trans-ontology of Enrique Dussel. *Sophia*, 50, 603–624.

Ives, C. (1994). Ethical pitfalls in imperial Zen and Nishida philosophy: Ichikawa Hakugen's critique. In J. W. Heisig & J. C. Maraldo (Eds.), *Rude Awakenings: Zen, the Kyoto School, and the Question of Nationalism* (pp. 16–39). Honolulu: University of Hawai'i Press.

Jackson, P. T. (2008). Foregrounding ontology: Dualism, monism, and IR theory: Review of 175.

Jaeggi, Rahel, & Smith, Alan E. (2014). *Alienation* (Neuhouser Frederick, Eds.). New York: Columbia University Press.

Jansson, A., & Andersson, M. (15–17 June 2011). Mediatization at the margins: Cosmopolitanism, network capital and spatial transformation in rural Sweden. Paper presented at International ACSIS Conference, Norrköping.

Jenco, L. K. (2007). "What does heaven ever say?" A methods-centered approach to cross-cultural engagement. *American Political Science Review*, 101(4), 741–755.

Jenny E. Carroll, Nullification as Law, 102 GEO. L.J. 579, 621–22 (2014).

Johan Karlsson, Democrats without borders: A critique of transnational democracy, University of Gothenburg 2008, Chapter 4. Retrieved January 21, 2013, from https ://gupea.ub.gu.se/bitstream/2077/18348/1/gupea_2077_18348_1.pdf.

Johnson, D. W. (2018). Self in nature, nature in the lifeworld: A reinterpretation of Watsuji's concept of Fūdo. *Philosophy East & West*, 68(4), 1134–1154. doi: 10.1353/pew.2018.0100.

Jones, J. T. (2017). *The Patronising Disposition of Unaccountable Power: A Report to Ensure the Pain and Suffering of the Hillsborough Families Is Not Repeated*. London: Printed in the UK by the APS Group on behalf of the Controller of Her Majesty's Stationary Office.

Kaase, M. (1999). Interpersonal trust, political trust and non-institutionalised political participation in Western Europe. *West European Politics*, 22(3), 1–21. doi: 10.1080/01402389908425313.

Kalmanson, L. (2010). Levinas in Japan: The ethics of alterity and the philosophy of no-self. *Continental Philosophy Review*, 43(2), 193–206.

Kangas, A., & Salmenniemi, S. (2016). Decolonizing knowledge: Neoliberalism beyond the three worlds. *Distinktion: Journal of Social Theory*, 1–17.

Karlsson, Johan. (2008). *Democrats Without Borders: A Critique of Transnational Democracy*. Gothenburg: University of Gothenburg.

Kasulis, P. T. (1981). *Zen Action/Zen Person*. Honolulu: University of Hawaii Press.

Kasulis, P. T. (1994). Researching the strata of the Japanese self. In R. T. Ames, W. Dissanayake, & T. P. Kasulis (Eds.), *Self as Person in Asian Theory and Practice*. New York: State University of New York Press.

Kellner, D. (1989). *Critical Theory, Marxism and Modernity*. Baltimore: John Hopkins University.

Kelly, G. A. (1976, Autumn). Politics & philosophy in Hegel. *Polity*, 9(1), 3–18.

Kendall, G., Woodward, I., & Skrbis, Z. (2009). *The Sociology of Cosmopolitanism: Globalization, Identity, Culture & Government*. New York: Palgrave McMillan.

Kern, J. H. (1896). *Manual of Indian Philosophy*. Strassberg: Karl J. Trubner.

Koehler, H. (1990). *Democracy and Human Rights: Do Human Rights Concur with Particular Democratic Systems?* Vienna: International Progress Organisation.

Koenigsberg, R. A. (2005). Civilization and self-destruction: The psychology of war and genocide. Institute for Conflict Analysis and Resolution, George Mason University.

Konishi, Sho. (2013). *Anarchist Modernity: Cooperatism and Japanese-Russian Intellectual Relations in Modern Japan* (Harvard East Asian Monographs, no. 356.). Cambridge, MA: Harvard University Asia Center, distributed by Harvard University Press.

Kristjansson, K. (2010). *The Self and Its Emotions*. Cambridge: Cambridge University Press.

Krueger, J. (2013). Watsuji's phenomenology of embodiment and social space. *Philosophy East and West*, 63(2), 127–152.

Krueger, J. (2014). The space between us: Embodiment and intersubjectivity in Watsuji and Levinas. In L. Kalmanson, F. Garrett, & S. Mattice (Eds.), *Levinas and Asian Philosophy* (pp. 53–78). Pittsburch: Duquesne University Press.

Krueger, J. (2018). Watsuji's phenomenology of aidagara: An interpretation and application to psychopathology. In S. Taguchi & A. Altobrando (Eds.), *Tetsugaku Companion to Phenomenology and Japanese Philosophy*. Springer.

Krueger, J. (2020). Watsuji, intentionality, and psychopathology. *Philosophy East and West*, 70(3), 757–780.

Kuzminski, A. (2008). *Pyrrhonism: How the Ancient Greeks Reinvented Buddhism*. Lanham, MD: Lexington Books.

Laclau, E., & Mouffe, C. (2001). *Hegemony and Socialist Strategy: Towards a Radical Democratic Politics* (2nd ed.). London: Verso.

Laclau, Ernesto, & Mouffe, Chantel. (2001 [1985]). *Hegemony and Socialist Strategy* (2nd ed.). London: Verso.

Lacroix, J., & Pranchère, J. (2018). Critiques of human rights in contemporary thought. In Human Rights in History. *Human Rights on Trial: A Genealogy of the Critique of Human Rights* (pp. 25–58). Cambridge: Cambridge University Press. doi: 10.1017/9781108334884.002.

LaFleur, W. (1978). Buddhist emptiness in the ethics and aesthetics of Watsuji Tetsurô. *Religious Studies*, 14, 237–250.

LaFleur, W. (1990). A turning in Taishô: Asia and Europe in the early writings of Watsuji Tetsurô. In J. T. Rimer (Ed.), *In Culture and Identity: Japanese Intellectuals During the Interwar Years* (pp. 234–256). Princeton: Princeton University Press.

LaFleur, W. (1994). An ethics of as-is: State and society in the Rinrigaku of Watsuji Tetsurô. In L. Vandermeersch (Ed.), *La société civile face à l'État dans les traditions chinoîse, japonaise, coréenne et vietnamienne* (pp. 464–543). Paris: Études thématiques 3, École franç.

Latimer, J., & Skeggs, B. (2011). The politics of imagination: Keeping open and critical. *The Sociological Review*, 59(3).

Latour, Bruno. (1993 [1991]). *We Have Never Been Modern* (Catherine Porter, Trans.). Cambridge, MA: Harvard University Press.

Latour, Bruno. (2005). *Reassembling the Social: An Introduction to Actor-Network Theory*. Oxford: Oxford University Press.

Lazarus, N. (2005). The politics of postcolonial modernism. In A. Loomba, S. Kaul, M. Bunzl, A. Burton, & J. Esty (Eds.), *Postcolonial Studies and Beyond* (pp. 423–437). Durham: Duke University Press.

Lefebvre, H. (1974). *The Production of Space* (D. Nicholson-Smith, Trans.). Oxford: Blackwells.

Lenkersdorf, C. (1996). *Los Hombres verdaderos: Voces y testimonios de los tojolabales*. Mexico: Siglo XX1.

Levinas, E. (1990). *Difficult Freedom: Essays on Judaism* (S. Hand, Trans.). London: Athlone Press.

Levinas, E. (2002 [1974]). *Otherwise Than Being, or Beyond Essence* [utrement qu'être, ou au- delà de l'essence] (A. Lingis, Trans.). Pittsburgh: Duquesne University Press.

Liederbach, Hans Peter. (2012). Watsuji Tetsurô on Spatiality: Existence Within the Context of Climate and History. Retrieved May 12, 2016, from https://www.kwansei.ac.jp/s_sociology/attached/0000021707.PDF.

Loy, D. (2003). *The Great Awakening: A Buddhist Social Theory*. Somerville, MA: Wisdom Publications.

Lugones, M. (2003). *Pilgrimages/Peregrinajes: Theorizing Coalition Against Multiple Oppressions*.

Luo, Zhitian. 2008. From 'Tianxia' (all under heaven) to 'the world': Changes in late Qing intellectuals' conceptions of human society. *Social Sciences in China*, XXIX(2), 93–105.

Lyotard, J.-F. (1984 [1979]). *The Postmodern Condition: Report on Knowledge* (G. Bennington & B. Massumi, Trans.). Manchester: Manchester University Press.

Macdonald, T., & Macdonald, K. (2019). Towards a 'pluralist' world order: Creative agency and legitimacy in global institutions. *European Journal of International Relations*. doi: 10.1177/1354066119873134.

Macfie, A. L. (2003). *Eastern Influences on Western Philosophy: A Reader*. Edinburgh: Edinburgh University Press.

MacIntyre, A. (1984). *After Virtue: A Study in Moral Theory* (2nd ed.). Notre Dame, IN: University of Notre Dame Press.

Maffesoli, M. (1996). *The Time of the Tribes: The Decline of Individualism in Mass Society*. London: SAGE.

Mahbubani, K. (2017, May 21). It's a Problem That America Is Still Unable to Admit It Will Become #2 to China. Theworldpost-A partnership of HuffPost and The Berggruen Institute. Retrieved May 21, 2017, from http://www.huffingtonpost.com/kishore-mahbubani/g20-china-globalization- growth_b_11727004.html.

Mair, Peter, Ruling the Void, & Paul F. Whiteley. (2010, June). Is the party over? The decline of party activism and membership across the democratic world. *Party Politics*, 17(1).

Malcomson, S. L. (1998). The varieties of cosmopolitan experience. In P. C. Robbins (Ed.), *Cosmopolitics: Thinking and Feeling Beyond the Nation* (pp. 233–245). Minneapolis: University of Minnesota Press.

Maraldo, J. C. (2002). Between individual and communal, subject and object, self and other: Mediating Watsuji Tetsurô's hermeneutics. In M. Marra (Ed.), *Japanese Hermeneutics: Current Debates on Aesthetics and Interpretation* (pp. 76–86). Honolulu: University of Hawaii Press.

Marchart, O. (2007). *Post-Foundational Political Thought: Political Difference in Nancy, Lefort, Badiou and Laclau.* Edinburgh: Edinburgh University Press.

Marinopoulou, Anastasia. (2017). *Critical Theory and Epistemology: The Politics of Modern Thought and Science.* Manchester: Manchester University Press.

Marková, I. (2003). Constitution of the self: Intersubjectivity and dialogicality. *Culture and Psychology*, 9(3), 249–259.

Marsh, D., & Akram, S. (2015). Political participation and citizen engagement: Beyond the mainstream. *Policy Studies*, 36(6), 523–531.

Maruyama, Masao. (1966). *Thought and Behaviour in Modern Japanese Politics.* London: Oxford University Press.

Masayuki, Shimizu. (1999). Watsuji Rinrigaku to Nippon no kaishaku Watsuji's ethics and his interpretation of Japan. In Sato, et al. (Eds.), *Yomigaeru Watsuji Tetsurō Reviving Watsuji Tetsurō.* Kyōto: Nakanishi-ya-shuppan.

Matsumoto, Koji. (1991). *The Rise of the Japanese Corporate System.* London: Kegan Paul.

Mayaram, S. (2009). Rereading global cities: Topographies of an alternative cosmopolitanism in Asia. In S. Mayaram (Ed.), *The Other Global City* (pp. 1–32). New York: Routledge.

Mayeda, G. (2006). *Time, Space and Ethics in the Philosophy of Watsuji Tetsurô, Kuki Shûzô, and Martin Heidegger.* New York: Routledge.

McAdams, D. P., Hoffman, B. J., Day, R., & Mansfield, E. D. (1996). Themes of agency and communion in significant autobiographical scenes. *Journal of Personality*, 64, 339–377.

McAdams, Dan P. (1996). Personality, modernity, and the storied self: A contemporary framework for studying persons. *Psychological Inquiry*, 7, 295–321.

McCarthy, E. (2010). Ethics embodied: Rethinking selfhood through continental, japanese, and 178.

McCarthy, T. (2009). *Race, Empire, and the Idea of Human Development.* Cambridge: Cambridge University Press.

McKnight, A. (2013). Jury nullification as a tool to balance the demands of law and justice. *Brigham Young University Law Review*, 2013(4), 1102–1132.

McLaren, P. (1989). *Life in Schools: An Introduction to Critical Pedagogy in the Foundations of Education.* London: Longman.

McSorley, K. (2015). Cosmopolitanism and the body. In A. Marinopoulou (Ed.), *Cosmopolitan Modernity* (pp. 203–220). Bern: Peter Lang International Academic Publishers.

Mendelson, T. (2013). Nāgārjuna's Philosophy of Emptiness and Political Philosophy: Liberty in Action. Melbourne: PhD thesis, School of Historical and Philosophical

Studies, Faculty of Arts, The University of Melbourne. Retrieved May 14, 2017, from https://minerva- access.unimelb.edu.au/bitstream/handle/11343/39771/3114 28_MENDELSON%20file%20propert ies.pdf?sequence=1.

Mendieta, E. (2009). From imperial to dialogical cosmopolitanism. *Ethics and Global Politics*, 2(3), 241–258.

Mercier, H., & Sperber, D. (2017). *The Enigma of Reason: A New Theory of Human Understanding*. Harvard: Allen Lane.

Merleau-Ponty, M. (1988). *In Praise of Philosophy and Other Essays (Studies in Phenomenology and Existential Philosophy)* (J. Wild, J. M. Edie, & J. O'Neill, Trans.). Evanston, IL: North Western University Press.

Merton, R. K. (1968). *Social Theory and Social Structure*. New York: Free Press.

Midgley, Mary. (1996). *Utopias, Dolphins and Computers: Problem of Philosophical Plumbing*. London and New York: Routledge.

Mignolo, W. (2000a). The many faces of cosmo-polis: Border thinking and critical cosmopolitanism. *Public Culture*, 12(3), 721–748.

Mignolo, W. (2000b). *Local Histories/Global Designs: Colonality, Subaltern Knowledges, and Border Thinking*. Princeton, NJ: Princeton University Press.

Mignolo, W. (2001). Local histories and global designs: An interview with Walter Mignolo. *Discourse*, 22(3), 7–33.

Mignolo, W. (2002). The many faces of cosmo-polis: Border thinking and critical cosmopolitanism. In C. A. Breckenridge, S. Pollock, H. K. Bhabha, & D. Chakrabarty (Eds.), *Cosmopolitanism* (pp. 157–187). Durham, NC and London: Duke University Press.

Mignolo, W. (2007). The de-colonial option and the meaning of identity in politics. *Anales Nueva Época*, 9(10), 43–72.

Mignolo, W. (2008). The geopolitics of knowledge and the colonial difference. In M. D. Moraña (Ed.), *Coloniality at Large: Latin America and the Postcolonial Debate* (pp. 225–258). Durham: Duke University Press.

Mignolo, W. (2010). Delinking: The rhetoric of modernity, the logic of coloniality and the grammar of decoloniality. In W. A. Mignolo (Ed.), *The Decolonial Option* (pp. 303–368). London: Routledge.

Mignolo, W. (2011). Cosmopolitan localism: A decolonial shifting of the Kantian's legacies. *Localities*, 1, 11–45.

Mignolo, W. (2012). *Local Histories/Global Designs: Colonality, Subaltern Knowledges, and Border Thinking*. Princeton, NJ: Princeton University Press.

Mignolo, W., & Schiwy, F. (2003). Transculturation and the colonial difference: Double translation. In T. M. Streck (Ed.), *From Translation and Ethnography: The Anthropological Challenge of Intercultural Understanding* (p. 179). Tucson: University of Arizona Press.

Mignolo, W. D. (2007). Delinking: The rhetoric of modernity, the logic of coloniality and the grammar of de-coloniality. *Cultural Studies*, 21(2), 449–514.

Mignolo, W. D., & Tlostanova, M. V. (2006). Theorizing from the borders: Shifting to geo- and body-politics of knowledge. *European Journal of Social Theory*, 9(2), 205–221.

Mignolo, W., & Vázquez, R. (2013). Decolonial AestheSis: Colonial Wounds/ Decolonial Healings. Retrieved June 8, 2014, from http://socialtextjournal.org/p eriscope_article/decolonial-aesthesis-colonial- woundsdecolonial-healings.

Mignolo, Walter D. (2018). Decoloniality and phenomenology: The geopolitics of knowing and epistemic/ontological colonial differences. *The Journal of Speculative Philosophy*, 32(3), 360–387.

Miller, D. (2002). Cosmopolitanism: A critique. *Critical Review of International Social and Political Philosophy*, 5(3), 80–85.

Mills, C. (2000[1959]). *The Sociological Imagination*. Oxford: Oxford University Press.

Mills, C. W. (1997). *The Racial Contract*. London: Cornell University Press.

Milstein, B. (2015). *Commercium: Critical Theory from a Cosmopolitan Point of View*. London: Rowman & Littlefield International Ltd.

Mohanty, C. (2003). *Feminism Without Borders: Decolonizing Theory, Practicing Solidarity*. Durham and London: Duke University Press.

Mol, A. (2010). Actor-network theory: Sensitive terms and enduring tensions. *Kölner Zeitschrift für Soziologie und Sozialpsychologie*, 50(1), 253–269.

Morgensen, S. L. (2011). *Spaces Between Us: Queer Settler Colonialism and Indigenous Decolonization*. Minneapolis: University of Minnesota Press.

Morrow, R. A. (2013). Defending Habermas against eurocentrism: Latin America and Mignolo's decolonial challenge. In T. Bailey (Ed.), *Global Perspectives on Habermas* (pp. 117–136). London: Routledge.

Mouffe, Chantal. (2018). *For a Left Populism*. New York: Verso.

Moya, Paula. (1997). Postmodernism, 'realism' and the politics of identity: Cherrie Moraga and Chicana feminism. In M. J. Alexander & C. T. Mohanty (Eds.), *Feminist Genealogies, Colonial Legacies, Democratic Futures* (pp. 125–150). New York: Routledge.

Moya, Paula. (2001). Chicana feminism and postmodernist theory. *Signs*, 26(2), 441–483.

Mulhall, Stephen, & Swift, Adam. (1993). Liberalisms and communitarianisms: Whose misconception? *Political Studies*, 41, 650–656.

Mungiu-Pippidi, A., et al. (2015). Public Integrity and Trust in Europe: European Research Centre for Anti-Corruption and State-Building. Retrieved January 9, 2019, from https://spa.sdsu.edu/documents/PUBLIC_INTEGRITY_AND_TRUST _IN_EUROPE.pdf.

Murchison, Melanie. (2013, June 11). *Law, Morality and Social Discourse: Jury Nullification in a Canadian Context*. Queen's University Belfast Law Research Paper No. 21.

Murphy, M. (2015). The critical cosmopolitanism of Watsuji Tetsurō. *European Journal of Social Theory*, 18(4), 507–522.

Murray, D. W. (1993, March). What is the western concept of the self? On forgetting David Hume. *Ethos*, 21(1).

Nagami, I. (1981). The ontological foundations in Tetsurô Watsuji's philosophy: Kû and human existence. *Philosophy East and West*, 31(3), 282–296.

Nāgārjuna. (1999). *Nāgārjuna's Middle Way: Mūlamadhyamakārikā* (M. Siderits & S. Katsura, Trans.). Boston: Wisdom Books.

Nāgārjuna. (2007). *Ratnāvalī' in Nāgārjuna's Precious Garland* (J. Hopkins, Trans., & Commentary). Snowlion: Ithaca.

Nakamura, Hajime. (1991). *Ways of Thinking of Eastern Peoples: India, China, Tibet, Japan*. Revised English translation Philip P. Wiener. Delhi: Motilal Banarsidiss Publishers.

Nandy, A. (1987). Cultural frames for social transformation: A credo. *Alternatives*, 12, 113–116.

Nandy, A. (1994). *The Illegitimacy of Nationalism: Rabindranath Tagore and the Politics of Self*. Delhi: Oxford University Press.

Nandy, A. (1995). The other within: The strange case of Radhabinod Pal's judgement on cupability. In *The Savage Freud and Other Essays on Possible and Retrievable Selves* (pp. 53–80). Princeton, NJ: Princeton University Press.

Nandy, A. (1998). Defining a new cosmopolitanism: Towards a dialogue of asian civilisations. In K.-H. Chen (Ed.), *Trajectories: Inter-Asia Cultural Studies* (pp. 142–149). London: Routledge.

Nash, K. (2006). Political culture, ethical cosmopolitanism and cosmopolitan democracy. *Cultural Politics*, 2(2), 193–212.

Ndlovu-Gatsheni, S. J., & Zondi, S. (2016). *Decolonizing the University, Knowledge Systems and Disciplines in Africa*. Durham: Carolina Academic Press.

Neilson, D. (2015). Class, precarity, and anxiety under neoliberal global capitalism: From denial to resistance. *Theory & Psychology*, 25(2), 1–18.

Nelson, B. (1976). On orient and occident in Max Weber. *Social Research*, 43(1), 114–129.

Nelson, B. (1981). *On the Roads to Modernity*. New York: Rowman & Littlefield.

Neumann, Iver B. (2002). Returning practice to the linguistic turn: The case of diplomacy. *Millennium: Journal of International Studies*, 31(3), 627–651.

Ngcoya, M. (2015). Ubuntu: Toward an emancipatory cosmopolitanism? *International Political Sociology*, 9, 248–262.

Nhat Hanh, T. (1999). *The Heart of the Buddha's Teaching: Transforming Suffering into Peace, Joy and Liberation*. New York: Broadway Books.

Nicolini, D. (2009). Articulating practice through the interview to the double. *Management Learning*, 40(2), 195–212.

Nisbet, R. (2006). *Sociology as an Art Form*. New Brunswick: Transaction.

Nishida, Kitaro. (1965). Nihonbunka no Mondai (The problem of Japanese culture). In *Nishida Kitaro Zenshu* (Vol. 14). Tokyo: Iwanami Shoten.

Nussbaum, M. C. (1997). Kant and stoic cosmopolitanism. *Journal of Political Philosophy*, 5(1), 1–25.

Odin, S. (1993). The social self in Japanese philosophy and American pragmatism: A comparative study of Watsuji Tetsurō and George Herbert Mead. *Philosophy East and West*, 42(3), 475–501.

Odin, S. (1996). *The Social Self in Zen and American Pragmatism*. New York: State University of New York Press.

Oke, N. (2009). Globalizing time and space: Temporal and spatial considerations in discourses of globalization. *International Political Sociology*, 3, 310–326.

O'Neill, O. (2002). A Question of Trust. Reith Lectures 2002. BBC. Retrieved January 17, 2019, from https://www.immagic.com/eLibrary/ARCHIVES/GEN ERAL/BBC_UK/B020000O.pdf.

Opoku, Kofi Asare. (2013[1993]). African traditional religion, an enduring heritage. In Jacob K. Olupona & Sulayman S. Nyang (Éds.), *Religious Plurality in Africa*. Berlin, New York: De Gruyter Mouton.

Ortner, Sherry B. (1984, January). Theory in anthropology since the sixties. *Comparative Studies in Society and History*, 26(1), 126–166, 181.

Oser, J., & Hooghe, M. (2018). Democratic ideals and levels of political participation: The role of political and social conceptualisations of democracy. *The British Journal of Politics and International Relations*, 20(3), 711–730.

Owen, David. (1995). *Nietzsche, Politics and Modernity*. London: SAGE Publications.

Pagden, A. (2000). Stoicism, cosmopolitanism, and the legacy of european imperialism. *Constellations: An International Journal of Critical and Democratic*, 7(1), 3–22. doi: 10.1111/1467- 8675.00167.

Papastephanou, M. (2002). Kant's cosmopolitanism and human history. *History of the Human Sciences*, 15(1), 17–37.

Papastephanou, M. (2012). *Thinking Differently About Cosmopolitanism: Theory, Eccentricity, and the Globalized World*. Boulder: Paradigm.

Pappas, G. F. (2017). The limitations and dangers of decolonial philosophies: Lessons from Zapatista Luis Villoro. *Radical Philosophy Review*, 1–31.

Parekh, B. (2000). *Rethinking Mutliculturalism: Cultural Diversity and Political Theory*. Cambridge, MA: Harvard University Press.

Park, Young-Do, & Han, Sang-Jin. (2014). Another cosmopolitanism: A critical reconstruction of the neo-confucian conception of Tianxiaweigong (天下爲公) in the age of global risks. *Development and Society*, 43(2), 185–206.

Parkes, Graham. (1991). The early reception of Nietzsche's philosophy in Japan. In Graham Parkes (Ed.), *Nietzsche and Asian Thought*. Chicago: University of Chicago Press.

Parkes, Graham. (1997). The Putative fascism of the Kyoto School and the political correctness of the modern academy. *Philosophy East and West*, 47(3), 305–336.

Parkes, Graham. (2009). Heidegger and Japanese fascism: An unsubstantiated connection. *Pli: The Warwick Journal of Philosophy*, 20, 226–248.

Parr, T., & Friston, K. J. (2018). The anatomy of inference: Generative models and brain structure. *Frontiers in Computational Neuroscience*, 12, 90. doi: 10.3389/fncom.2018.00090.

Parsons, Talcott. (1937). *The Structure of Social Action*. New York: The Free Press.

Parsons, Talcott. (1977a). *Social Systems and the Evolution of Action Theory*. New York: Free Press. Parsons, Talcott. (1977b). Some problems of general theory in sociology. In *Social Systems and the Evolution of Action Theory* (pp. 229–269). New York: Free Press.

Perniola, M. (2013). *20th Century Aesthetics: Towards a Theory of Feeling* (M. Verdicchio, Trans.). London: Bloomsbury.

Pharr, S., & Putnam, R. (2000). *Disaffected Democracies: What's Troubling the Trilateral Countries?* Princeton, NJ: Princeton University Press.

Pichler, F. (2012). Cosmopolitanism in a global perspective: An international comparison of open-minded orientations. *International Sociology*, 27(1), 21–50.

Pieterse, J. N., & Parekh, B. (1995). *The Decolonization of Imagination: Culture, Knowledge and Power*. London: Zed Books.

Piketty, T. (2018, December 20). Manifesto for the Democratisation of Europe. Retrieved from http://piketty.blog.lemonde.fr/2018/12/10/manifesto-for-the-democratisation-of-europe/

Piketty, Thomas. (2014). *Capital in the Twenty-First Century*. Cambridge, MA: Harvard University Press.

Pilgrim, Richard. (1985). *Japanese Religion*. Englewood Cliffs, NJ: Prentice Hall.

Pin-Fat, V. (2015). Cosmopolitanism without foundations. In S. G. Padmanabhan (Ed.), *Politics and Cosmopolitanism in a Global Age* (pp. 83–102). New Delhi: Routledge.

Piovesana, Gino K. (1969). *Contemporary Japanese Philosophical Thought*. New York: St. John's University Press.

Pollock, Sheldon, Bhabha, Homi K., Breckenridge, Carol A., & Chakrabarty, Dipesh. (2000). Cosmopolitanisms. *Public Culture*, 12(3), 577–589.

Poster, M. (1989). *Critical Theory and Poststructuralism: In Search of a Context*. London: Cornell University Press.

Price, M. (2017 [2016]). Un/shared space: The dilemma of inclusive architecture. In J. Boys (Ed.), *Disability, Space and Architecture: A Reader* (pp. 155–172). Abingdon, Oxon: Routledge.

Priest, G. (2009). The structure of emptiness. *Philosophy East and West*, 59(4), 467–480.

Priest, G. (2013). Nāgārjuna's Mūlamadhyakamakārikā. *Topoi*, 32, 129–134.

Priest, G., & Garfield, J. (2002). Nāgārjuna and the limits of thought. In G. Priest (Ed.), *Beyond the Limits of Thought* (pp. 249–270). Oxford: Clarendon Press.

Putman, H. (1996). Must we choose between patriotism and universal reason? In J. Cohen (Ed.), *For Love of Country: Debating the Limits of Patriotism: Martha Nussbaum with Respondents* (pp. 91–97). Boston: Beacon.

Rainsborough, M. (2016). Rethinking Kant's shorter writings: Kant's philosophy of history. In R. V. Jiménez, R. L. R. Hanna, J. R. Rosales, & N. S. Madrid (Eds.), *Kant's Shorter Writings* (pp. 473–492). Cambridge: Cambridge Scholars Publishing.

Ranicère, J. (2004). *The Politics of Aesthetics* (G. Rockhill, Trans.). London: Continuum.

Rancière, J. (2006). *Hatred of Democracy* (S. Corcoran, Trans.). London: Verso.

Rapport, N. (2012a). *Anyone, the Cosmopolitan Subject of Anthropology*. Oxford: Berghahn Books.

Rapport, N. (2012b). The cosmopolitan world. In R. Fardon, O. Harris, & T. Marchand (Eds.), *The Sage Handbook of Social Anthropology* (pp. 523–537). London: Sage Publications.

Read, H. (1955). *Icon and Idea: The Function of Art in the Development of Human Consciousness*. Cambridge, MA: Harvard University Press.

Reckwitz, Andreas. (2002). Toward a theory of social practices: A development in culturalist theorizing. *European Journal of Social Theory*, 5(2), 243–263.

Reckwitz, Andreas. (2005). Toward a theory of social practices: A development in culturalist theorizing. In M. Gabrielle (Ed.), *Practicing History: New Directions in the Historical Writing after the Linguistic Turn*. New York: Routledge (Rewriting Histories).

Reiss, H. (1990). *Kant: Political Writings* (H. Reiss, Ed.). Cambridge: Polity Press.

Ricoeur, P. (1981). *Hermeneutics & The Human Sciences* (J. B. Thompson, Ed., & J. B. Thompson, Trans.). Cambridge & Paris: Cambridge University Press & Editions de la Maison de Science de l'homme.

Robbins, B. (1998). Introduction part I: Actually existing cosmopolitanism. In P. Cheah & B. Robbins (Eds.), *Cosmopolitics: Thinking and Feeling Beyond the Nation* (pp. 1–19). Minneapolis, MN: University of Minnesota Press.

Roberts, H. (2004). Cynic shamelessness in late sixteenth-century French texts. *The Modern Language Review*, 99(3), 595–607.

Robertson, R. (1992). *Globalization: Social Theory and Global Culture*. London: Sage.

Rofel, L. (2012). Between Tianxia and postsocialism: Contemporary Chinese cosmopolitanism. In G. Delanty (Ed.), *Routledge Handbook of Cosmopolitanism Studies*. London: Routledge.

Rothstein, B. (2019). Epistemic democracy and the quality of government. *European Politics and Society*, 20(1), 16–31.

Ruggie, J. G. (1993). Territoriality and beyond: Problematizing modernity in international relations. *International Organization*, 47(1), 139–174.

Ruggie, J. G. (2000). *Constructing the World Polity*. London: Routledge.

Rumford, C. (2013). *The Globalization of Strangeness*. New York: Palgrave Macmillan.

Saadawi, N. E. (1998 [1983]). *Memoirs from the Women's Prison* (M. Booth, Trans.). Berkeley: University of California Press.

Said, E. (1978). *Orientalism*. New York: Pantheon.

Said, E. (1983). *The World, the Text and the Critic*. Cambridge, MA: Harvard University Press.

Said, E. (1993). *Culture and Imperialism*. New York: Vintage.

Saito, A. (1984). *Buddhapālita-mula-madhyamaka-vrtti*. Australian National University.

Sakai, N. (1993). Return to the west/return to the east: Watsuji Tetsuro's anthropology and discussions of authenticity. In M. Miyoshi & H. Harootunian (Eds.), *Japan in the World* (pp. 237–270). Durham, NC: Duke University Press.

Sandbeck, Lars. (2011). God as immanent transcendence in Mark C. Taylor and John D. Caputo. *Studia Theologica: Nordic Journal of Theology*, 65(1), 18–38.

Sandel, Michael J. (1982 [1998]). *Liberalism and the Limits of Justice*. Cambridge, MA: Cambridge University Press.

Sandelands, L. (1998). *Feeling and Form in Social Life*. Lanham, MD: Rowman & Littlefield.

Santina, P. D. (2002). *Causality and Emptiness: The Wisdom of Nāgārjuna.* Singapore: Buddha Dharma Education Association.

Schlereth, T. (1977). *The Cosmopolitan Ideal in Enlightenment Thought: Its Form and Function in the Ideas of Franklin, Hume, and Voltaire, 1694–1790.* Notre Dame: University of Notre Dame Press.

Schueth, S., & O'Loughlin, J. (2008). Belonging to the world: Cosmopolitanism in geographic contexts. *Geoforum*, 39, 926–941.

Schwartzberg, M. (2015). Epistemic democracy and its challenges. *Annual Review of Political Science*, 18(1), 187–203.

Sellars, J. (2007). Deleuze and cosmopolitanism. *Radical Philosophy: Philosophical Journal of the Independent Left.* Retrieved March 18, 2017, from https://www.rad icalphilosophy.com/article/deleuze-and-cosmopolitanism.

Sen, A. (2006). *The Argumentative Indian: Writings on Indian History, Culture and Identity* (2nd ed.). London: Penguin Books.

Sen, A. K. (1999). Democracy as a universal value. *Journal of Democracy*, 10, 3–17.

Seth, S. (2004). Reason or reasoning? Clio or Siva? *Social Text*, 22(1).

Seth, S. (2013). "Once was blind but now can see": Modernity and the social sciences. *International Political Sociology*, 7, 136–151.

Sevilla, A. L. (2015). *Exporting the Ethics of Emptiness: Applications, Limitations, and Possibilities of Watsuji Tetsurô's Ethical System* [Dissertation]. Japan: Graduate University of Advanced Studies.

Sevilla, A. L. (2017). *Watsuji Tetsurô's Global Ethics of Emptiness: A Contemporary Look at a Modern Japanese Philosopher.* Cham, Switzerland: Palgrave Macmillan.

Shapin, S. (1996). *The Scientific Revolution.* Chicago: University of Chicago Press.

Sheard, C. M. (1993, March). Kairos and Kenneth Burke's psychology of political and social communication. *College English*, 55(3), 291–310.

Shields, J. M. (2011a). The art of Aidagara: Ethics, aesthetics, and the quest for an ontology of social existence in Watsuji Tetsurō's Rinrigaku. *Asian Philosophy*, 19(3), 265–283.

Shields, James Mark. (2011b). *Critical Buddhism: Engaging with Modern Japanese Buddhist Thought.* Farnham, Surrey, and Burlington, VT: Ashgate.

Shigemi, I. (2013). Japanese philosophers go west: The effect of maritime trips on philosophy in Japan with special reference to the case of Watsuji Tetsurō (1889–1960). *Japan Review*, 25, 113–144.

Shonin, E., Singh, N., Van Gordon, W., & Griffiths, M. D. (2015). There is only one mindfulness: Why science and Buddhism need to work together. *Mindfulness*, 6, 49–56.

Shotter, John. (1993). *Cultural Politics of Everyday Life: Social Constructionism, Rhetoric and Knowing of the Third Kind.* Toronto: University of Toronto Press.

Simmel, Georg, & Hughes, Everett C. (1949, November). The sociology of sociability. *American Journal of Sociology*, 55(3), 254–261.

Simpson, L. C. (2014). Critical interventions: Towards a hermeneutical rejoinder. In M. Xie (Ed.), *The Agon of Interpretations: Towards a Critical Intercultural Hermeneutics* (pp. 252–274). Toronto and London: University of Toronto Press.

Sirimanne, C. R. (2016). Buddhism and women: The Dhamma has no gender. *Journal of International Women's Studies*, 18(1), 273–292.

Skrbis, Z., & Woodward, I. (2013). *Cosmopolitanism: Uses of the Idea*. London: Sage.

Smith, A. (1978). Lectures on jurisprudence. In R. L. Meek, D. D. Raphael, & P. Stein (Eds.), *The Glasgow Edition of the Works and Correspondence of Adam Smith* (Vol. 5). Oxford: Oxford University Press. Oxford Scholarly Editions Online (2014). doi: 10.1093/actrade/9780198281887.book.1.

Smith, L. T. (1999). *Decolonizing Methodologies: Research and Indigenous Peoples*. New York and London: Zed Books.

Smith, W. (2007). Cosmopolitan citizenship: Virtue, irony and worldliness. *European Journal of Social Theory*, 10(1), 37–52.

Sobré-Denton, M., & Bardhan, N. (2013). *Global Citizens: Cultivating Cosmopolitanism for Intercultural Communication*. New York: Routledge.

Somers, Margaret R. (1994). The narrative constitution of identity: A relational and network approach. *Theory and Society*, 23(5), 605–649. doi: 10.1007/BF00992905.

Sousa Santos, B. de. (2014). *Epistemologies of the South: Justice Against Epistemicide*. London: Routledge.

Sousa Santos, Boaventura de, Nunes, Joao Arriscado, & Meneses, Maria Paula. (2008). Introduction: Opening up the canon of knowledge and the recognition of difference. In de Boaventura Sousa Santos (Ed.), *Another Knowledge Is Possible: Beyond Northern Epistemologies* (pp. xviii–Lxxii). New York: Verso.

Spariosu, M. (2014). Some prospects of intercultural hermeneutics in a global framework. In M. Xie (Ed.), *The Agon of Interpretations: Towards a Critical Intercultural Hermeneutics* (pp. 187–209). Toronto, London: University of Toronto Press.

Spiegel, Gabrielle. (2005). Introduction. In Gabrielle Spiegel (Ed.), *Practicing History: New Directions in the Historical Writing After the Linguistic Turn*. New York: Routledge (Rewriting Histories).

Spivak, G. C. (1988). Can the subaltern speak? In L. Grossberg & C. Nelson (Eds.), *Marxism and the Interpretation of Culture* (pp. 271–313). Urbana: University of Illinois Press.

Standing, G. (2014). Why the Precariat Is Not a "Bogus Concept". Open Democracy. Retrieved February 18, 2018, from https://www.opendemocracy.net/guy-standing/why-precariat-is-not-%E2%80%9Cbogus-concept%E2%80%9D.

Steger, M. B. (2008). Neo-isms: What's new about political ideologies in the global age. *Global*, 185.

Steger, M. B. (2009). Globalisation and social imaginaries: The changing ideological landscape of the twenty-first century. *Journal of Critical Globalisation Studies*, 1, 9–30.

Stiglitz, J. E. (2012). *The Price of Inequality: How Today's Divided Society Endangers our Future*. New York: W.W. Norton & Co.

Stoker, G. (2006). *Why Politics Matters: Making Democracy Work*. Basingstoke: Palgrave MacMillan.

Strydom, P. (2010). Immanent transcendence: Critical theory's left-Hegelian heritage. Retrieved August 2, 2016, from academica.edu: https://www.academia.edu/6085904/Reconstructive_Explanatory_Critique_On_Axel_Honneths_.

Strydom, P. (2011). *Contemporary Critical Theory and Methodology*. London and New York: Routledge.

Sugimoto, Y. (2012). Kyōsei: Japan's cosmopolitanism. In G. Delanty (Ed.), *Routledge Handbook of Cosmopolitanism Studies* (pp. 452–462). London: Routledge.

Suiter, J. (2018). Deliberation in action: Ireland's abortion referendum. *Political Insight*, 9, 30–32.

Swale, Alistair D. (2009). *The Meiji Restoration: Monarchism, Mass Communication and Conservative Revolution*. Basingstoke: Palgrave Macmillan UK.

Szerszynski, B., & Urry, J. (2006). Visuality, mobility and the cosmopolitan: Inhabiting the world from afar. *British Journal of Sociology*, 57(1), 113–131.

Tagore, S. (2008, Fall). Tagore's conception of cosmopolitanism: A reconstruction. *University of Toronto Quarterly*, 77(4), 1070–1084.

Takolander, Maria. (2007). *Catching Butterflies: Bringing Magical Realism to Ground*. Bern: Peter Lang.

Tan, C. (2015). Beyond rote-memorisation: Confucius' concept of thinking. *Educational Philosophy and Theory*, 47(5), 428–439.

Tan, C., & Tan, L. (2016). A shared vision of human excellence: Confucian spirituality and arts education. *Pastoral Care in Education*, 34(3), 156–166.

Tan, Charlene. (2013). *Confucius*. London: Bloomsbury.

Tan, Charlene. (2016). A confucian conception of critical thinking. *Journal of Philosophy of Education*, 51. doi: 10.1111/1467-97.

Tatsuo, Arima. (1969). *The Failure of Freedom: A Portrait of Modern Japanese Intellectuals*. Cambridge: Harvard University Press.

Taylor, Charles. (1985). *Human Agency and Language: Philosophical Papers* (Vol. 1). Cambridge: Cambridge University Press.

Taylor, Charles. (1989). Cross-purposes: The liberal-communitarian debate. In Nancy Rosenblum (Ed.), *Liberalism and the Moral Life*. Cambridge, MA: Harvard University Press.

Taylor, Charles. (1992). *The Ethics of Authenticity*. London: Harvard University Press.

Taylor, Charles. (2004). *Modern Social Imaginaries*. Durham, NC: Duke University.

Taylor, Charles. (2015 [1975]). *Hegel and Modern Society*. Cambridge: Cambridge University Press.

Taylor, P. (1999). *Modernities: A Geopolitical Interpretation*. Cambridge: Cambridge Polity Press.

Tetsuo, Najita, & Harootunian, H. D. (1993). Japanese revolt against the west: Political and cultural criticism in the twentieth century. In Peter Duus (Ed.), *The Cambridge History of Japan Six* (pp. 711–774). Cambridge: Cambridge University Press.

Theocharis, Y., & Van Deth, J. W. (2018). The continuous expansion of citizen participation: A new taxonomy. *European Political Science Review*, 10(1), 139–163.

Thiong'o, N. W. (1981). *Decolonising the Mind: The Politics of Language in African Literature*. Suffolk, UK: Boydell.

Thomas, N. J. (2014). The multidimensional spectrum of imagination: Images, dreams, 186.

Thompson, D. (2004). Election time: Normative implications of temporal properties of the electoral process in the United States. *American Political Science Review*, 98(1), 51–63. doi: 10.1017/S0003055404000991.

Thong, H. S. (1996). *An Anthology of Vietnamese Poems from the Eleventh Through the Twentieth Centuries* (H. S. Thong, Ed., & Trans.). New Haven, CT, London: Yale University Press.

Tlostanova, M. (2017). *Postcolonialism and Postsocialism in Fiction and Art: Resistance and Re-existence*. Basingstoke: Palgrave Macmillan.

Tobin, J. J. (Ed.). (1992). *Remade in Japan: Everyday Life and Consumer Taste in a Changing Society*. New Haven: Yale University Press.

Toscano, Alberto. (2012). Seeing it whole: Staging totality in social theory and art. *The Sociological Review*, 60(S1), 64–83.

Touraine, A. (1985). An introduction to the study of social movements. *Social Research*, 54(4), 749–787.

Trungpa, C., Baker, J., & Casper, M. (1987). *Cutting Through Spiritual Materialism*. Boston: Shambhala.

Turner, B. (2002). Cosmopolitan virtue: Globalization and patriotism. *Theory, Culture & Society*, 19(1), 45–63.

UNESCO. (2013). *World Social Science Report 2013 Changing Global Environments: Changing Global Environments*. Paris: Unesco Publishing.

van Deth, J. (2014). A conceptual map of political participation. *Acta Politica*, 49(3), 349–367.

Vaughan-Williams, N. (2007). Beyond a cosmopolitan ideal: The politics of singularity. *International Politics*, 44, 107–124.

Vazquez, R., & Mignolo, W. (2013). Decolonial AestheSis: Colonial Wounds/ Decolonial Healings. Periscope. Retrieved June 8, 15, from https://socialtextjo urnal.org/periscope_article/the-decolonial- aesthesis-dossier/.

Venn, C. (2006). *The Postcolonial Challenge Towards Alternative Worlds*. London: Sage.

Verba, S., Schlozman, K., & Brady, H. (1995). *Voice and Equality: Civic Voluntarism in American Politics*. Cambridge, MA: Harvard University Press.

Walker, R. (1992). *Inside/Outside: International Relations as Political Theory (Cambridge Studies in International Relations)*. Cambridge: Cambridge University Press. doi: 10.1017/CBO9780511559150.

Walker, R. B. J. (1991). On the spatiotemporal conditions of democratic practice. *Alternatives*, 16, 243–262.

Ward, E. (2013). Human suffering and the quest for cosmopolitan solidarity: A Buddhist perspective. *Journal of International Political Theory*, 9(2), 136–154.

Watsuji, T. (1918). *Guzo Saiko*. Tokyo: Iwanami.

Watsuji, T. (1988 [1935]). *Climate and Culture: A Philosophical Study*. Originally published as Fûdo ningen-gakuteki kôsatsu (G. Bownas, Trans.). Tokyo: Monbushō, 1961 Reprinted in 1988 by Greenwood Press.

Watsuji, T. (1996 [1937, 1942, 1949]). *Watsuji Tetsuro's Rinrigaku: Ethics in Japan* (S. Yamamoto & R. E. Carter, Trans.). Albany: State University of New York.

Watsuji, Tetsurō Zenshū (WTZ). (1991–1992). 27 volumes, (ed). Abe Yoshishige, et al. Tokyo: Iwanami shoten.

Bibliography

Webb, A. K. (2015). *Deep Cosmopolis: Rethinking World Politics and Globalization.* Abingdon: Oxon: Routledge.

Whitebook, J. (1989). Intersubjectivity and the Monadic Core of the Psyche: Habermas and Castoriadis on the Unconscious. *Revue européenne des sciences sociales,* 86(27), 225–244.Retrieved May 18, 2016.

Wiener, A. (2014). *A Theory of Contestation.* Heidelberg, New York, Dordrecht, London: Springer.

Wike, R., Simmons, K., Stokes, B., & Fetterolf, J. (2017, October). *Globally, Broad Support for Representative and Direct Democracy: But Many Also Endorse Nondemocratic Alternatives.* Pew Research Center.

Wilkinson, M. (2013). The specter of authoritarian liberalism: Reflections on the constitutional crisis of the European Union. *German Law Journal,* 14.

Williams, David. (2014). *The Philosophy of Japanese Wartime Resistance: A Reading, with Commentary, of the Complete Texts of the Kyoto School Discussions of "The Standpoint of World History and Japan."* London and New York: Routledge.

Wintour, P. (2017, June 15). Growing Awareness of Colonial Past Fuels Radicalisation, Says Czech Minister. The Guardian. Retrieved June 15, 2017, from https://ww w.theguardian.com/world/2017/jun/15/growing-awareness-of-colonial-past-fuel s- radicalisation-says-czech-minister.

Wiredu, K. (1995). *Conceptual Decolonization in African Philosophy.* Ibadan, Nigeria: Hope Publications.

Wood, D. (2017). Decolonizing knowledge: An epistemographical mise en place. *Tabula Rasa: Revista de Humanidades,* 26, 1–21. Retrieved February 18, 2017, from https://www.academia.edu/31494242/Decolonizing_Knowledge_An_Epist emographical_Mise_e n_Place.

Woons, M., & Weier, S. (Eds.). (2017). Interview with Walter D. Mignolo. In *Critical Epistemologies of Global Politics* (pp. 11–25). Bristol, England: E-International Relations.

Wu, Jeffrey. (2001). The philosophy of as-is: The ethics of Watsuji Tetsurō. *Stanford Journal of East Asian Affairs,* 1, 96–102. Retrieved April 12, 2018, from http:// www.stanford.edu/group/sjeaa/journal1/japan2.pdf.

Xiong, Y. (2012). Social inequality and inclusive growth in China: Significance of social policy in a new era. *Journal of Poverty and Social Justice,* 20(3), 277–290.

Yoko, Arisaka, & Kitaro, Nishida. (1996, Spring). The Nishida Enigma: 'The principle of the new world order.' *Monumenta Nipponica,* 51(1), 81–105.

Yoshida, Kazuhisa. (2009). The predicament of speaking about cultural differences: Two readings of Watsuji Tetsuro's cultural typology and the context of American multiculturalism. doi: 10.15057/17330.

Yoshino, Kosaku. (1992). *Cultural Nationalism in Contemporary Japan.* London: Routledge.

Yuasa, Yasuo. (1987). *The Body: Toward an Eastern Mind-Body Theory* (Shigenori Nagatomo & Thomas P. Kasulis, Trans.). Albany: State University of New York Press.

Zamora, L. P., & Faris, W. B. (1995). *Magical Realism: Theory, History, Community.* Durham, NC: Duke University Press.

Zaorálek, L. (2017, June 15). *Growing Awareness of Colonial Past Fuels Radicalisation: Future of Europe Summit.* Prague: Ministerstvo zahraničních věcí ČR. Retrieved June 15, 2017, from https://www.youtube.com/watch?v=Zn4S9rY14zc.

Zhu, Jing, & Thagard, Paul. (2002). Emotion and action. *Philosophical Psychology*, 15(1).

Žižek, S. (2005). Author's afterword: Why Hegel is a Lacanian. In S. Žižek, R. Butler, & S. Stephens (Eds.), *Interrogating the Real*. London: Continuum.

Zolo, D. (1997). *Cosmopolis: Prospects for World Government*. Cambridge: Polity Press.

Index

Adorno, Theodor, 59, 60, 62
Allen, Amy, 55, 63
Anzaldúa, Gloria, 43, 131, 132, 158
Arnason, Johann, 69

Beck, Ulrich, 38–39, 64–67, 101–2;
    cosmopolitization, 39, 66;
    globalization, 39; individualization,
    39, 63; reflexive modernity, 65–66;
    second modernity, 39, 66–67
Beck-Gernsheim, Elisabeth, 38
being human-social (infinite) finite
    being, 3, 17, 53, 146, 164, 167
Bellamy, Richard, 145–46
Benhabib, Seyla, 34–36, 63
Bhabha, Homi K., 35, 43, 64, 72, 132
Bhambra, Gurminder K, 102
Brzezinski, Zbigniew, 28
Buddhism, 44–46; Mahāyāna-middle
    path, 106–8; noble truths, 45

Castoriadis, Cornelius, 57, 136–37;
    critique of, 164–65; on the
    imaginary/imagination, 154–55
Confucianism, 5, 31, 44, 46–49;
    Dao, 47–48, 80, 97; five cardinal
    relationships, 47, 88; li, 47, 48, 80;
    Ren, 46, 48; tianxia, 46, 50

contradictions of the human condition,
    5, 8, 12, 13
cosmopolitanism: anthropological, 35—
    36; beginning in self, 12–13, 18–19,
    151–73; Citizen of the world, 30,
    37; cosmopolitanism as an answer to
    contradictions of human condition,
    51–53; cosmopolitan theory as
    diametric duality, 19, 50–51, 61,
    74–75, 100–102, 166; cosmopolitics,
    35; critique non-western forms,
    14–15, 49–51; Cynic philosophy,
    30; democratic theory, 37–38; early
    Christianity, 13, 30, 32; history of
    Western, 32–38; how a cosmopolitan
    thinks, 16–18, 14–16, 50–52, 47–49,
    101–25; Immanuel Kant, 13, 30,
    32–34, 33n6, 37; introduction to,
    12—14; multidisciplinary, 13–14;
    non-western traditions, 14–15,
    44–49; standard narrative, 12–14, 30;
    Stoics, 13, 30, 44, 45, 46; tasks of
    critical cosmopolitan social theory, 5,
    17–20. See also post-western centric
    critical cosmopolitan social theory
critical theory, 55–78; anti-dogmatic,
    59; construct keys, before which
    reality springs open, 60; critique of,

About the Author

Michael Murphy was awarded his doctorate from Royal Holloway, University of London, in 2018. He is recognised as an expert with UNESCO Inclusive Policy Lab and is a member of the Labour Academic Network of leading global scholars supporting the UK Labour party's policy work. His current research extends his work in Post-Western Critical Cosmopolitan Social Theory into an investigation of the social foundations of democratic Life. Alongside this he is carrying out research for his next book on 'Love and the Political.